NATO ASI Series

Advanced Science Institutes Series

A series presenting the results of activities sponsored by the NATO Science Committee, which aims at the dissemination of advanced scientific and technological knowledge, with a view to strengthening links between scientific communities.

The Series is published by an international board of publishers in conjunction with the NATO Scientific Affairs Division

A Life Sciences	Plenum Publishing Corporation
B Physics	London and New York
C Mathematical and Physical Sciences	Kluwer Academic Publishers Dordrecht, Boston and London
D Behavioural and Social Sciences	
E Applied Sciences	
F Computer and Systems Sciences	Springer-Verlag Berlin Heidelberg New York
G Ecological Sciences	London Paris Tokyo Hong Kong
H Cell Biology	Barcelona Budapest
I Global Environmental Change	

NATO-PCO DATABASE

The electronic index to the NATO ASI Series provides full bibliographical references (with keywords and/or abstracts) to more than 30000 contributions from international scientists published in all sections of the NATO ASI Series. Access to the NATO-PCO DATABASE compiled by the NATO Publication Coordination Office is possible in two ways:

- via online FILE 128 (NATO-PCO DATABASE) hosted by ESRIN, Via Galileo Galilei, I-00044 Frascati, Italy.

- via CD-ROM "NATO Science & Technology Disk" with user-friendly retrieval software in English, French and German (© WTV GmbH and DATAWARE Technologies Inc. 1992).

The CD-ROM can be ordered through any member of the Board of Publishers or through NATO-PCO, Overijse, Belgium.

Series F: Computer and Systems Sciences Vol. 119

The ASI Series F Books Published as a Result of
Activities of the Special Programme on
ADVANCED EDUCATIONAL TECHNOLOGY

This book contains the proceedings of a NATO Advanced Research Workshop held within the activities of the NATO Special Programme on Advanced Educational Technology, running from 1988 to 1993 under the auspices of the NATO Science Committee.

The volumes published so far in the Special Programme are as follows (further details are given at the end of this volume):

129569

Automating Instructional Design, Development, and Delivery

Edited by

Robert D. Tennyson

Learning and Cognition, Department of Educational Psychology
University of Minnesota, 178 Pillsbury Drive S.E.
Minneapolis, MN 55455, USA

Springer-Verlag
Berlin Heidelberg New York London Paris Tokyo
Hong Kong Barcelona Budapest
Published in cooperation with NATO Scientific Affairs Division

Proceedings of the NATO Advanced Research Workshop on Automating
Instructional Design, Development, and Delivery, held in Sitges, Spain,
March 23–27, 1992

CR Subject Classification (1991): K.3, J.4

ISBN 3-540-57022-5 Springer-Verlag Berlin Heidelberg New York
ISBN 0-387-57022-5 Springer-Verlag New York Berlin Heidelberg

CIP data applied for

© Springer-Verlag Berlin Heidelberg 1994
Printed in Germany

Typesetting: Camera-ready by authors/editors
45/3140 - 5 4 3 2 1 0 - Printed on acid-free paper

Preface

This workshop was organized and presented by an international group of scholars interested in the advancement of automating instructional design. Although the principal leader for this effort was myself, each of the committee members devoted equally in time and effort in the total preparation and conducting of the workshop. Members of the organizing committee included Dr. Klaus Breuer from disce and the University of Paderborn (Germany), Dr. Begoña Gros from the University of Barcelona, and Dr. Daniel Muraida and Dr. Michael Spector from the Armstrong Laboratory (USA). Dr. Gros participated as the co-director of the workshop and was directly responsible for the preparation and operation of the workshop in Sitges, Spain.

The workshop was held in Sitges, a short distance from Barcelona, March 23-27, 1992. Because of preparations at that time for the 1992 summer Olympic Games in Barcelona, the workshop was moved to a more convenient location. The theme of the workshop included three main topics: planning, production, and implementation. Dr. Peter Goodyear, from the Lancaster University (England), presented the invited keynote address. During the four day workshop, 14 papers were presented and discussed. Following each of the three topic areas, Drs. Gros and Breuer led discussions critiquing the ideas presented.

The organizing committee is grateful to the University of Minnesota, Department of Educational Psychology and the University of Barcelona, Department of Theory of Education, and disce (Germany) for co-sponsoring the workshop and providing computing equipment, communications, mailing, and printing of materials. A special thank you also goes to the NATO Scientific and Environmental Affairs Division office for assistance in every aspect of conducting this workshop. As editor, I would like to thank the editorial staff at Springer-Verlag, including Dr. Wösner and his assistant, Mr. J. Andrew Ross, for their help in making the final editing and manuscript preparations.

Finally, the authors wish to thank Ms. Chris Larson for the word processing and camera ready editing of the final version of this book.

University of Minnesota   Robert D. Tennyson
October 1993

Introduction and Keynote Paper

Contents

Part 3. Implementation

1

Automation and Instructional System Development

Robert D. Tennyson[1], J. Michael Spector[2], and Daniel J. Muriada[2]

[1]Learning and Cognition, Department of Educational Psychology, University of Minnesota, 178 Pillsbury Dr. S.E., Minneapolis, MN 55455, USA
[2]Armstrong Laboratory, AL/HRTC, Brooks AFB, TX 78235-5601, USA

Abstract: This chapter introduces the book's theme for elaborating and disseminating information on the automation of instructional system development. The focus is to promote the use of artificial intelligence and advanced interactive technologies in the design, development, and delivery of instructional computing systems. The specific goals are to: (a) share the lessons learned from the NATO Advanced Research Workshop in the area of automated instructional design; (b) facilitate international cooperation in the implementation of advanced instructional development systems; and (c) stimulate further R&D by presenting state-of-the-art knowledge with regard to automated instructional design.

Keywords: automating instructional development, planning ISD, instructional system development, delivery, production, evaluation

1.1 Introduction

The theme of this book is that applying advanced hardware and software technologies to the design, development and delivery of instruction can result in improved student learning and enhanced courseware authoring efficiency. Efforts to realize these benefits of automation will be most effective if they are informed by cognitive learning theory and are guided by established instructional emphases on student motivation, specification of objectives and evaluation of results.

Each of three instructional system development phases (i.e., planning, production, and implementation) will be examined in this book from four viewpoints: (a) motivation for automation; (b) theoretical issues involved in automation; (c) implementation issues involved in automation; and (d) evaluation of the automation process and results.

The three main topics listed below form the basis for this book. They represent the full range of issues concerning the automation of instructional design, development and delivery. Each part of the book will conclude with a formal synopsis of information and findings gathered from the main presentations and the small group discussions. These summaries were prepared by Begoña Gros with assistance from Klaus Breuer.

The book begins with Goodyear's keynote address that reviews a number of issues involved in automating the design, development, and delivery of instruction. He focuses on theoretical issues in the automation of instructional development and provides illustrations from work in the European Community's advanced learning technologies program, DELTA.

1.2 Automating Instructional Design (Planning Phase)

Part 1 will address questions associated with the planning of an automated instructional development system. Each of the authors offer answers to the following questions:

(a)   Which instructional design functions can and should be automated?

(b)   What are the implications of cognitive learning theory (e.g., constructivism, learner control, levels of interaction, etc.) for the design of interactive courseware?

(c)   What approaches (e.g., advisor, critic, guide, etc.) to the automation of instructional design have proven to be of some value?

(d)   How is progress to be evaluated?

The four chapters in this part provide a range of topics from generic models to specific applications. First, Tennyson introduces a historical overview of the ISD field by discussing the four generations of instructional system development. The purpose is to introduce the scope of the field by chronologically the growth of ISD from relative simple models to advanced systems that exhibit a self-organizing nature based on situational concerns. He concludes his chapter with a complete overview of authoring activities as a knowledge base for ISD.

The chapter by van Merriënboer, Krammer, and Maaswinkel provides findings from a research-based effort to implement a specific instructional theory. Their concern was with the automating of a computer-based system that would plan and execute an instructional program. Gonzalez and Vavik discuss a broader range of findings from evaluation activities associated with several development activities in Norway. Both chapters offer a rich set of findings and experiences that can be generalized when reviewing the issues of automation.

Part 1 concludes with an important focus of this book: The importance of evaluation in system design and development. Gros and Rodríquez present appropriate criteria for the evaluation of the automation of instructional development.

1.3 Automating Instructional Development (Production Phase)

In Part 2 the authors have dealt with problems associated with the production of an automated ISD. The specific questions addressed by the workshop included the following:

(a)   Which instructional development functions can and should be automated?
(b)   What theoretical issues are relevant to attempts to automate instructional development of computer-based simulations?
(c)   What are the implementation issues involved in the development of a system to automate the production of computer-based simulations?
(d)   How is progress to be evaluated?

The first chapter in this part, by Sancho, addresses issues of educational software development by taking into account the context of the learning environment. Sancho deals with philosophical themes that shape the interface between a proposed automated system the audience. Issues discussed range from organizational concerns to the specification of teaching and learning strategies. In this same vane of philosophical themes, Muraida proposes that evaluation most be an integral component of producing an automated system. Muraida develops the thesis that analysis of an automated ISD be carried out so that instructional designers are sensitive to the influences of different contexts on the nature of instructional development.

The two concluding chapters by Tennyson and Breuer (Chap. 9) and Wasson (Chap. 10) demonstrate two different approaches to the automation of ISD. Wasson reviews in detail expert system methods employed by what might now be considered the conventional approach to automating ISD. That is, taking existing instructional development models and producing systems based on production rule programming techniques. The assumption is that the existing ISD models provide the necessary structure by which to produce an automated system.

In contrast, Tennyson and Breuer propose, for ISD Expert, a neural network approach that advances the concept of self-organizational theory. That is, the system is much more dynamic because it does not assume the existence of a given system of ISD. Tennyson and Breuer present a model based upon the fourth generation of ISD presented in Chap. 3. ISD Expert advances automation in both content structure of instructional development as well as in the approach taken for the production of a system.

1.4 Automating Instructional Delivery (Implementation Phase)

In Part 3 of the book, questions dealing with the implementation of automated ISD are addressed. In both cases, the authors are presenting information based on actually experiences in setting-up and attempting to run an automated ISD. Questions covered by the authors and the workshop included the following:

(a)   When are computer-based, multi-media presentations useful and instructionally effective?

(b)   In which instructional settings are particular delivery modalities (tutorial, learner control, mixed initiative, guided discovery, etc.) and combinations effective?

(c)   What implementation issues are involved in creating effective and adaptive delivery modalities?

(d)   What are the relevant evaluation criteria?

In Chapter 11, Baker describes the design, production, and, finally, the implementation of an automated ISD--SHIVA. A system developed by a European consortium in France. Employing a basic second generation ISD model (i.e., a linear model of instructional development), SHIVA does a number of automatic processes while providing an option that adapts the instructional sequence to students' responses. The importance of the SHIVA project in the context of advancing information on automating ISD was the extensive formation evaluation performed by the developers.

Likewise, the University of Twente project described by Krammer and Dijkstra, offer an automated system employing a conventional system. In this case, Krammer and Dijkstra use an instructional strategy model for teaching concepts as the model of the system rather than actual ISD model as used for SHIVA. Also, the developers included evaluation as part of the development project so that generalizable outcomes could be realized.

The concluding chapter by Spector presents an extended argument for taking an integrated approach towards optimizing the use of the new interactive learning technologies for the basis of delivering complex instruction. The integration should include multi-phase ISD models (i.e., fourth generation models), learning theory, and the variety of technologies available.

1.5 Conclusion

Recent advances in computer-based interactive technologies have important implications for automated learning environments.   Incorporating these new technologies effectively into computer-based instructional settings, however, is not a simple task.

Often persons with inadequate knowledge of instructional technology, instructional design, and education psychology are asked to create effective instruction using a new technology. To insure that learning is effective when using new technologies it is important to plan instruction in accordance with established principles of learning theory, to carefully integrate instructional strategies, to provide flexible levels of advising for authors and students, to provide meaningful student interactions, to provide effective student modeling, and to design interfaces that are appropriate both to the task at hand and to the individual performing the task.

The challenge is great but the potential to provide vastly improved learning environments is greater. This workshop and book explore what can be done using new technologies in accord with principles of cognitive science. As such, the book is a blend of theory and application. The emphasis is on what is possible and what works. This book proceeds on the assumption that teachers are powerful and intelligent persons who mold minds and shape lives. Putting powerful and intelligent instructional design and development tools in the hands of such persons will have an extremely positive effect on learning.

Additional, this book provides new knowledge in the area of automating instructional design, development, and delivery by bringing together the best practitioners and academicians in Europe and North America. Illiteracy in industrialized countries is increasing at a time when technology demands skilled and education populations. To insure that education keeps pace with advances in technology we must find means to make the process of designing, developing, and delivering instruction more effective and more efficient.

As Europe and North America become a more integrated society maintaining a modern educational basis throughout the two continents will remain a high priority issue. Sharing research findings and developments that can already produce meaningful improvements in the educational system was and still is a basic motivating factor for the workshop and this book.

2

Foundations for Courseware Engineering

Peter Goodyear

Department of Educational Research and Centre for Studies in Advanced Learning Technology (CSALT), Lancaster University, Bailrigg, Lancaster, LA1 4YL, England

Abstract: This chapter reviews a number of key issues involved in automating the design, development and delivery of instruction. It uses an examination of these issues to assess the strength of the foundations that might be available for Courseware Engineering. It focuses on theoretical issues in the automation of instructional design, and provides illustrations from recent work in the European Community's advanced learning technologies programme, DELTA.

Keywords: courseware engineering, automation, instructional design

2.1 Introduction

My goal in this chapter is to sketch out some of the issues that emerge when one attempts to unpack what is involved in automating instructional system development (ISD). If a coherent picture begins to emerge, then the processes it depicts can reasonably be dubbed "Courseware Engineering." My secondary goal is to examine the foundations for Courseware Engineering, to see what they might consist of and whether they might be strong enough to meet the demands that will be placed upon them.

Figure 1 gives a schematic view of the intellectual concerns of the NATO ARW on "Automating instructional design, development and delivery." The workshop set out to address three phases in the lifecycle of courseware (design or planning," development or "production," and delivery or "implementation"). Four cross-cutting issue-sets were identified: motivational,

	Design (Planning)	Development (Production)	Delivery (Implementation)
Nature of the activity	a) Design of learning events, environments or resources b) From training analysis to detailed specifications, (or just the core design activities?) c) Design of all kinds of learning events, environments and resources (or just courseware?)	Transformations of the outputs of the design process into inputs adequate for effective execution of the delivery process	a) Teaching, Training or Instruction "face-to-face" b) Delivery through courseware
What would automation mean?	• Automatic transformation of (say) a list of training objectives into a specification for a sequence of instructional events • Computer-based ID advisor or consistency checker • Tools for more efficient, effective and/or enjoyable design work	(If courseware) • Automatic transformation of specifications into code • "Authoring" tools, shells	Courseware (economical replication of educational work)
Motivation for automation (Why would we want to automate?)	• ID is routine • ID is expensive • Good ID is crucial to everything else	• Development is routine	• Teaching is routine • Good teachers are scarce (courseware is economically distributable)
Theoretical Issues involved in automation	• Understanding the practice of ID • Understanding how to design ITSs (systems that do their own design, development & delivery)	• Understanding the development process for different courseware types	• Understanding interactive learning
Implementation Issues involved in automation	• Capturing ID expertise • Formalising ID phenomena • HCI of computer-aided ID	• Technology of code generators • Interfacing upstream & downstream modules • Integrating resources (ULMs) • HCI of authoring tools	• Effect of range of software genres • HCI of delivery systems • Representation of subject matter, learner(s), instructional strategies
Evaluation of the automation process (How would we know if automation had helped? Or, how should we study the process and results of automation?)	• Cost:effectiveness measures • More consistent, complete, unambiguous designs • Re-usable designs • User satisfaction	• Match between design intentions and delivery? • Development ratios • User satisfaction	• Improvements in learning • Cost:effectiveness measures • Learner satisfaction measures

Fig. 2.1. Automating Instructional Design, Development and Delivery: a space of issues.

theoretical, implementational and evaluational. Figure 1 helps define an issue space, and leads directly towards a closer examination of the meaning of the rough headings with which we began.

What I plan to do in this chapter is (a) interpret the nature of the activities involved in the three phases of the courseware lifecycle, (b) try to identify what automation might mean, in the context of each of those phases, (c) raise a number of questions about automation (under the four headings defining the issue sets) and, (d) focus particularly on:

- *theoretical* issues involved in the automation of *design,*
- *implementational* issues involved in the automation of *delivery*,
- *evaluation* issues in the automation of *development*.

The chapter concludes with some observations about courseware engineering derived from our recent work on EC DELTA projects such as TOSKA, SAFE/Simulate, DisCOURSE and OSCAR.

2.2   ISD: The Nature of the Activities

What is the nature of the first of the three phases identified? At heart, it consists of the design of learning events, learning resources and/or learning environments. It consists of the data-gathering, planning and other decision-making activities involved in specifying what these events, resources or environments should be. In theory, it should not include the actual running of learning events or the actual creation of learning resources or environments. In practice, this distinction is blurred by two phenomena. Firstly, a significant amount of instruction is interactive – to the extent that design can be said to take place dynamically, "on-the-fly." Secondly, iterative design and implementation techniques, such as rapid prototyping, necessarily interleave design and development activities. I will return to this shortly. For now, we can at least imagine that a coherent design phase exists, and recognize that this might be thought of as (a) all activities in the courseware development lifecycle from initial training analysis through to specification of functional and non-functional requirements, and detailed interface design, or (b) some core sub-set of these activities – such as those found in the practices of mainstream Instructional Design. This distinction is necessary when we come to address the requirements for, and feasibility of, automating design. Equally necessary is some clarity about the kinds of learning events, resources and environments whose design we contemplate automating. It is reasonable to consider automating the design of lectures, just as it is reasonable to consider hand-crafted design of intelligent tutoring systems [17]. The key is to be clear about the scope for decoupling design activities from delivery activities, for much apparent disagreement about the possibilities for automation can be traced to a conflation of these things.

What is involved in development? The answer is straightforward. Development is the transformation of the outputs of the design process into inputs which are adequate for the effective execution of the delivery process.

As for delivery, this might be teaching, training or instruction on a conventional "face-to-face" basis, or it might be delivery through courseware. It might be many other things besides: tutorial, seminar, discussion group, self-study text, tutor videotape, etc. For the purposes of this chapter, I will assume that the activity to be automated is not already automated --that we are considering ways of replacing or supplementing established delivery methods with courseware. I will apply this interpretation, henceforth, to both development and delivery phases, making the assumption that what is being developed is courseware.

2.3 What Would Automation Mean?

Automation is action which is performed mechanically, without human intervention. In cognitive science, it can also mean activity which, through repeated practice, can be engaged in without major demands on working memory. For our present purposes, I suggest we need two definitions of automation, one strong, the other weak. The strong definition takes automation to mean the *replacement* of human activity. The weak definition casts automation as *support* for a human agent, who is in control. It may be possible to reconcile these two views, by attending to the grain-size of the activity involved: replacing human agency in some sub-tasks of a process is a way of giving support. Nevertheless, the replacement:support distinction is evocative resilient and likely to persist in debate for some time.

(a)   Automation of design: (strong sense) would involve the automatic transformation of (say) a list of training objectives into a specification of a sequence of instructional events. In the weak sense, we can conceive of tools such as a computer-based instructional design adviser (see e.g., Gros & Rodriquez, Chap. 6) or a consistency checker: tools which relieve some of the cognitive burden on the instructional designer and contribute to making design more efficient, effective or enjoyable.

(b)   Automation of the development of courseware: (strong sense) implies the automatic transformation of specifications into code. In the weak sense, tools to support development include such things as authoring languages, authoring systems, user-interface management systems, shells of various kinds, etc.

(c)   Automation of delivery, I am taking to mean the use of courseware.

2.4 The Motivation for Automation

The general motivation for automation rests on two attributes of the process to be automated: it should be routine and it should be expensive. "Routine" means that the process is sufficiently consistent, sufficiently free from unpredictable or idiosyncratic events and sufficiently well understood. "Expense" need not be interpreted in a narrow financial way (though automation is a non-trivial and correspondingly expensive task in itself). Expense may include the subjective costs borne by people engaged in mindless, repetitive, demeaning *or* demanding, intellectually strenuous activity. It may also include the opportunity costs of under-utilizing expensive talents or the costs of errors consequent upon over-taxing designers or developers.

2.5 Theoretical Issues in the Automation of Design

What kind of theoretical concerns are bound up in automation? The most fundamental, and most powerful in their effects on the success of the enterprise, relate to the acquisition of a sound understanding of the practices involved. Theorizing the practices of courseware design (and development) represents the key element in providing a foundation for courseware engineering. In this chapter, I must limit my discussion to the following: an examination of some crucial inadequacies in the use of taxonomies for classifying instructional objectives, and an examination of the status of normative models of the instructional design process. There are many other aspects of theorization to be tackled. Among the more intriguing are questions posed in the intelligent tutoring systems field – such as how we might design systems that carry out their own instructional design, development and delivery tasks [5].

2.5.1 Taxonomies of Instructional Objectives

A major labor-saving device in the toolkit of the instructional designer is a taxonomy of learning objectives. Such taxonomies save labor (reduce the decision-making needed) through supporting a process of abstraction. Instead of taking a learning objective as unique, and deducing the learning processes that might be implicated in its attainment, and deducing the instructional events that might precipitate and support those learning processes, the instructional designer can re-use past design decisions by de-emphasizing the unique qualities of the learning objective and focusing on what it has in common with other, previously encountered, learning objectives. Classifying a learning objective in terms of an established taxonomy is the standard method of abstraction. This gives great importance to the adequacy of the taxonomy.

All taxonomies are open to criticism. After all, they are simplifications meant to be appropriate for certain kinds of task. From the viewpoint of another kind of task, a taxonomy may seem inappropriate or incomprehensible. So one needs to be careful not to dismiss a mental tool on inappropriate grounds. Nevertheless, it seems to me that the kinds of taxonomies current in instructional design provide some rather shaky foundations [3,12,41,20,18].

Let us examine, for example, a taxonomic system which divides instructional objectives or "learning outcomes" into categories such as the following:

- verbal information
- intellectual skill
  - concrete concept
  - defined concept
  - rule
  - higher-order rule
- cognitive strategy
- motor skill
- attitude

and which asserts that each of these types of learning outcome requires a different instructional treatment [41]. A key question has to be "what is the nature of the distinctions being drawn between the categories in such a taxonomy?." Wager and Gagné hold that these are different kinds of *performance* expected of a learner [41]. It's clear that by "performance" they do not mean just (observable) behavior, since their distinctions make reference to mental processes. For example "verbal information" is distinguished from the ability to recite, verbatim, a piece of prose, by specifying that constructive mental processes must be involved in the former. The learner must be able to give semantically equivalent, but lexically different, accounts of what they know ("putting it into their own words"), in order for the learning outcome to be labelled "verbal information" [41].

The problem I have with this, is that in any instance of the demonstration of such a learning outcome, it may be extraordinarily difficult to show that certain mental processes have been involved. The difficulty (some would say impossibility) of demonstrating that behavior x draws on mental process y and cognitive structure z is well documented (e.g., [43]). These long-standing reservations about the status of cognitive structures are being given new weight in debates about situated cognition and the dynamic, reconstructive nature of memory (e.g., [6,33]). This means that the category "verbal information" is defined through of a mixture of (a) *verifiable statements* about observable behaviors, (b) *hypotheses* about the nature of the cognitive processes underlying those behaviors.

If we turn to another of Gagné's distinctions, that between concrete and defined concepts, we find another dimension to the taxonomy. Thus, "..it would not be possible to identify a concept like *first cousin* by pointing to instances; nor would this be true of *city* or *cooking*" [41, p. 38, original italics). In Gagné ([12] Chaps. 5 & 6) further instances and non-instances of the concept of "defined concept" are given:

(a)   Jungle, City, Cousin, Diagonal

(b)   Tree, House, List (e.g., of numbers), Striated Muscle (instances are in list (a); non-instances, list (b)).

Part of what (for Gagné) distinguishes defined from concrete concepts is something new, which appears to be something intrinsic to the phenomena being conceptualized. There is something intrinsic to a tree that allows it to be learned as a concrete concept, whereas a jungle or a city cannot be learned by observation but have to be learned through verbal definition [12, pp. 129-130]. I say "appears" because in actuality, if there is a principle at work here, it involves a relation between a perceiver-learner and the phenomenon being perceived and learned. It amounts to saying, "in 'normal' circumstances, cities or jungles are too *big* to be observed." I find this an unsatisfactory kind of claim. It cries out for all sorts of counter-examples, of the form "if only you arranged things thus….it would be very easy to see how x could be a concrete concept." Since the making of such arrangements happens to lie at the heart of instructional activity, the solidity of the distinctions becomes very questionable. One is led to the view that things are not *necessarily* concrete or defined concepts, not *necessarily* higher-order rules rather than cognitive strategies, but that instructional assumptions and instructional arrangements can render them so. But this choice is a problem for us, because the very purpose of the taxonomy is meant to be to help us prepare the ground for *making* such choices. The intimacy of the relation between what is to be learned and the manner of its learning undermines the ostensible utility of the taxonomy.

This leads one to ask whether there can be a taxonomy of learning outcomes or instructional objectives which is sufficiently independent of learning processes and instructional activity that it can be used as the starting point for making predictions about learning processes and decisions about instructional activities. On what would such a taxonomy be based? This seems to me a major issue for research, and one in which a perspective shift: from instructor's view to learner's view, is long overdue. We need to achieve an understanding of learned capabilities which is informed by study of the actual practices embodying those capabilities (how "just plain folks" actually do what they do [19]) and by clearer knowledge of the contexts in which those capabilities are acquired and demonstrated.

A more radical proposal would be to say that since (a) we can have no reliable knowledge of a learner's mental states and mental processes and (b) it is un-controversial to see the learner as an active, construing, meaning-making participant in the learning:teaching interaction, instructional design should shift its focus from manipulating the learner to generating an interpretable, consistent behavior on the part of the instructional system. I find this a more convincing paradigm for courseware design, particularly when we come to design tasks outside the old core of tutorial and drill-and-practice programs. In the design of knowledge-based systems, simulations or exploratory tools, key design requirements revolve around the need for systems to be comprehensible. What's needed is a creative fusion of ideas and practices from the instructional design and human:computer interface fields.

2.5.2 Theorizing the Practice of Instructional Design

The second concern which I have space to air, questions the adequacy of our notions of instructional design. Models of instructional design abound in the literature [2,28] Most if not all of these models are normative, in the sense that they say how design should be done, rather than how it is done in practice. They are prescriptive rather than descriptive. This is fine, given the goals of (a) systematizing a dilute version of instructional design so that it might be embodied in an expert system [21], or (b) teaching the rudiments of instructional design to novices. It is problematic, however, when our goals include (c) helping novice instructional designers acquire the heuristic knowledge of experienced designers (how can we model their development path?), or (d) building ID support tools that will integrate with the complex practices of contemporary design work [13].

The research need here is based on recognizing the good sense of designing computer tools or computer systems based around what users actually need and do, rather than around textbook accounts of what they *should* do. Such research needs to recognize the material circumstances which impact upon, and contextualize, design work. It needs to avoid the task-idealization underlying statements like:

An instructional design, like other designs, involves selecting among alternative means to achieve *certain ends*. These ends are instructional goals [26] (my emphasis).

Implied by such a view is the existence of well-specified instructional goals and an image of the task as a search through a space of instructional designs. This idealization needs to be contrasted with what we know about the practice of instructional design, from such sources as the Startup project [37] and similar surveys of design work [e.g., 42]. The following key points are based on data from those reports.

- *ID practice should be seen as a dialectic between (a) available solutions and (b) the definition and refinement of instructional goals*

Experienced designers are able to modify and re-use designs, design components, and learning materials; their knowledge of the availability of design *solutions* shapes their evolving understanding and definition of learning objectives. This portrays ID neither as a top-down, objectives-driven activity, nor as a bottom-up, opportunistic activity, but as a skilful interweaving of the two. Tools and methods are needed which support, and structure, such practices.

- *The top level goal of an instructional designer is not to produce an optimal plan for instruction but to no longer have an instructional design problem.*

To think otherwise is to abstract the designer from the material circumstances in which they work.

- *Constraints on the instructional designer are not just constraints of the instructional situation (such as what delivery platform some courseware must run on). Constraints also include the time and resources available for the design stage, relations between design and the rest of production, and the imperatives of the production process.*

The designer works in a context in which success is determined not by the quality of the learning that results from the courseware but by whether the client organization comes back to commission another product. The key organizational imperative which impacts on the designer is repeat business. What determines whether the client comes back with repeat business? There is no evidence to suggest that hard data about improvements in the efficiency or effectiveness of learning plays any part in determining whether or not the client organization (a) views the courseware project as a success, and (b) comes back with repeat business [37]. Among producers themselves there is no clear picture:

> While there is general agreement among producers that the quality of the courseware they produce is of paramount importance, there is no consensus regarding the meaning of that term [37, p. 105].

Hard evidence about gains in efficiency and/or effectiveness is not used, because it is rarely gathered. At least in the areas covered by the Startup and USAF surveys [42], we can be fairly confident that evaluation is almost always limited to:

(a) Integrity checking (does the software crash?)
(b) Drivability (can a user navigate through the software?)
     Evaluation rarely involves representative learners.

Knowing that courseware designers rarely if ever get reliable feedback on the efficacy of their designs is important if we want to understand the forces which shape the practices of instructional design, which must itself be a pre-requisite for designing tools that are compatible with practice.

2.6 Evaluation Issues in the Automation of Courseware Development

The focal question here is: how do we know that automation has helped? In particular, how do we judge whether the delivery courseware matches its specification? This is already recognized as a major problem in mainstream software engineering (e.g., [34] & [36]). The use of formal specification methods is put forward as one solution, but it needs to be recognized that (a) formal specification methodologies are still little used and little tested in real production settings, (b) formal notations can be hard to learn and use – a problem in mainstream software development groups which is likely to impact much more strongly on courseware development teams, given the current mix of skills [37], (c) much of the complexity involved in specifying and validating courseware derives from the inherently interactive nature of the product. Formal methods applicable to highly interactive systems are even less developed than those for conventional data processing systems.

The relation between a system and its specification is also a major theme in ITS R&D. In so far as ITS work emphasizes the generalizability of results, rather than restricting itself to the building of individual systems [22], it is of crucial importance to attend to the relations between (a) an implemented system (b) the theory-base that the system is meant to be instantiating. Some projects (e.g., Memolab, [10]) have paid scrupulous attention to such relations, making them an important object of study. But even in such projects, the complexity of the behavior of the system and the length of the causal chain between theory and behavior make a demonstration of the relations extremely problematic. The same is true even in quite simple research-oriented CAI systems, such as those designed to implement and compare alternative pedagogic strategies (e.g., [25]). In such studies the interpretation of findings is made extremely difficult by the problems of distinguishing between (a) the alternate pedagogical strategies under test (b) the specification of those strategies, (c) their implementation in the system(s) used, (d) the run-time behavior of the system(s), (e) the run-time behavior as apprehended by the subject:learners in the experiments.

Alternatively, or additionally, we can adopt a view of evaluation which is illuminative rather than judgmental [38] and say that what we really need, at this stage, are studies of the process and results of automation, unfettered by strong prescriptions about what *ought* to be happening. How, for example, do we evaluate the impact of new tools or automation on the roles and skills in involved in courseware development [8,37].

2.7 Implementation Issues in the Automation of Delivery

In many discussions of courseware design and development methods, scant attention is paid to the *variety* of ways in which computers can support learning [16]. It is far from clear that instructional design methods that are tuned to the production of drill-and-practice software work equally well for (say) computer simulations. Since courseware can include such *genres* as tutorial CBT, simulations, modelling tools, hypermedia, interactive video, intelligent tutoring systems and intelligent or interactive learning environments, it can be argued that a common/standard courseware engineering methodology will not be sufficient to the task and that the design knowledge base for courseware engineering is severely restricted in its scope. Implementation issues arising from decisions about delivery media will necessarily feed back to earlier stages in the courseware lifecycle. This suggests, once more, a need for iterative development methods that allow, and discipline, progressive refinement of both requirements and candidate solutions.

2.8 Tools and Methods in the "Upstream" Phases of Courseware Production

A strong theme in this chapter has been the necessity of grounding the automation of instructional design and development activities in a realistic account of the practices of instructional designers and developers. The same message holds true for courseware engineering. As was and is the case with software engineering, advances towards and in courseware engineering will need to be informed by robust models of the practices involved. In this last main section of the chapter I want to draw out a few illustrations from the EC DELTA programme of R&D in advanced learning technologies [8,14,27]. I will start with a few points about courseware engineering models and go on to look at some work on abstraction and re-use of instructional designs.

2.8.1 Courseware Engineering Models

The "conventional wisdom" on courseware development methodology is encapsulated in the "waterfall model" (e.g., [1,29,30]) This posits that the process consists of discrete stages of requirements analysis, specification, design, implementation, system integration and operation. Interpretations of the model vary in a number of ways, most crucially in terms of the feedback that may or may not be allowed from one stage to another. Some interpretations, realized as working procedures or quality assurance procedures in courseware companies, involve a client signing-off (approving) a specification before design work begins, after which point changes to the specification are prohibited.   This is meant to reduce the probability of expensive implementation changes consequent upon revisions to the specification or other "upstream" documents.

The main difficulty with the "waterfall" approach arises when the client either (a) has difficulty understanding the documents that contain the requirements analysis, specification or design detail, and/or (b) has a poorly articulated understanding of their requirement in the first place.   "Small wonder that software developers live in fear of the sentence, 'I know this is what I asked for, but it isn't really what I wanted'" [34, p.49; cf.24].

The difficulty of helping a client understand what a product will be like, through using paper-based specification documents, has done much to stimulate the use of rapid prototyping methods, both in software engineering and in courseware development [7, 34, 36].   Rapid prototyping consists of a number of fast iterations through a specify-design-implement-review loop, in which both developers and the client can refine their understanding of the client's requirement through the use of prototype products that increasingly resemble the desired system.

The rapid prototyping model has at least two major strengths. First, it is more consistent than the waterfall model with the kinds of practices I described earlier in this chapter - practices which represent a dialectic between problems and solutions rather than an orderly march from the former to the latter.   Second, it is being empowered by highly productive new tools that support rapid prototyping; especially rapid prototyping of user interfaces.

A special case of rapid prototyping is Boehm's spiral model [4].   Implications of the spiral model for courseware engineering have been described in [7].   Elaborating a little on their formulations, the spiral model for courseware engineering can be thought of as follows:

(a)   the essence of courseware engineering is seen to be *model refinement* – a process through which a model (or more usually a set of models) of the desired system is made increasingly more concrete and specific

(b)   the system under construction is partitioned in terms of a number of design components (e.g., a subject matter or "domain" component, a teaching strategies or "pedagogic" component, a student attributes or "learner model" component and a user interface component).

(c)   refinement of each design component proceeds through a "loop" of activities (Figure 2.2)

(d)   each loop consists of the following stages: risk assessment, refinement, compliance testing, integrity checking

(e)   looping is terminated when compliance testing and integrity checking reach defined thresholds.

Risk assessment is a key motivating feature of Boehm's spiral model. Periodic risk assessment is used to determine what should be refined next (a "riskiest things first" strategy minimizes overall costs). If there is little risk associated with leaving one of the design component models at its current level of abstraction, then little or no work is done on its refinement at that stage in the development program. Work concentrates on refinement of higher-risk components.

Refinement means making the current model more concrete or specific. An example might be moving down a level in a task-decomposition hierarchy (spelling out the details of how someone is meant to carry out the task for which they are to be trained). Another example might be instantiating a domain-independent teaching strategy (e.g., "give example" becomes "give an example of a widget-testing device").

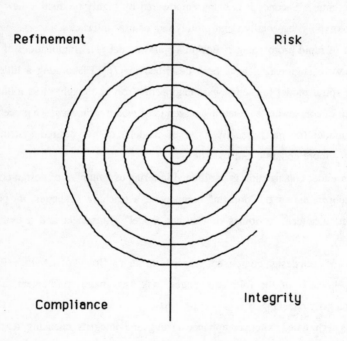

Fig. 2.2. Spiral model for courseware engineering.

Compliance testing: involves checking the new state of the model against the current understanding of requirements. This involves the communication of key aspects of the model to personnel (critically, personnel from the client organization). Tools and methods to support such communication are still very rudimentary and represent a major area for R&D work. They include prototyping methods – which are reasonably well advanced as far as the user-interface is concerned but are primitive or absent when communication about other design components is concerned.

Integrity checking: means that periodic checks are made on the possibility of integrating (a) the several design components, (b) the system with its operating environment.

2.8.2 Abstractions of Instructional Methods

The spiral model means that courseware engineers need to be able to work, at the outset, at relatively abstract levels. They need to be able to model instructional activities etc. at much more abstract levels than is common in conventional courseware authoring, where the work is tied very closely to the presentation level or final "look and feel" of the delivered system. Such levels of abstraction are not unfamiliar in the instructional design field. As an instance, Salisbury [32] talks about approaches to drill-and-practice courseware using terms like "two pool drills," "three pool drills," "progressive state drills," and "variable item interval drills." Courseware engineering tools should support work at such levels of abstraction, rather than, as now, forcing the expression of such design ideas in the concrete form of the screen displays that the learner will see. An approach to the provision of support for working at higher levels of abstraction can be found in GTE (for a review of GTE, see Wasson, Chap. 10).

2.8.3 Re-use of Learning Materials and "Half-fabricates"

The view of instructional design, and, more generally, of courseware engineering, as involving a dialectic between problems and solutions has implications for supporting the re-use of solutions. This has manifested itself within DELTA research projects in terms of repositories of (a) Units of Learning Material (ULMs) and (b) "half-fabricates" or "semi-finished" materials. ULMs are low-level "building blocks" such as still images, video clips, text fragments, etc that can be stored in a library (such as an object-oriented database), indexed in terms of a ULM description language, browsed and incorporated into courseware. DELTA projects such as ESM-BASE [23], and SHIVA [11] have made extensive use of this approach and their follow ups (eg OSCAR) are currently developing and testing database and other courseware engineering tools. Working at various levels of abstraction can be supported by storing and re-using not only ULMs but also more complex artefact, such as instructional designs, learner modelling management systems [35], bug libraries, and instructional case libraries. Ground-breaking work on the infrastructure for re-use of "half-fabricates" has been completed in the OS-ID sub-project of SAFE [9].

2.8.4 Documentation of Instructional Design(s)

The iterative elaboration of design component models places heavy demands on project management and especially on methods for the effective communication of ideas. In the OSCAR project we have been exploring the sharing and re-use of instructional design documents [39]. This draws on, and extends, work on IDE, the Instructional Design Environment [31]. Our work in this area, both within the OSCAR project and beyond, has a number of goals. One is to facilitate communication within a design team, and between the design team and the system implementors. By extension, this gives shared on-line documentation a key role in managing courseware engineering projects. A second goal is to support the recording of design decisions (especially in documenting the design rationale). This supports a third goal, one shared with IDE, namely supporting the re-use of designs. The fourth goal is, we believe, more original and is concerned with the direct effects on learning of exposure to instructional design rationales.

This represents a convergence of two streams of ideas. From expert systems research we take the notion of explanation and self-explaining systems – that usable intelligent systems have to be able to provide some explanation of their reasoning. From research in metacognition we take the idea that a learner who consciously reflects on her own learning processes will learn more effectively. This suggests that we experiment with CAI or ICAI systems that can provide explanations not only of their "domain" of expertise (physics, helicopter blade maintenance or whatever), but also of their pedagogical decisions. This can be done if systems designers are caused to make explicit the rationale behind the pedagogical decisions embedded in, or made by, their systems. Couching such a rationale in language that is meaningful to the learner would represent a fair test of its adequacy [15].

2.9 Conclusion

In this chapter I have used the schema for the ARW as a starting point for exploring issues in the nascent field of Courseware Engineering. I paid particular attention to design, since design is so central and fundamental an activity, with manifold implications. I sketched some starting points for theorizing the practices of instructional design, since a degree of compatibility with practice is essential to successful tools and innovative methodologies. As courseware design and development grow in complexity, so it becomes necessary to create models (however provisional) of what we are doing, in order that we can communicate and collaborate in our work. I outlined some characteristics of a spiral model for a Courseware Engineering lifecycle. Finally, I described some approaches to aspects of Courseware Engineering consistent with the spiral model.

Acknowledgements

This chapter could not have been written without many fruitful discussions I have had over a number of years in DELTA project teams and with courseware developers. I would especially like to thank Robin Johnson (TOSKA and DisCOURSE projects), Bob Lewis, Joan Machell and

Lucinda Beier (Startup Project) at Lancaster; also members of the SAFE/Simulate team, particularly Jos van Berkum, Ton de Jong, Wouter van Joolingen, Melanie Njoo, Ken Tait; staff of Dida*el and Knowledge Technologies associated with GTE (Kris van Marcke, Stefano Cerri, Angus McIntyre), and participants in the NATO ARWs at Maratea (1991) and Sitges (1992). This work was partially supported by EC DELTA grants for the projects SAFE/Simulate, TOSKA, OSCAR and DisCOURSE). Final thanks to Mike Spector: "now at least we know what we don't know."

References

1.   Alessi, S., & Trollip, S.: Computer-based instruction: Methods and development (2nd ed.). Englewood Cliffs, NJ: Prentice Hall 1991

2.   Andrews, D., & Goodson, L.: A comparative analysis of models of instructional design. Journal of Instructional Development,3, 2-16 (1980)

3.   Bloom, B. et al.: Taxonomy of educational objectives I: Cognitive domain. London: Longman 1956

4.   Boehm, B.: A spiral model of software development and enhancement. IEEE Computer, 21, 61-72 (1988)

5.   Burns, H., Parlett, J., & Redfield, C. (Eds.): Intelligent tutoring systems: Evolutions in design. Hillsdale, NJ: Lawrence Erlbaum 1991

6.   Clancey, W.: Representations of knowing: In defense of cognitive apprenticeship. Artificial Intelligence in Education, 3, 139-168 (1992)

7.   de Hoog, R., de Jong, T., & de Vries, F.: Outline of a SIMULATE authoring methodology. Amsterdam: Dept. of Social Science Informatics 1991

8.   DELTA Office: Research and technology development of telematic systems for flexible and distance learning. Brussels: Delta Office 1992

9.   Derks, M., & Bulthuis, W.: A framework for authoring tool integration, In Precise Consortium, Learning technology in the European Communities (pp. 549-562). Dordrecht: Kluwer 1992

10.   Dillenbourg, P.: The lift in the pyramid: A metaphor for designing educational computing systems that develop metacognitive skills. Paper at the NATO ASI on Syntheses of Instructional Science and Computing Science for Effective Instructional Systems, Calgary (July 1990)

11.   Elsom-Cook, M. The ECAL teaching engine: Pragmatic AI for education. In Precise Consortium, Learning technology in the European Communities (pp. 329-340). Dordrecht: Kluwer 1992

12.   Gagné, R.M.: The conditions of learning (4th ed.). New York: Holt, Rinehart & Winston 1985

13. Goel V., & Pirolli, P.:M otivating the notion of generic design within information processing theory: The design problem space. Report No: UC-TR-DPS-1, University of California at Berkeley 1988

14. Goodyear, P.: Development of learning technology at the European level: The DELTA programme. Educational & Training Technology International, 26, 335-341 (1989)

15. Goodyear, P,, O'Malley, C., & Mayes, T.: Pedagogical visibility in Intelligent Tutoring Systems, as yet unfunded research proposal, Lancaster University 1991

16. Jonassen, D.: Instructional designs for microcomputer courseware. London: Lawrence Erlbaum 1988

17. Jones, M., & Wipond, K.: Intelligent environments for curriculum and course development. In P. Goodyear (Ed.), Teaching knowledge and intelligent tutoring (pp. 379-398). Norwood, NJ: Ablex 1991

18. Kyllonen, P., & Shute, V.: A Taxonomy of learning skills. In P. Ackerman, R. Sternberg, & R Glaser (Eds.) Learning and individual differences (pp. 117-163). New York: Freeman 1989

19. Lave, J.: Cognition in practice. Cambridge: Cambridge University Press 1988

20. Merrill, M.D.: Applying component display theory to the design of courseware. In D. Jonassen (Ed.) Instructional designs for microcomputer courseware (pp. 61-96). London: Lawrence Erlbaum 1988

21. Merrill, M.D., & Li, Z.: An instructional design expert system. Journal of Computer-Based Instruction, 16, 95-101, (1989)

22. Ohlsson, S.: System hacking meets learning theory: Reflections of the goals and standards of research in artificial intelligence and education. Artificial Intelligence in Education, 2, 5-18, (1989)

23. Olimpo, G. et al.: On the concept of reusability in educational design. In Precise Consortium, Learning technology in the European Communities (pp. 535-545) Dordrecht: Kluwer 1992

24. Oliver, G.: A commercial producer's perspective. Paper presented at the NATO ARW on Advanced Authoring Systems, Maratea (May 1991)

25. Pieters, J., Simons, P., & de Leeuw, L. (Eds.) Research on computer based instruction. Amsterdam: Swets & Zeitlinger 1991

26. Pirolli, P., & Greeno, J.: The problem space of instructional design. In J. Psotka et al. (Eds.), Intelligent tutoring systems: Lessons learned (pp. 181-202). Hillsdale, NJ: Lawrence Erlbaum 1988

27. Precise Consortium: Learning technology in the European Communities. Dordrecht: Kluwer 1992

28. Reigeluth, C.M.: Instructional design: What is it and Why is it?. In C.M. Reigeluth (Ed.) Instructional design: Theories and models (pp. 3-36). Hillsdale, NJ: Lawrence Erlbaum 1983

29. Roblyer, M.: Fundamental problems and principles of designing effective courseware. In D. Jonassen (Ed.), Instructional designs for microcomputer courseware (pp. 7-34). London: Lawrence Erlbaum 1988

30. Royce, W.: Managing the development of large software systems: Concepts and techniques. Proceedings of WestCon, (August 1979)

31. Russell, D., Moran, T., & Jordan, D.: The instructional design environment. In J. Psotka et al. (Eds), Intelligent tutoring systems: Lessons learned. Hillsdale, NJ: Lawrence Erlbaum 1988

32. Salisbury, D.: Effective drill & practice strategies. In D. Jonassen (Ed), Instructional designs for microcomputer courseware (pp. 103-124). London: Lawrence Erlbaum 1988

33. Sandberg, J., & Weilinga, B.: Situated cognition: A paradigm shift? Artificial Intelligence in Education, 3, 129-138 (1992)

34. Schach, S.R.: Software engineering. Boston, MA: Aksen Associates 1990

35. Self, J.: Tools for building learner models. In Precise Consortium, Learning technology in the European Communities (pp. 317-328). Dordrecht: Kluwer 1992

36. Sommerville, I.: Software engineering (3rd ed.) Wokingham, UK: Addison Wesley 1989

37. Startup Project: Production of multimedia materials for education and training in Europe. Paris: OTE 1991

38. Thorpe, M.: Evaluating open and distance learning. Harlow, UK: Longman 1988

39. Valley, K.: Requirements analysis and specification of a courseware authoring project management toolset. OSCAR Deliverable 2. Brussels: Delta Office 1992

40. van Marcke, K.: A generic tutoring environment. Proceedings of ECAI-90 (1990)

41. Wager, W., & Gagné, R.M.: Designing computer-aided instruction. In D. Jonassen (Ed.), Instructional designs for microcomputer courseware (pp. 35-66). London: Lawrence Erlbaum 1988

42. Walsh, W. et al.,: A survey of Air Force computer based training (CBT) planning, selection and implementation issues. Report AL-TP-1991-0059, Air Force Systems Command, Brooks Air Force Base, TX 1992

43. Winograd, T.: Frame representations and the declarative/procedural controversy. In D. Bobrow, & A. Collins (Eds.), Representation and understanding: Studies in cognitive science (pp. 185-210). Hillsdale, NJ: Lawrence Erlbaum 1975

3

Knowledge Base for Automated Instructional System Development

Robert D. Tennyson

Learning and Cognition, Department of Educational Psychology, University of Minnesota, 178 Pillsbury Dr. S.E., Minneapolis, MN 55455, USA

Abstract: Described is a knowledge base for automating instructional system development (ISD). The knowledge base is formulated from four generations of ISD models. First generation models (ISD[1]), founded in behavioral learning, employed systems theory to enhance subject matter expert instructional design. Second generation models (ISD[2]) evolved into increasingly complex ISD systems that required trained technicians to develop instruction. Third generation models (ISD[3]), with increased concern for evaluation, required the special skills of expert instructional designers to manipulate phases of ISD. Fourth generation models (ISD[4]), employing advancements from cognitive science, are applying intelligent programming techniques to automate ISD for subject matter expert instructional development.

Keywords: instructional development, intelligent systems, rule-based systems, instructional design, systems approach, cognitive science

3.1 Introduction

Instructional system development (ISD) refers to a set of procedures to guide instructional designers in the evaluation, analysis, design, production, and implementation of learning environments. This systematic guidance is represented in the form of operational instructional system development (ISD) models. Attributes defined in ISD models are supported by a diverse set of characteristics: system structure, evaluation activities, learning theory, instructional development (ID) processes, author subject matter and ID expertise, and authoring activities (see Table 3.1). Foundations for the ISD models are offered by the available descriptive theories of learning and prescriptive theories of instruction [8]. Figure 3.1 illustrates the foundational support of ISD models by linking instructional development to instructional theory to learning theory to philosophy of learning [22].

Learning Philosophy ↔	**Learning Theory** ↔	**Instructional Theory** ↔	**Instructional Implementation Models**
Logical explanation of the phenomena of learning:	Descriptive models of the how and why of learning.	Prescriptive variables and conditions to implement learning theory.	Systems that provide the means to produce learning environments.
			Teacher-dependent
Nature (Genetic Influences)	How: Description of how the mental system operates.	The purpose of instructional theory is to improve learning.	Teacher-independent
Nurture (Environmental Influences)			The purpose of instructional models is to enhance the learning environment.
	Why: Description of why the mental system performs.		

Fig. 3.1. Foundations of instructional system development (ISD).

Defining the direct linkages between the philosophies of learning and the respective learning and instructional theories helps maintain application integrity of ISD models. For example, it is not possible to implement cognitive psychology into instructional strategies if the educational philosophy remains rooted in a view of the human organism that learns solely from externally controlled environments.

This chapter presents the developmental growth of ISD by defining four generations of ISD models which exhibit advancements coming from sources both internal and external to the field of educational technology. Discussing the updates of disciplines or fields by identifying distinguishable generations is an appropriate approach to chronicle major developments. For example, Guba and Lincoln [10] discussion four generations of evaluation; distinguishing the four generations by identifying the evolving role activities of the evaluator.   In another educational field, Bunderson, Olson, and Li [2] provide a literature review describing four generations of computer-based testing (with the fourth generation managed by intelligent systems).

The purposes of this chapter are to (a) summarize the variables and conditions of the four generations of ISD and (b) operationally define the contemporary ISD[4] models in terms of their theoretical foundations and authoring activities.   Although many of the defined authoring activities are extensions from the previous three generations, the focus will be on the those activities both changed and added by new developments in such areas as cognitive science, educational research, and educational technology. The authoring activities provide the first level of specification for rule-based automated instructional design systems.

3.2 Instructional System Development

This section will summary the growth of the instructional design field by identifying the variables and conditions of instructional development. The field of instructional design was initiated by the United States Department of Defense during World War II to improve the efficiency of certain types of high-level technical training programs (e.g., pilot training) [16]. By the 1950s, behavioral learning theory-based instructional design principles for the improvement of teaching were introduced. Skinner's [18] approach to the behavioral learning paradigm set the initial theoretical foundation for instructional theory and ISD.   Skinner proposed a concept for models of instruction that consisted of formal and generalizable methods of instructional design supported by clearly defined principles of behavioral learning.   The behavioral paradigm defined by Skinner [19] for instructional theory contained the following three principles:

- Small incremental steps of content presentation
- Overt (active) learner responding
- Immediate reinforcement of correct responses

This instructional approach assumes that the student can make only correct responses. However, in practice, the approach seems useful only in those learning situations that are relatively short in duration and that do not have complex associations. To account for more complex behavioral situations that might imply the possibility of error and/or having multiple possible answers, Crowder [4] elaborated on Skinner's paradigm by integrating Pressey's [15] multiple-choice testing/teaching machine with the following two principles:

- Knowledge of results feedback on both correct and incorrect responses
- Branching in response to errors and/or mistakes

The behavioral paradigm for instructional theory maintained that learning of a task was basically the reinforcement of correct responses to given stimuli. The behavioral paradigm remained basically the foundational learning theory through the first three generations of ISD models (see Table 3.1).

To assist in the preparation of appropriate instructional materials to improve learning, ISD models were constructed around general systems theory principles which identified a number of general (ill-defined) activities to be performed by an instructional developer. In one of the first ISD models, Glaser [7] identified the following five interactive components (see Figure 3.2):

- Preparing behavioral objectives
- Designing a pretest
- Producing instructional program
  Designing a posttest
- Conducting a formative evaluation

From that original set of procedures, ISD models rapidly expanded as educational technology advanced in the media areas of computer and video instructional delivery systems. The growth of the models was, however, based solely on procedures thought to enhance development of instruction, not necessarily on the support of advancements in learning theory. That is, the ISD models expanded in complexity independently of developments learning theories.

For example, Gropper [9] added six ISD components to Glaser's original five:
- Learner assessment (i.e., other measures beyond the pre-and posttests)
- Sequencing of goals and content
- Learner analysis
- Instructional strategies
- Media selection
- Implementation and maintenance

By the end of the 1970s, Andrews and Goodson [1], in a review of ISD models, identified four more generally used ISD components. These were:
- Needs analysis
- Alternatives
- Constraints
- Costs

In all, Andrews and Goodson [1] reviewed over 60 different ISD models from which they selected 40 to analyze, using the complete set ISD components listed above as comparison variables.

In summary, the initial ISD models directly exhibited the theoretical foundations of behavioral learning theory in their principles of instruction. The growth in the models was not a direct result of developments in learning research but rather in ways to enhance both the efficiency of the instructional development process and the quality of the product. Thus, ISD models development from two separate and independent fields: Initially, from the foundations of learning principles and, secondly, from standard systems theory. The first field provided the learning theory foundation while from the second evolved processes for product development.

Research and theory advancements in cognitive science and educational technology and research in the past two decades provide a means to update both the learning theory foundation and the operational procedures of ISD models. These developments also offer recommendations for changes and adjustments within the system itself.

3.2.1 Overview of Changes

Beginning in the early 1970's, learning psychologists with an interest in classroom learning [11] began to discuss the shortcomings of the behavioral paradigm to the demands of classroom learning needs.   Offered as substitutes to the behavioral paradigm were learning theories proposed from cognitive-based theories. The description of the learning process shifted from the stimulus-response-reinforcement paradigm to an acquisition, storage, and retrieval of knowledge paradigm (see Figure 3.1).

As a result of the cognitive shifts in learning and instructional theories, the emphasis in instructional development procedures also gradually shifted from the behaviorally-based to the following:
- Organization of information (i.e., knowledge base),
- Acquisition and employment of knowledge (i.e., pedagogy base),
- Representations of knowledge in memory,
- Situational or contextual nature of learning,
- Constructing of knowledge and skills from employment of higher-order cognitive strategies.

Examples of the effect of cognitive psychology on the learning paradigm shift can be seen in how it has influenced several instructional theories. Gagné's instructional theory, as defined in his conditions of learning, shows a profound transformation from a behavioral paradigm with emphasis on associative and assimilation theory [5] to a cognitive theory with concern for understanding of the internal processes of learning and thinking [6].

Merrill's work, likewise, reflects a direct shift in the underlying learning theory in his approach to instructional development. In his Component Display Theory [12], Merrill drops the notion of behavioral objectives in favor of such components as a student model (knowledge stored in memory) and a knowledge base (domain of information).

In another example, Tennyson's instructional theory makes a direct trace of each of eight instructional variables through the knowledge base to specific learning processes [21]. While more recently expanding the knowledge base to include not only declarative (knowing that) and procedural (knowing how) knowledge but also contextual knowledge (knowing why, when and where). His instructional theory links directly cognitive processes with specific instructional strategies, with the instructional strategies ranging from expository presentations (to improve declarative knowledge) to self-directed strategies (to improve creative processes).

During this same time period, educational technologists were focusing their work on the direct interaction of media attributes with learning and instruction [17]. Because of the learning paradigm shift from behavioral to cognitive, instructional technologists became increasingly concerned with the "why" of media in the improvement of learning as well as the "how" [3]. This interest was accelerated with the rapid growth of microcomputers starting in the late 1970s.

An emerging paradox in educational technology was the fear that the exciting advances in hardware and software would dominate the ISD process to the exclusion of other concerns. For example, in applications of artificial intelligence (AI) methods to instructional computing, the focus was on software intelligence with only a narrow foundation in learning philosophy. For example, the technology emphasis by ICAI (intelligent, computer-assisted instruction) developers tended to reduce attention on most other educational concerns of ISD in favor of simple instructional methods and strategies [14].

However, the potential impact of educational technology on the ISD process is readily seen in several areas. These include methods of information analysis (e.g., expert systems), learner interaction with media (e.g., mixed initiative, natural language dialogue), means of learner assessment during learning (e.g., error analysis diagnosis), and control of the learning environment (e.g., learner control, advisement, coaching).

3.2.2 Attributes of ISD Models

The field of instructional system development has evolved over the past several decades from a relatively simple set of procedures that could be performed by a teacher to a complex set of authoring activities requiring highly skilled instructional development experts. The developments of ISD can be defined through four distinct generations employing six instructional development model attributes: system design, evaluation, learning theory, ID processes, ID author, and authoring activities. These are summarized below and compared in Table 3.1.

- System design. Systems theory implies some form of defined interaction between variables. These interactions can be of a logical order controlled by predefined relationships or a fluid nature relative to a given situation. In ISD application, the system designs have ranged from linear to integrated based on the increased complexity of the variables and conditions associated with instructional development. To account for increased complexity, system designs reflect more problem solution techniques associated with human expertise or artificial intelligent methods.

Table 3.1. Summary of Attributes for Four Generations of ISD

Attributes	Generation			
	ISD[1]	ISD[2]	ID[3]	ISD[4]
System	Linear	Flow-chart	Phases	Integrated
Evaluation	Formative	Formative/ Summative Summative	Feasibility Formative Formative Maintenance Maintenance	Situational Feasibility Summative
Learning Theory	Behavioral	Behavioral	Behavioral (Cognitive)	Cognitive (Behavioral)
Process	Step-by-Step (simple)	Step-by-Step (complex)	Phase-by-Phase	Knowledge Base
Author	Content Expert (system novice)	Technician (content novice)	ID Expert (content novice)	Content/ System (tool) Expert
Authoring Activities	Ill-defined	Operational Definitions	Expert Defined	Explicit Rules

- Evaluation. Traditionally, ISD has incorporated advancements coming from the field of program evaluation. Although, the development of evaluation concepts have come within the context of general education, they have been readily adopted into ISD. For example, the concept of formative evaluation was first proposed as a means to evaluation students needing remedial assistance. However, the concept of formative evaluation provided the first means for making ISD a system with a quality control revision cycle. Presently, evaluation exhibits a dominate influence that provides the prescriptions for instructional development depending on the situational environment. The additional forms of evaluation added over the growth of ISD include: summative (final report on effectiveness of the product), feasibility (determining the scope of a possible ID effort), and maintenance (an on-going assessment of a product to evaluate continued employment).

- Learning theory. ISD was from the start the means by which learning theory could be directly implemented into classroom instructional design. Behavioral theory as the foremost learning theory in the 1960s, became by default, the learning foundation for the first generation of ISD. By the 1980s, cognitive psychology was becoming the preferred learning theory foundation for ISD. However, each of the generations has been affected by competing learning theories. For example, both the third and fourth generations can accommodate a combination of any useful learning theory.

- Process. Implementation of the system's design is accomplished through specification of a given models's procedures. With the relatively simple nature of the first generation's system design, the process of ID consisted of a linear sequence of step-by-step procedures. As ISD expanded, the step-by-step procedures of the flow-chart system evolved into a linear set of phases more or less organized by the conditions of the given ID task; with the contemporary generation collapsing numerous overlapping procedures into an integrated process prescribed by a situational evaluation.

- Author. Design of instruction in the first generation of ISD was in the hands of the teacher or subject matter expert. By following the steps in the models, a teacher could design instruction that reflected the attributes of behavioral psychology. However, with elaboration of ISD into a complex process of multiple steps and layers, the field moved away from subject matter experts employing the models to the need for highly trained technicians to work with content experts. The authoring of instruction evolved into the third generation by the increasing demanded that ID required experts that could adjust to individual situations. To implement ISD required an ID expert who could do more that just follow a static set of procedures. Although, the technician and ID expert authoring models resulted in instructional products, the need for ISD continues to expand such that once again it is necessary to consider that subject matter experts directly participate in authoring. The four generation is in large part a result of the need to construct a means by which the large body of content experts can efficiently be instructional developers. Employing computer programming methods associated primarily with artificial intelligence, the contemporary view of the author is a subject matter expert that becomes a competent technician with computer-based ISD tools.

- Authoring Activities. To establish computer-based tools for authoring, the rules of instructional development need to be made explicit. The first ID rules were by nature only ill-defined concepts that described procedures in board terms that could fit most classroom situations. As the field of ISD grew, the concepts became increasingly defined and specific. With research verification of many of the concepts and expert manipulations, rules of development have become much more explicit. Therefore, it is now possible to put ID procedures into specific authoring rules.

3.2.3 Four Generations of ISD

Using the six attributes defined above, the four distinct generations of instructional system development can be described as follows:

- First generation, **ISD**[1] (Figure 3.2). The main focus of the first generation ISD models was to provide subject matter experts with a systematic approach to the development of instruction employing the behavioral paradigm of learning. The first systematic models consisted of four step-by-step components: preparing objectives, developing a pretest, producing instructional activities and developing a posttest. The system was completed with a formative evaluation loop for purposes of revision.

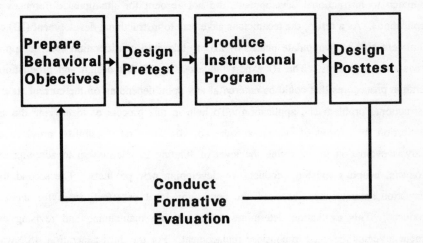

Fig. 3.2. ISD[1], first generation of ISD.

- Second generation, **ISD[2]** (Figure 3.3). Advancements in instructional technology led to the need to increase the variables and conditions of ISD models. The second generation expanded the employment of systems theory to control and manage the increasingly complex ISD process. The new variables included reference to curricular goals, assessing the student population, reviewing and selecting materials, deciding on the delivery system, and issues associated with implementation. Each of the boxes represented in Figure 3.3 are further elaborated with secondary layers of development. The behavioral learning paradigm remained, but was of secondary importance to the focus of the system--developing instruction independent of the content expert author. To expand the dissemination of such produced materials, summative evaluation was added to the models to document effectiveness. Additionally, the increasing complexity of ISD lead to the shift of authoring from the content expert to a trained technician. Instructional development was now considered a team activity with the ID technician working with a subject matter expert.

- Third generation, ISD^3 (Figure 3.4). In practice, ISD^2, because of the linear, step-by-step approach to instructional development, did not account for situational differences among applications. As a result, the technicians gave way to instructional development (ID) experts who were able to manipulate phases of ISD to take into consideration specific application needs and constraints. The ID expert models assumed that design and production were iterative procedures that could be entered at any point depending on the current state of the instructional problem and application. To help in this process of identifying the specific application, two forms of evaluation were added. The first, feasibility, provided a cost-analysis evaluation to determine the level of funding in relationship to adopting existing products, adapting existing products, or developing new products. The second form of evaluation, maintenance, assessed the continuing level of effectiveness for the existing products. This evaluation determines costs between maintaining and revising existing products versus the need to consider replacement. For the third generation, ISD was now totally in the hands of ID experts that were employing models that used evaluation at each phase of the process.

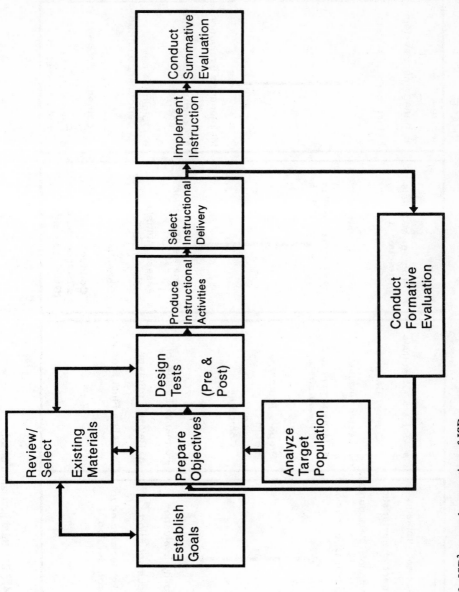

Fig. 3.3. ISD², second generation of ISD.

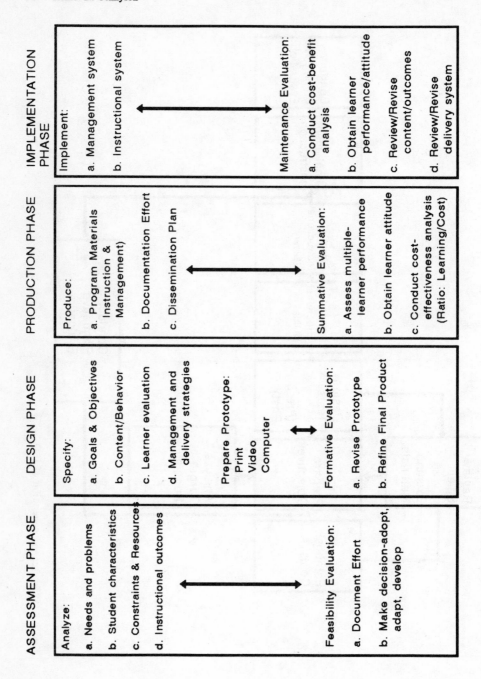

Fig. 3.4. ISD[3], third generation of ISD.

- Fourth generation, **ISD⁴** (Figure 3.5). Advancements from cognitive science and educational technology have continued to alter and expand the variables and conditions of ISD, making instructional development yet more complex. Employing technologies from the field of artificial intelligence, fourth generation ISD models propose to handle the complexity of ISD and situational application differences through the development of knowledge based systems of the ID. The knowledge base is embedded within an automated ISD system. Instead of a system consisting of a confederation of abstract (i.e., ill-defined) or expert controlled procedures, the fourth generation models propose systems of explicit rules controlled by contextual or situational problem solving evaluations. The author in this generation would once again be a subject matter expert who is also a competent (i.e., skilled) user of a given automated system (much like a writer using a word processing system). The initial evaluation in ISD⁴ performs the function of a diagnosis of the given problem situation followed by an ID prescription generated from the knowledge base.

3.3 Knowledge Base for ISD⁴

In this next section I will provide a summary of the main characteristics of the Fourth Generation ISD Models (ISD⁴). This is done in two parts. The first part defines the structure of the ISD⁴ models while the second part elaborates on the authoring activities associated with the elements of the fourth generation models.

ISD⁴ represents almost three decades of research and theory development in which instructional design has evolved from a subject matter expert activity to a sophisticated technology system employing advances from cognitive science, educational research, and educational technology. The first generation (ISD¹) consisted of four steps in the development of content expert-dependent materials following a behavioral learning theory for instructional prescription. As the need for accountability grew in education in the 1960s, ISD models expanded to include control of more aspects of the instructional materials production.

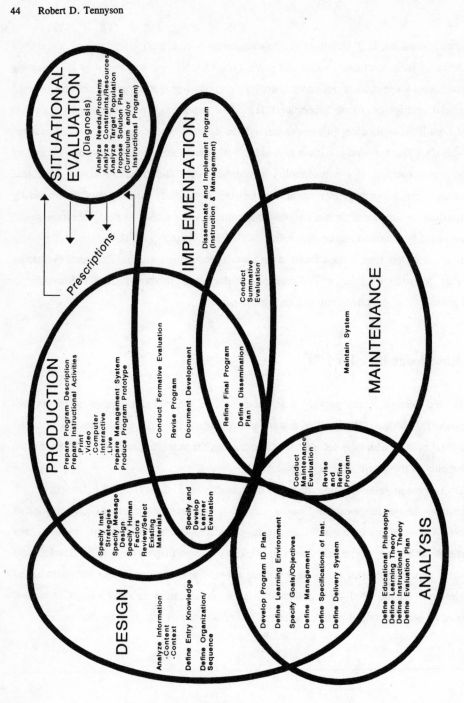

Fig. 3.5. ISD⁴, fourth generation of ISD.

The second generation (ISD^2) formalized a set of procedures designed to enhance instructional materials production by a system of highly manipulated steps. ISD^2 required a trained technician to successful execute the complex system.

Throughout the 1970s, ISD^2 models continued to expand in complexity because of external client requirements for improved quality control of products. By the late 1970s, instructional development had become so complex that application demands dictated that modifications to ISD^2 models had to made by ID experts who knew where, when, and why to make such changes. The market place demanded ID experts that could employ the general phases of ISD (i.e., analysis, design, production, evaluation, and implementation) but within the context of specific environments. This third generation (ISD^3) was characterized as consisting of phases of instructional development controlled by an ID expert. Additionally, the ID experts became increasingly specialized because of the rapid growth in electronic media (e.g., computer-based or video-based materials development ID expert).

Thus, within two decades, the field of instructional design went from a simple ISD model implemented by subject matter experts to one that was dominated by highly skilled ID experts employing complex systems of learning theories, evaluation plans, and media-based delivery systems. However, even with the expansion caused by new technologies and elaborated control factors for instructional development, advancements in cognitive psychology and artificial intelligence forced updating of the underlaying foundations of ISD. Cognitive psychology influenced just about every aspect of instructional development, requiring basic adjustments in all variables and conditions of the authoring activities. Additionally, artificial intelligence (AI) technologies were providing the means for employing ISD by a broader market of instructional developer novices. The fourth generation (ISD^4) models reflect both ID content updates and format in which to employ ISD.

Additionally, ISD^4 departs from the previous generations by focusing on explicit rules, in terms of authoring activities, rather than on the ID process (see Spector, Chap. 13). ISD^3 represents a system characterized as heuristic/iterative/linear while ISD^4 is dynamic/iterative/nonlinear. By concentrating on the authoring activities of instructional development, ISD^4 advances the flexibility and employment of instructional design principles and theory.

3.3.1 Structure of ISD⁴

Initial developments in ISD⁴ followed standard AI techniques that reduced instructional development activities into explicit rules. There are currently several such systems now in various stages of development (see Wasson's chapter). The first such computer-based systems used conventional computer software programming methods and focused on ISD² procedures. These attempts are not within the definition of ISD⁴ because the content is from ISD² and the programming uses conventional computer science methods.

A system that is a forerunner of ISD⁴ is Merrill's ID² system which uses production rule techniques with an instructional theory influenced by cognitive psychology [13]. However, other work in AI is looking at systems which are much more fluid and make use of heuristic and "fuzzy" logic. These types of systems are broadly defined as neural networks. The connections in neural networks, unlike production rules, can be fashioned at the moment of situational need. The ISD⁴ model represented in Figure 3.5 is an example of employing neural networks in constructing an AI ISD system. The elements or bubbles in Figure 3.5 show considerable flexibility and connections that represent concepts that can be networked based on at the moment need. The system's theme is based on the interaction of a situational evaluation (diagnosis) with prescribed authoring activities. Depending on the experience of the user, the authoring activities would exhibit more or less help in the actual proposed development effort [20].

The model illustrated in Figure 3.5 identifies six main elements of content. For purposes of maintaining continuity with the previous three generations, the main elements use the same basic labels. Given the overall title of the system which includes the term development, only one change was needed in labelling the elements of ISD⁴. The label of "production" was substituted for the more frequent label used in the previous generations, "development." The label production seems more appropriate because of the increased use of electronic media in instructional design. In the first two generations, the term development referred to construction of non-electronic based materials. Although, the systems eventually included possible selection of electronic delivery systems, they did so only as direct transfers from non-electronic designs. That is, the unique attributes of the given electronic medium were not utilized.

Evaluation is further integrated into ISD^4 by making it the interface between the author and the system. The assumption is that the situation can be diagnosed and then the system will prescribe the solution without the author directly participating. In the absence of an AI automated system, ISD^4 would still require the author be an expert in ISD authoring activities. In this context, the difference between ISD^4 with ISD^3 is both the updated content and the integration of the development elements (which is not done in ISD^3).

In terms of content, Sect. 3.3.2 will address that issue (for the AI system, see [20]). Integration of the five development elements represents the fluid nature of ISD. In the previous generations, each development activity was constrained with a rigid taxonomy that assumed a linear progression from one step (i.e., ISD^2) or phase (i.e., ISD^3) to the next. Given the notion of neural networks, development activities can be connected by context rather than by content attributes. For example, if the context is a Design situation, then authoring activities would include variables associated with the elements of Analysis, Production, and Implementation (see Figure 3.5). Also, for situations diagnosed as Production, elements of Design, Implementation, and Maintenance may be included. Rarely would an instructional situation prescribe all of the authoring activities within the domain of ISD.

3.3.2 Authoring Activities

The fourth generation of Instructional System Development (ISD^4) models represent application of artificial intelligence methods to the automation of instructional development. The three previous generations evolved the content and procedures of the activities associated with the production of instructional materials. With each generation the content and procedures increased in amount and complexity of instructional development. ISD^4 models can be classified as either production rule expert systems or neural networks. The difference is how the two expert systems approach the problem of instructional development.

ISD^4 models (ISD$^{4.1}$) that make use of production rule methods are basically linear programs that begin with an instructional problem and proceed with the solution of that problem following a sequence of IF THEN decisions. At the conclusion of the program, a solution is offered.

In contrast, ISD^4 models ($ISD^{4.2}$) that employ neural network methods start with a diagnosis of a given situation and then propose a prescription. No assumption is made concerning a given sequence of activities to be prescribed. In neural network methods, after a solution is proposed, the system works to validate the solution and then stores the prescription as contextual knowledge. The uniqueness of this programming methodology is that new contextual strategies can be added to the knowledge base. This is important for instructional development because each effort consists of individual differences that require tailoring of the ISD variables and conditions.

That is, $ISD^{4.1}$ models represent a given approach to problem solving such that the linear sequence of the rules dictate the process of instructional development. This form of modelling is a direct application of the conventional approach to ISD that begins with a task analysis followed in order with design, development, and implementation phases. Given the structure of the rule based system, it is not possible to proceed with the solution until completing the system. There is no solution until the program is finished.

$ISD^{4.2}$ models initially prescribe a solution as part of the situational evaluation. This form of AI allows more interface with the author than is possible with the $ISD^{4.1}$ models. The prescription offered from the situational evaluation does not assume any predetermined sequence of ISD. Situational evaluation in $ISD^{4.2}$ occurs in the front-end of the ID process rather than as a continuous step-by-step procedure that becomes increasingly inflexible as the ID activity proceeds (as in $ISD^{4.1}$).

$ISD^{4.2}$ consists of two main components (Figure 3.5): (a) a situational evaluation component that assesses the situation and then offers an expert prescription; and, (b) a knowledge base that includes five domains of interactive instructional development elements. These elements are by their nature overlapping in their respective activities. That is possible because the concepts (which are authoring activities) are both constant and variable in their attributes. Constant implies that specific context applications do not adjust the attributes. On the other hand, variable concepts adjust their attributes based on the context. Thus, rather than a step-by-step linear instructional development process as in the previous generations, ISD^4 prescribes authoring activities to fit the given situation. That is, each prescription would present a different model of ID. For example, the previous generations included review of existing materials, but did so without reference to the interaction with the other processes. In ISD^4, on the other hand, reviewing existing materials could be directly part of a production prescription (see Figure 3.5). This possibility of mixing and matching authoring activities is more dynamic because of the vary system is nonlinear. A prescription from ISD^4 would resemble a highly interactive GANTT chart instead of a flow-chart. An additional feature of ISD^4 is the computer science method of fast prototyping. Fast prototyping allows for the development of a minimally structured system but with no "frills." Elaboration only comes later after a functional system is developed and evaluated. The concept of fast prototyping improves the economics of instructional development.

Situational Evaluation

The first component in the generic ISD^4 model is the situational evaluation system. The purpose of this evaluation is twofold: (a) assessment of the situation (an interface between the author and the system) and (b) construction of a prescription (a set of authoring activities). Employing neural network methods (i.e., ISD$^{4.1}$), the prescription can be adjusted to the experience of the author. For example, for the novice author, the prescription would be a set of concrete authoring activities directly derived from the knowledge base. In contrast, for the ID expert author the prescription would assume participation by the author in the assessment process and solution construction. Concepts and authoring activities for the situational evaluation include as a minimum the following:

CONCEPTS	AUTHORING ACTIVITIES
-Analyze Needs/Problems	Identify discrepancies between desired and actual learning. Determine consequences of learning discrepancies.
-Analyze Constraints & Resources	Identify the scope of the need/problem (i.e., curricular, instructional, course, module and/or lesson). Define the constraints restricting resolution of need/problem.

-Analyze Target Population	Determine learner characteristics: educational background, age, ability, need for motivation, present skill levels, number of students, geographic location, culture.
	Determine learner differences: cognitive style, aptitude, learning style, affective factors, motivation, perception, etc.
-Propose Solution Plan	Validate the situational diagnosis. Consider whether to: buy and use existing materials, modify existing materials, or develop a new materials. Estimate costs and resource requirements for each alternative.

In contrast with previous generations of ISD, the content in the ISD^4 knowledge base is represented as domains (i.e., elements) of concepts independent of any formal connecting structure. That is, the domains are fluid clusters of concepts representing authoring activities. Each of the domains are labelled with a conventional ID term to maintain consistence with the established ID field. That is, to have an automated system, there needs to be an existing content base. The rules for the content base can be either of the production rules type employed in ISD4.1 or the heuristic rules type used in ISD$^{4.2}$. Heuristic rules are for the most part based on context or situation whereas production rules are independent of any context. Heuristic rules allow for the construction of new prescriptions (the very heart of the neural network method) while the production rules are more rigid structures.

The five domains and the seven interactive subdomains are arranged in Figure 3.5 to illustrate a neural network rather than a hierarchy or taxonomy of ID procedures. For example, in the first three generations, the sequence of ID procedures flowed from the analysis to the implementation: The maintenance activity was introduced for those learning environments with heavy use of media. For ISD^4, the assumption of a linear process of instructional development was changed to represent the more fluid nature of ISD. For example, most ISD situations evolve around the maintenance of established curricular programs. Only occasionally would there be an instructional development effort requiring each of the five domains.

The domains defined for ISD[4] represent contemporary advancements in the instructional development field. These advancements are seen at the concept level rather than the domain definitional level. For example, cognitive psychology has directly influenced the instructional strategies by providing more strategies to deal with higher-order cognitive processing. Also, electronic media has influenced both the delivery of instruction and how students can experience creative activities. At the domain level, the definitions and authoring activities are as follows:

Analysis

The analysis domain includes a variety of concepts associated with establishing the foundational aspects for a proposed or existing learning environment. Once these foundational elements are determined, they can serve across the entire range of development activities within a given curricular situation.

CONCEPTS	AUTHORING ACTIVITIES
-Define Philosophy & Theory of Learning	These conditions influence each domain in the ID process. Specify the educational philosophy and the educational learning theory.
-Define Instruction Theory	Given the rich knowledge base of the system, defining the instructional theory would aid the author in adjusting the system's prescription.
-Define Evaluation	A program evaluation plan establishes plan the quality control of the development effort (include formative, summative, and maintenance).

Analysis-Design

This subdomain represents those concepts that are interactive between the analysis and design domains.

CONCEPTS	AUTHORING ACTIVITIES
-Develop Program	Establish the following: ID team, ID Plan authoring activities/time schedule (pert chart), and budget.

-Define Learning Environment	Establish the physical conditions of the learning environment: resources and constraints.
-Specify Goals	State curricular level descriptions of knowledge and cognitive processes to be learned (i.e., declarative, procedural, & contextual knowledge; cognitive complexity & cognitive constructivism)
-Specify Objectives	State objectives for the learning environment (e.g., verbal information, intellectual skills, contextual skills, cognitive strategies, creative processes).
-Define Management	Establish the conditions of control and responsibility of learning within the environment. Ranging from complete program control to learner control.
-Define Specifications of Instruction	Document conditions and specifications of learning environment: length, structure, & proportion to be presented by allowable media.
-Define Delivery System	Identify the means of delivering instruction (e.g., print, video, computer, interactive, live, etc.).

Analysis-Maintenance

Concepts that interact between the analysis and maintenance domains.

CONCEPTS	AUTHORING ACTIVITIES
-Conduct Maintenance Evaluation	Implement plan to continuously evaluate the learning environment.
-Revise and Refine Program	Update the instructional program based findings of the evaluation.

Design

Design specifications of the learning environment are established.

CONCEPTS	AUTHORING ACTIVITIES
-Analyze Information (Macro)	Define the content/task to be learned at the curricular level (most abstract description). Define the context in which higher-order cognitive objectives are to be learned.
-Analyze Information (Micro)	Perform appropriate information analysis based on learning objectives (i.e., content/task analysis, contextual module analysis).
-Define Entry Knowledge	Identify and determine learner entry knowledge. Specify the student model: affective area, cognitive area (i.e., background knowledge, prerequisite knowledge, and prior knowledge).
-Define Organization/ Sequence	Determine sequence of information through: (a) course, (b) module, of Information (c) lesson. (Use the information analysis from micro level.)

Design-Production

Interaction of concepts associated with the initial design and production of the learning environment.

CONCEPTS	AUTHORING ACTIVITIES
-Specify Instructional Strategies	Identify appropriate instructional strategies linked to objectives (expository, practice, problem-oriented, complex-dynamic problems, self-directed experiences).
-Specify Message Design	Select display characteristics (e.g., graphics, text, color, manipulation) in relation to information.
-Specify Human Factors	Identify considerations for mediated instruction (e.g., menus, function keys, prompts, special help).
-Review/Select Existing Materials	Identify employment of existing materials.

Design-Production-Implementation

This three way interaction involves the specification of the learner evaluation system for the learning environment.

CONCEPTS	AUTHORING ACTIVITIES
-Specify and Develop Learner Evaluation	Establish learner evaluation: assessment system and assessment system and criteria and level of diagnosis (e.g., preventive, reactive, advisement, coaching, etc.). Determine use of pretests, progress checks, and posttests. Determine how assessments are to be administered (e.g., written, oral, via computer, etc.). Link the evaluation process to the objectives.

Production

This domain involves those concepts directly associated with the development of the learning environment.

CONCEPTS	AUTHORING ACTIVITIES
-Prepare Program	Acquire subject matter content. Description Review content for adherence to design specifications and for accuracy and completeness.
-Prepare Instructional Activities	Produce the necessary instruction (i.e., print, video, computer, interactive, live, etc.). Package all necessary materials to implement the learning environment (including directions and costs).
-Prepare Management System	Produce the management in respect to the conditions of the defined learning environment. Includes all necessary documents for implementation and maintenance.
-Produce Program Prototype	Production of the prototype materials and interface with the management system.

Production-Implementation

This subdomain includes those concepts associated with the final preparation of the learning environment.

CONCEPTS	AUTHORING ACTIVITIES
-Conduct Formative Evaluation	Conduct evaluation of prototype curricular/instructional program (e.g., one-on-one tryout). Conduct simulated tryout. Revise on the basis of simulation test. Perform technical and mechanical tryout and revision.
-Revise Program	Revise on the basis of findings from the formative evaluation.
-Document Development Activities	Prepare a report of the formative evaluation and revisions.

Production-Implementation-Maintenance

This subdomain includes those activities necessary to finalize the program.

CONCEPTS	AUTHORING ACTIVITIES
-Refine Final Program	Continuous refinement of the program until criteria of the design specifications have been met.
-Define Dissemination Plan	Prepare the plan for dissemination of the program. When introducing a new system most consider effects on existing environment.

Implementation

This domain provides the means to put the curricular/instructional program in to operation.

CONCEPTS	AUTHORING ACTIVITIES
-Disseminate and Implement Program	Reproduce program for learning environment. Establish/ modify support services. Distribute program. Collect data on learner performance and other learner indices.

Implementation-Maintenance

The purpose of this subdomain is to development and implement the summative evaluation plan.

CONCEPTS   AUTHORING ACTIVITIES

-Conduct Summative   Analyze assessment data (e.g., performance, time, costs)
   Evaluation   to prepare benefits analysis and/or costs analysis.

Maintenance

This domain provides the means to support the quality control of the entire learning environment.

CONCEPTS   AUTHORING ACTIVITIES

-Maintenance System   Design a system to maintain the quality of the learning
                                environment (e.g., content, objectives, media, etc.).

3.4 Conclusion

The purpose of this chapter was twofold: First, to review the variables and conditions of four generations of ISD; and, second, to define the structure and authoring activities of ISD^4. As in other fields of study and disciplines which have shown theoretical and application advancements and changes, it is convenient to distinguish the major advancements by characterizing specific generations. In the past several decades, the field of instructional system development has grown from a basically simple system of four components with an evaluation cycle to a complex set of domains requiring an ID expert for employment. Besides changes in basic instructional development procedures, the field has shifted in its overall learning theory foundation--from behavioral to cognitive--and increased its use of highly sophisticated electronic delivery systems.

ISD^1 expanded in complexity to the point that a trained technician was required to employ the system. Thus, ISD^2 moved instructional development into a wholly new field within the education and training environment. When the environment for ISD employment expanded, adjustments to the procedures of instructional development needed to be done to take into account unique, situational application needs and problems. Rather than viewing ISD as a rigid flowchart of activities, the field moved from specific models to individualized ID experts who manipulated phases of ISD in response to specific applications. ISD^3 represents the field as dominated by ID experts.

Forces for change in education, including cognitive science and electronic technology, are creating a demand for ISD that can not in total be met by a discipline controlled by experts. Access to ISD needs to be broaden but within the scope of users that will not or cannot become ID experts. Computer-based intelligent techniques offer an opportunity to development ISD automated systems that empower the novice in ID to fully employ ISD to any learning environment. ISD4 models can accommodate both ID novices and experts by providing systems with advanced authoring activities in efficient employment.

The second section of this chapter proposed the characteristics of ISD^4 models in terms of the operating systems (i.e., production rule or neural network) and proposed the updated knowledge base of the authoring activities. The fourth generation of ISD is distinguished from the earlier generations by the nature of a diagnostic/prescriptive approach to instructional development. Although the ISD^4 model as presented exhibits an intelligent programming structure, the concept of the fluid nature of ISD could be implemented by competent individuals in education. That is, the content of ISD^4 and the interactive nature of the various domains are independent of a given computer-based automated system.

At the present time, all four generations are in various levels of use. ISD^1 continues to be employed by subject matter experts (e.g., classroom teachers), especially as the general theme in education moves toward outcome based education (OBE). The second generation models still remain as the central core of graduate programs in instructional systems and technology. And as the graduate programs continue to increase the number of trained instructional developers, ISD^3 models will continue to flourish. Finally, the next generation of ISD will offer machine-dependent systems under various conditions of user control. ISD^4 models are only now being conceived and developed, as these become applied, the cycle of improvement will offer enhancements not yet realized.

References

1. Andrews, D. H., & Goodson, L. A.: A comparative analysis of models of instructional design. Journal of Instructional Development, 3, 2-16 (1980)
2. Bunderson, V., Olson, J., & Li, Z.: Four generations of computer-based testing. In R. Linn (Ed.), Handbook on educational measurement (pp. 114-146). New York: Academic Press 1989
3. Clark, R. E.: Reconsidering research on learning from media. Review of Educational Research, 53, 445-459 (1983)
4. Crowder, N. A.: Automatic tutoring by intrinsic programming. In A. Lumsdaine & R. Glaser (Eds.), Teaching machines and programmed learning (pp. 34-56). Washington, DC: National Education Association 1960
5. Gagné, R. M.: The conditions of learning. New York: Holt, Rinehart & Winston 1965
6. Gagné, R. M.: The conditions of learning (4th ed.). New York: Holt, Rinehart, and Winston 1985
7. Glaser, R.: Psychology and instructional technology. In R. Glaser (Ed.), Training research and education. Pittsburgh: University of Pittsburgh Press 1962
8. Glaser, R.: The reemergence of learning theory within instructional research. American Psychologist, 45, 29-39 (1990)
9. Gropper, G. L.: A technology for developing instructional materials. Pittsburgh: American Institutes for Research 1973
10. Guba, E. G., & Lincoln, Y. S.: The countenances of Fourth-generation evaluation: Description, judgment, and negotiation. Evaluation Studies Review Annual, 11, 70-88 (1986)
11. McKeachie, W. J.: Instructional psychology. Annual Review of Psychology, 25, 161-193 (1974)
12. Merrill, M. D.: Component display theory. In C. M. Reigeluth (Ed.), Instructional design theories and models: An overview of their current status (pp 123-156). Hillsdale, NJ: Erlbaum Associates 1983
13. Merrill, M. D., & Li, Z.: An instructional design expert system. In S. Dijkstra, B. van Hout Wolters, & P. C. van der Sijde (Eds.), Research on instruction: Design and effects (pp. 21-44). Englewood Cliffs, NJ: Educational Technology Publications 1990
14. Park, O., & Seidel, R. J.: Instructional design principles and AI techniques for development of ICAI. Computers in Human Behavior, 3, 273-287 (1987)
15. Pressey, S. L.: A simple apparatus which gives tests and scores and teaches. School and Society, 23, 373-392 (1926)
16. Reiser, R. A.: Instructional technology: A history. In R. M. Gagné (Ed.), Instructional technology: Foundations (pp. 11-48). Hillsdale, NJ: Erlbaum Associates 1987
17. Salomon, G.: Interaction of media, cognition, and learning. San Francisco: Jossey-Bass 1979
18. Skinner, B. F.: Science and human behavior. New York: Macmillan 1953
19. Skinner, B. F.: The science of learning and the art of teaching. Harvard Educational Review, 24, 86-97 (1954)

20.   Tennyson, R.D.: A framework for an automated instructional design advisor. In J. M. Spector, M. Polson, & D. Muraida (Eds.), Automating instructional design: Concepts and issues. Englewood Cliffs, NJ: Educational Technology Publications 1992

21.   Tennyson, R.D., & Breuer, K.: Instructional theory: Psychological perspectives. In R.D. Tennyson & F. Schott (Eds.), Instructional design: International perspectives, Vol. I: Theory and research. Hillsdale, NJ: Erlbaum Associates 1993.

22.   Tennyson, R.D., & Cocchiarella, M. J.: An empirically based instructional design theory for teaching concepts. Review of Educational Research, 36, 40-71 (1986)

4

Automating the Planning and Construction of Programming Assignments for Teaching Introductory Computer Programming

Jeroen J. G. van Merriënboer, Hein P. M. Krammer, and Rudolf M. Maaswinkel

Department of Instructional Technology, University of Twente,
P.O. Box 217, 7500 AE Enschede, The Netherlands

Abstract: This chapter describes CASCO, an automated system for the planning and construction of programming tasks for introductory computer programming. The generated tasks have the form of completion assignments, which consist of an incomplete example program with (a) instructions to complete, extend or change the program so that it meets certain specifications, (b) explanations on new features that are illustrated by parts of the incomplete program, and (c) questions on the working and the structure of the program. The planning and construction of the completion assignments is based on a model in terms of programming plans, student profile, and problem database.

Keywords: intelligent task generation, computer programming, instructional strategies, intelligent tutoring systems (ITS), student modelling

4.1 Introduction

The goal of this chapter is to describe a system for intelligent *task generation* in the domain of teaching computer programming to novice programmers. Task generation refers to the dynamic construction of student exercises, cases, problems or assignments in such a way that they are tailored to the particular needs of individual students. Research on intelligent task generation in computer-based instructional systems began as early as the end of the 60's (e.g., [9]) and has, amongst others, been conducted in the fields of elementary arithmetic (IDEBUGGY, [3]; LMS, [8]), teaching economics (SMITHTOWN, [7]), and trouble shooting of electronic circuits (MHO, [6]). With regard to the field of introductory computer programming, the authors are not familiar with other research pertaining to the dynamic construction of programming assignments. However, there has been done important work on the selection of programming assignments from an existing database of problems, such as in the Stanford BIP project (Basic Instructional Program, [2, 13]).

The tasks that will be constructed by our system are "completion assignments." These kind of assignments serve a central role in the *Completion Strategy*: An instructional strategy for teaching introductory computer programming which focuses on the completion of increasingly larger parts of well-designed, well-readable but incomplete computer programs [12]. In several experiments [10, 11], the Completion Strategy yielded higher learning outcomes than more traditional strategies that were focusing on the students' unconstrained generation of new computer programs. In this strategy, students are offered a series of programming assignments which may consist of the following five elements:

1. A programming problem as described in a problem text - this is the only element that is required for *all* completion assignments.
2. An example program - usually the student is offered an incomplete example program that yields a partial solution to the posed programming problem; however, the student may also be offered a complete example program or no example program at all.
3. Task instructions - either to solve the programming problem (if no example program is provided), to complete the incomplete example program, or to extend or change a complete example program so that it meets a new problem specification.
4. Explanations on new features of the programming language that are illustrated by--parts of--the example program.
5. Questions on the working and the structure of the example program.

The structure of this chapter is as follows. In the second section, a brief description is given of the different knowledge bases of CASCO (an acronym for the system, meaning Completion ASsignment COnstructor), that is, its domain model, its overlay student profile, and its database of programming problems. In section three, a general four-stage approach to the construction of completion assignments is described. Section four provides a brief evaluation of the system. The significance of the presented approach and our plans for future developments are presented in the last section.

4.2 Knowledge Bases

In CASCO, three main knowledge bases can be distinguished: A domain model consisting of an interrelated set of programming plans, a simple overlay student profile, and a problem database.

4.2.1 Domain Model

The domain model, that is, the model of the knowledge that must be taught, consists of a comprehensive library of programming plans on which several ordering relations are defined. Our notion of programming plans is identical to that of Johnson and Soloway [5]. Programming plans may be seen as stereotyped sequences of computer instructions, or more specifically, as schematic descriptions of the structure of pieces of code that should be used in order to reach particular programming goals. High level plans may, for instance, be used to separate input, process and output; then, the problem can be further decomposed into parts that can be performed with other plans and finally, low level plans may be used to combine elementary language commands with their arguments using the correct syntax.

A simple example of a medium-level plan is the "counter-loop plan" to count how many times a loop has been passed. It consists of two parts: An initialization part before the loop, and an update within the loop. In the initialization part a counting variable is set to zero (*counter : = 0), and in the update part this same variable is increased by one (*counter : = counter + 1). A programming plan may contain parameters and free variables (usually labelled by asterisks, in this case *counter), and may refer to other plans or may itself contain labels (labelled by #, in this case #initialize:, and #update:) to which other plans can refer, and contains itself a reference to another plan which contains a loop.

The main relations defined on the set of plans are (a) *part-of/prerequisite* relations, (b) *conflict* relations, and (c) *pedagogical priority* relations. In the teaching of Pascal, a part-of relation occurs, for example, between the "counter-loop plan" and the low-level "assignment plan" (the statement for assigning a value to a variable which is a part of the looping plan); a prerequisite relation may be argued to occur between a plan using the IF statement and a plan using the CASE statement. A conflict relation occurs, for example, between plans using a WHILE statement and plans using an IF statement, because it is known that students often interchange these statements. According to the conflict relation, one category of plans should not be presented before students have some proficiency in applying the other category of plans. Pedagogical priority relations indicate the desirability to teach a plan early in the learning process; for instance, according to the "structured programming" approach a plan using a PROCEDURE should have a higher pedagogical priority than a plan using a GOTO and a LABEL. Obviously, other types of relations, such as difficulty relations, may also be defined on the set of plans (e.g., a looping plan using the WHILE-statement is more difficult than a looping plan using the FOR-statement). However, we assume that difficulty relations are mainly a function of part-of/prerequisite relations and conflict relations.

4.2.2 Student Profile

As shown in Figure 4.1, the student profile is a partitioning of the domain model, according to a dimension describing the--estimated--state of the learning process (i.e., a classical overlay model). We hesitate to call it a student model, because it uses a declarative, "propaedeutic" representation of the knowledge and is not able to solve the same problems that students do. The profile may be perceived of as consisting of four sets of plans. The first set is formed by the

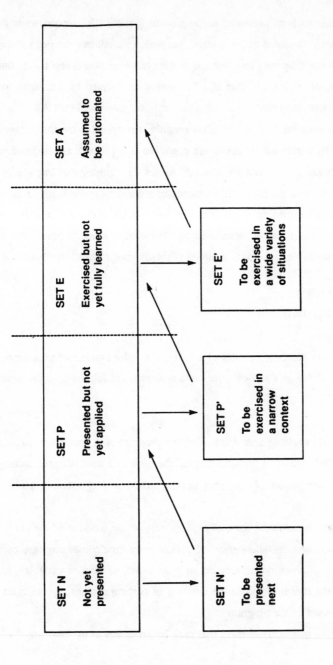

Fig. 4.1. The student profile as a partitioning of the domain model, and its relation to the candidate sets of plans for tutorial actions.

plans that have not yet been presented to the student (Set N). The second set is formed by the plans that have been presented to the student, but which the student has not yet applied (Set P). The third set is formed by the plans that the student has exercised a few times, but that are not yet fully learned, or, automated (Set E). The last set is formed by the plans that have been correctly applied for many times and are assumed to be automated (Set A).

Transitions between the four sets of plans roughly correspond to the three stages that may be distinguished in the acquisition of a complex cognitive skill [1] such as computer programming: The declarative stage (transitions from Set N to Set P), the stage of knowledge compilation (transitions from Set P to Set E), and the procedural stage (transitions from Set E to Set A). But, whereas most cognitive theories for skill acquisition will argue that different levels of expertise must be modelled by different techniques for knowledge representation, the same type of knowledge representation (i.e., programming plans) is used for all three levels of expertise.

4.2.3 Problem Database

Finally, the problem database consists of a large, but finite number of programming problems which can be presented to a student. For each problem, the following information is available in the database:

1. A problem text, providing a description of the programming problem in natural language.
2. A complete solution for this problem that has the form of a well-designed computer program, as well as a description of this program in terms of programming plans (i.e., a plan specification).
3. Additional information in the form of explanations on the working of the plans that are used in the program, and the application of syntax rules (including language commands) and discourse rules (indentation, proper use of procedures, naming of variables, etc.).
4. Questions on the structure and/or the working of particular plans, syntax rules or discourse rules that are used in the program.
5. A set of possible instructional tasks that may be presented to the student.

4.3 Construction of Completion Assignments

In CASCO's overall, cyclical approach to the planning and construction of completion assignments, four stages may be distinguished: (1) defining sets of candidate plans on which the tutorial actions will be based, (2) selecting one problem from the problem database, (3) constructing the completion assignment, and (4) updating the student profile in order to plan the selection of the next problem. The stages (1) and (2) pertain to *content planning* and are rather similar to the procedures used in BIP-II [2, 13], on the understanding that programming plans are used instead of (sub-)skills. Stage 4 pertains to *delivery planning* and is highly characteristic for the Completion Strategy. Each of the four stages will be briefly described in the next sections.

4.3.1 Stage 1: Construction of Candidate Sets

In this first stage, three sets of candidate plans for tutorial actions are generated from the student profile: (1) a set of candidate plans to be presented next (Set N'; a subset of Set N), (2) a set of candidate plans to be exercised in a "narrow" context (Set P'; a subset of Set P), and (3) a set of candidate plans to be further exercised in a wide variety of situations in order to reach automation (Set E'; a subset of Set E). These candidate sets are depicted in Figure 4.1.

Each of the sets has a maximum size and is generated on the basis of the relations that are defined on the set of plans in the domain model. For instance, a plan may only be added to the set of candidate plans to-be-presented next (Set N') if all plans that have a part-of/prerequisite relation with this plan are marked as belonging to the "automated" part of the student profile (i.e., they all belong to set A). As another example, a plan may only be added to the set of candidate plans to-be-exercised in a narrow context (Set P') if all plans that have a conflict relation with this plan are either not yet presented (i.e., they belong to set N) *or* belong to the automated part of the student profile (i.e., they belong to set A).

4.3.2 Stage 2: Problem Selection

In the second stage, one programming problem has to be selected from the problem database. As an important condition, the number of plans that may simultaneously be presented, exercised in a narrow context, and/or exercised in a wide variety of situations must be specified. For example, one may argue on pedagogical grounds that a suitable assignment may contain not more then six new elements: (a) not more than two plans from set N' (i.e., not more than two new plans may be simultaneously presented to the student), (b) not more than two--already presented--plans from set P' (i.e., not more than two plans may be simultaneously exercised by the student), and (c) not more than two--already exercised--plans from set E' (i.e., not more than two plans may be simultaneously trained in a varied context). For this particular example, 27 *combinations* are possible. These combinations include the "empty set"; in this case, all plans that are necessary to solve the problem are in Set A, that is, they are assumed to be already automated.

To select one problem from the problem database, for all problems in the database all possible combinations are investigated to determine the *expected* value of the number of plans in Set P' (i.e., the number of new plans that may be presented when this problem is used) as well as the expected value of the number of plans in Set E' (i.e., the number of already presented plans that may be exercised). Only the problems for which these values are equal to, or smaller than, the maximum number of new elements (in the example above: 6) are acceptable. Thus, in this first pass problems/combinations that require the presentation or use of too many plans are excluded.

For the remaining problems/combinations, a so-called *preference value* is calculated. This value is a function (actually, the sum of the standardized values) of the "deliverance possibility" and the "pedagogical priority." The deliverance possibility of a plan indicates if the plan is used in many problems; plans with a high deliverance possibility are usually preferred because they open the way to subsequently use many other problems. As already mentioned, the pedagogical priority of a plan indicates the desirability to teach that plan early in the learning process; for instance, plans applying a WHILE loop will probably receive higher pedagogical priority values than plans applying the GOTO statement. In the selection of the problem, the problem/combination is chosen that optimizes the preference value. Finally, the selected problem is marked in order to prevent a second presentation during the training process; thus, each problem is used only once.

4.3.3 Stage 3: Assignment Construction

The third stage is concerned with delivery planning: A completion assignment is constructed for the problem/combination that has been selected in stage 2. A completion assignment always consists of a problem text, that is, a problem specification in natural language. In addition, it usually contains an incomplete solution in the form of a well-designed computer program that offers a partial solution to the posed programming problem. Two special cases may occur. First, the problem specification may be presented with no solution at all; then, the student is confronted with a conventional programming problem. Second, the problem specification may be presented with a complete solution; then, the student is confronted with a fully worked-out example.

In addition, completion assignments may contain one or more of the following three elements: (1) *explanations* of new features of the programming language that are illustrated by-parts of-the incomplete program, (2) *questions* on the working and the structure of-parts of-the incomplete program, and (3) *instructions* to write, complete, extend, or change the program so that it meets a given problem specification.

Both explanations and questions may pertain to either new plans, syntactic rules, or discourse rules. Syntactic rules pertain to language-dependent programming principles, including the use of basic language commands. Some examples are: A program should end with "end", to every "begin" belongs an "end", text after "{" on the same line does not belong to the program, and so forth. Discourse rules are rules of thumb which prescribe how to derive programming code from a plan specification. These rules mainly have to do with the readability and comprehensibility of the program. Some aspects of interest are: the proper choice of names for variables and procedures, the structuring of the program by means of procedures and functions, the use of indentation, the addition of comments, and so forth.

The construction of the completion assignment is dependent on the contents of the candidate sets N', P' and E' as well as the plans that are necessary to solve the selected problem. The construction is governed by four rule sets: (1) example rules, (2) explanation rules, (3) question rules, and (4) task rules. The *example rules* are particularly important to the completion strategy and serve to instantiate an example with program code; in effect, they delete portions from the solution of the programming problem as specified in the problem database. For instance, one of the rules determines that *if* none of the plans that are necessary to solve the posed programming problem are in one of the three candidate sets N', P', or E' (i.e., they are all assumed to be automated), *then* all plans are deleted from the solution; thus, the student will be confronted with a conventional programming problem for which no partial solution is provided. The following rule may serve as a second example: *if* exactly one plan of the selected problem is in the candidate set P' (i.e., plans to be exercised in a narrow context), and no more than two plans are in the set N' (candidate plans to be presented for the first time), *then* delete this one plan from the solution.

The *explanation rules* and *question rules* serve to instantiate either explanations or questions pertaining to programming plans, syntax rules, or discourse rules that are used in the-incomplete-example program. An example of a simple rule that instantiates an explanation on a new plan is the following: *if* one or more plans of the presented example are in the candidate set N' (plans to be presented for the first time), *then* provide the pre-stored explanation on the working of the plan(s) and highlight the realization of this plan in the example that is provided to the student. The following rule may instantiate a question on a discourse rule: *if* one plan of the presented example is in set P', and no plans are in set N' or E', and a discourse rule is applied in the realization of this plan, *then* ask the pre-stored question on this discourse rule and highlight the realization of this discourse rule in the example program.

Finally, the *task rules* specify the instructional task that will be presented to the student. This may be either writing a complete program (if no example program is provided), completing an incomplete program, or extending or changing a program (if a complete example program is provided). The Figures 4.2 and 4.3 provide two examples of completion assignments that may be constructed by the system. It concerns the same programming problem, for which completion assignments are constructed early in the learning process and at the end of the learning process. In general, completion assignments that are constructed early in the learning process will contain example programs that are almost complete and many explanations; completion assignments that are constructed late in the learning process will contain example programs that are largely incomplete and few explanations.

4.3.4 Stage 4: Updating the Student Profile

The student will perform the tasks as required in the completion assignment, and his or her success/failure will lead to an update of the student profile. Here, failure is defined as a situation in which a student asks the system for a correct solution. Simply stated, the following situations may occur: (a) if a particular plan of the performed problem formed part of Set N', it will be added to Set P of the student profile, (b) if a plan formed part of Set P', and has been successfully applied by the student, it will be added to Set

Explanation on plan 'Running Total'

In the *italic* lines of the example program the plan 'Running Total' is used. It is generally used when you need to compute the sum of a series of values. Use a running-total variable (here: 'total_cigarettes'), set it to zero before the loop, and update it within the loop by adding the newly-to-add value to its own value.

Explanation on discourse rule **'Procedure Use'**

In the **bold** lines of the example program a 'procedure' is used. In order to improve the readability of your programs, place a set of lines wich belong logically together apart in a procedure. Give the procedure a name after the word PROCEDURE (here: smoking), start it with BEGIN and end it with END;, and refer to the procedure name from the main program.

Question on syntax rule 'MOD'

The operator 'mod' is used in this program for:

a. division of two values
b. integer division of two values
c. multiplication of two values
d. remainder after integer division of two values

Programming problem:

During World War II, there was a severe shortage of tobacco. Some chain-smoking people were gathering cigarette stumps in order to roll their own cigarettes. They needed, for example, four stumps to roll a "new" cigarette. Write a program to model this chain-smoking process. The program must take the number of collected cigarette stumps as input, and output the total number of cigarettes that could be smoked, as well as the number of stumps that is finally left over.

Example program:

```
program chainsmoking;

const needed=4; (i.e., # of stumps needed for 1 cigarette)
var  stumps, cigarettes, total_cigarettes, left_over: integer;

procedure smoking;
begin
   total_cigarettes:=0;
   repeat
      cigarettes:=stumps div needed;
      total_cigarettes:=total_cigarettes+cigarettes;
      left_over:=stumps mod needed;
      stumps:=cigarettes+left_over
   until stumps<needed
end; {smoking}

begin
   write('# of available stumps: ');
   readln(stumps);
   smoking;
   writeln(total_cigarettes,' cigarettes have been smoked,');
   writeln('and ', stumps,' stumps are left.')
end.
```

Fig. 4.2. Example of a completion assignment that is constructed early in the learning process, with a complete example program, two explanations and one question.

Programming problem:

During World War II, there was a severe shortage of tobacco. Some chain-smoking people were gathering cigarette stumps in order to roll their own cigarettes. They needed, for example, four stumps to roll a "new" cigarette. Write a program to model this chain-smoking process. The program must take the number of collected cigarette stumps as input, and output the total number of cigarettes that could be smoked, as well as the number of stumps that is finally left over.

Example program:

```
program chainsmoking;

const needed=4; (i.e., # of stumps needed for 1 cigarette)
var  stumps, total_cigarettes: integer;

procedure smoking;
var cigarettes, left_over: integer;

begin
  write('# of available stumps: ');
  readln(stumps);
  smoking;
  writeln(total_cigarettes,' cigarettes have been smoked,');
  writeln('and ', stumps,' stumps are left.')
end.
```

Question on discourse rule 'Local Variables'

Highlight in the example program the line(s) in which the 'local variables'-rule is used.

Instructional Task

Complete the procedure 'smoking' in order to reach a working program, and subsequently test this program.

Fig. 4.3. Example of a completion assignment that is constructed later in the learning process with a largely incomplete example program, one question and one instructional task.

E of the student profile, (c) if a plan formed part of Set E', and has been successfully applied for a specified number of times (e.g., five times in succession), it will be added to Set A of the student profile, and (d) if a plan formed part of either Set P' or E', and has *not* been successfully applied (i.e., the student asks the system for the correct solution), it will be added to Set N of the student profile. Based on the updated student profile, sets of new candidate plans are formed in order to construct the next completion assignment.

It should be noted that if a student does not succeed in the correct application of one or more particular plans, these plans will be simply re-presented and explained in subsequent problems. Essentially, they are handled in the same way as (new) plans that have not been presented before, although some extra explanation on their working can be provided to the student. But obviously, the errors that are made by the student may signify underlying misconceptions or "bugs." In the current system specification, such misconceptions are not properly taken care of - or at least, they are taken care of in an overly simplified manner. In the last section, some necessary extensions of CASCO are discussed in order to make a proper handling of misconceptions possible.

4.4 Evaluation

CASCO may be argued to fulfil the three requirements which Halff [4] proposed for the selection and sequencing of problems and examples in procedural tutors: Manageability, structural transparency, and individualization. Manageability refers to the fact that each exercise should be solvable and every example should be comprehensible. Clearly, the first stage in which the sets of to be presented, to be exercised, and to be automated plans are constructed is directed towards the manageability; in addition, new elements in examples (i.e., the incomplete solutions) are always explained in order to make them even more comprehensible. Structural transparency indicates that the sequence of generated exercises and examples should reflect the structure of the skills being taught. It is strived after by constructing completion assignments in which the most relevant and most important plans are first presented, exercised and automated;

they are expected to help the learner to develop a knowledge base of cognitive schemata that underlay a proficient performance of computer programming skills. Finally, individualization is realized by maintaining and using the student profile throughout the stages of our procedure to dynamically generate adaptive sequences of problems.

Yet, no empirical evaluation data are available on the performance of the system because its implementation is still on its way. The implementation proceeds through two phases. First, a stripped version of CASCO will be used to conduct a series of "simulation" studies. The main goals of these studies are to test and improve the stability of the system (i.e., tuning it in order to acquire appropriate sequences of programming assignments) and to determine the required size of the problem database. Second, formative evaluations using actual students will take place.

4.5 Conclusion

Whereas CASCO should be seen as only *one* of the subsystems of the instructional model that may form part of an Intelligent Tutoring System (ITS), the authors consider it to be a particularly important subsystem. It may be argued that the acquisition of a complex cognitive skill, such as computer programming, is mainly a function of the didactic value of the practice that is offered to the students; thus, the generation of suitable tasks is considered to be a core aspect of good teaching.

Currently, we are augmenting the design of the system to resolve some of its weaknesses and shortcomings. Its set-based approach may be seen as a first weakness. On the one hand, the use of sets makes is easy to talk and reason about the system's instructional functions and to specify and formulate the rules that govern the construction of completion assignments. But on the other hand, it should be obvious that the acquisition of programming skills is a relatively smooth, continuous process that is not adequately modelled by the use of a set-based student profile. To resolve this problem, "fuzzy-set theory" will be applied to describe the particular sets of the student profile and the sets of candidate plans for tutorial actions. Then, particular plans may "more-or-less" constitute a part of particular sets.

A second, more important shortcoming of the described system is its inability to adequately handle misconceptions or "bugs". In the present system, students' failures on the application of particular plans result in the repeated presentation of those plans in subsequent completion assignments, in a manner that is essentially identical to the presentation of new, not previously presented plans. Clearly, CASCO should be improved by augmenting it with a subsystem for *remediation*. This requires the availability of a library of misconceptions, as well as procedures to couple errors that are made in the application of particular plans, in particular circumstances, to these misconceptions. In case of misconceptions, they must be specified in the student profile and CASCO should both generate completion assignments with a high diagnostic value in order to discriminate between particular misconceptions (i.e., apply techniques for interactive diagnosis) and present special corrective feedback. By augmenting CASCO with such special facilities for remediation, its capability to generate highly adaptive instructional sequences of programming tasks will be substantially increased.

Finally, it should be noted that our fundamental interest is not in teaching computer programming per se, but in dynamic task generation for complex, design-related problem solving skills. It is our hope that the ideas and concepts underlying both the Completion Strategy and CASCO are also useful for dynamic task generation in other domains, such or writing essays, planning production processes, designing electronic circuits, or designing instruction and courseware. On the long term, our goal is the development of generic tools for dynamic task generation in such complex domains.

References

1.   Anderson, J. R.: Skill acquisition: Compilation of weak-method problem solutions. Psychological Review, 94, 192-210 (1987)
2.   Barr, A., Beard, M., & Atkinson, R. C.: The computer as a tutorial laboratory: The Stanford BIP project. International Journal of Man-Machine Studies, 8, 567-596 (1976)
3.   Burton, R. R.: Diagnosing bugs in a simple procedural skill. In D. H. Sleeman & J. S. Brown (Eds.), Intelligent Tutoring Systems. London: Academic Press 1982
4.   Halff, H. M.: Curriculum and instruction in automated tutors. In M. C. Polson & J. J. Richardson (Eds.), Foundations of intelligent tutoring systems (pp. 79-108). Hillsdale, NJ: Lawrence Erlbaum 1988

5. Johnson, W. L., & Soloway, E. M.: PROUST: An automatic debugger for Pascal programs. Byte, 10(4), 179-190 (1985)
6. Lesgold, A. M., Bonar, J. G., Ivill, J. M., & Bowen, A.: An intelligent tutoring system for electronics troubleshooting DC-circuit understanding. In L. B. Resnick (Ed.), Knowing and learning: Issues for the cognitive psychology of instruction. Hillsdale, NJ: Lawrence Erlbaum 1987
7. Shute, V., & Bonar, J. G.: An intelligent tutoring system for scientific inquiry skills. Proceedings of the 8th Cognitive Science Society Conference (pp. 353-370). Amherst, MA: Lawrence Erlbaum 1986
8. Sleeman, D. H.: A rule-based task generation system. Proceedings of the 7th International Joint Conference on Artificial Intelligence (pp. 882-887). Vancouver: Morgan Kaufman 1981
9. Uhr, L.: Teaching machine programs that generate problems as a function of interaction with students. Proceedings of the National ACM Conference (pp. 125-134). New York: Association for Computing Machinery 1969
10. Van Merriënboer, J. J. G.: Strategies for programming instruction in high school: Program completion vs. program generation. Journal of Educational Computing Research, 6, 265-285 (1990)
11. Van Merriënboer, J. J. G., & De Croock, M. B. M.: Strategies for computer-based programming instruction: Program completion vs. program generation. Journal of Educational Computing Research (in press)
12. Van Merriënboer, J. J. G., & Krammer, H. P. M.: The "completion strategy" in programming instruction: Theoretical and empirical support. In S. Dijkstra, B. H. M. van Hout-Wolters, & P. C. van der Sijde (Eds.), Research on instruction (pp. 45-61). Englewood Cliffs, NJ: Educational Technology Publications 1989
13. Wescourt, K., Beard, M., & Gould, L.: Knowledge-based adaptive curriculum sequencing for CAI: Application of a network Representation. Proceedings of the 1977 Annual Conference, Association for Computing Machinery (pp. 234-240). New York: Association for Computing Machinery 1977

5

Experiences and Prospects Derived from the Norwegian R&D Project in Automation of Instructional Design

José J. Gonzalez[1] and Lars Vavik[2]

[1]ModellData AS and Agder College of Engineering, PO Box 42, N-4871 Fevik, Norway
[2]ModellData AS and Stord College of Education, PO Box 5, N-5414 Rommetveit, Norway

Abstract: Argued is that an important parameter determining the extent of automation of instructional design is whether the issue is a closed or an open problem. Closed problems deal with topics where facts and heuristics are known and accessible. Open problems challenge the learner to localize, to find or even to discover crucial information concerning facts or heuristics. Closed problems do not raise particularly interesting theoretical issues. Open problems are a formidable demand both because of their intrinsic importance and their challenge to instructional science, learning theory and technology.

Keywords: CBT, CAL, automated instructional design, open learning, complex problems, problem solving, heuristic methods

5.1 Introduction

Fruitful theories of instructional design, development and delivery (IDDD) acknowledge the fact that real-life implementations have to adapt to many constraints. Some of these constraints are due to clashes between the modern basis of IDDD and ism's reigning in the environment where the particular implementation of IDDD occurs.

Instructional design, development and delivery has always been both science and art and will probably remain so despite increasing role of automation techniques. There are always imponderables that make implementation of IDDD more than just producing an instance of some preconceived stuff.

Understanding the practice of IDDD is a crucial issue for further advances in the area. The purpose of this paper is partly to describe experiences derived from the extensive Norwegian experiment within IDDD. Since 1984 Norway has had a comprehensive activity within computers/IT in schools and training, including R&D in CAL and software development.. The project, mainly financed by the Norwegian Ministry of Education and Research, has involved universities, institutes of technology and colleges of education as well as a dozen software and multimedia companies. An important part of the Norwegian project has been dedicated to research, development and use of advanced tools for automation of IDDD (Mosaikk, SimTek, Winix, WinSim). The tools have found application in CBT and CAL for a number of companies (Norwegian Hydro, the Norwegian state oil company Statoil, Shell and Falconbridge Mining Co.).

According to our experiences, an important parameter determining the extent of automation of instructional design is whether the issue is a closed or an open problem. Closed problems deal with topics where facts and heuristics are known and accessible. Open problems challenge the learner to localize, to find or even to discover crucial information concerning facts or heuristics.

Closed problems do not raise particularly interesting theoretical issues. Open problems are a formidable demand both because of their intrinsic importance and their challenge to instructional science, learning theory and technology.

5.2 Tasks versus Problems

We propose to view training as an activity involving carrying out tasks and solving problems. Methodology and the level of automation of instructional design depend upon the extent of each one (tasks versus problems). We follow Dörner [2] in distinguishing between the following:

- Knowledge of facts and knowledge about solving methods (heuristic methods).
- "Solving" (actually, carrying out) tasks and solving problems.

5.2.1 Cognition

Human knowledge seems to be structured as knowledge of facts (*episodic structure*) and knowledge of heuristic methods (*heuristic structure*). Obtaining factual knowledge is an important part of the learning process. Knowledge of facts allows the learners to orient themselves in some topic or domain. Such static knowledge is not sufficient to achieve goals. One has to master and apply heuristic methods to find out a way through the domain, i.e. to carry out tasks or solve problems.

5.2.2 Task Characteristics

The characteristics of tasks are as follows:

- Full knowledge of the topic exists.
- Knowledge is concentrated and available for use (i.e., we   know both who, or which entity, has the full knowledge and how to access this knowledge).
- Actions have certain and unambiguous effects (i.e., one has rule-based systems).

The characteristics given above imply that complete methods exist (or can be derived) to carry out tasks. Accordingly, at this level training consists in passing how-to procedures to the learners. Once the learner masters the procedures, achieving some goal is tantamount to apply a known method, i.e. to reproduce a familiar procedure.

In real life one seldom has situations dealing with pure tasks. Most situations involve some degree of problem solving. We turn now to the characteristics of problems.

5.2.3 Closed and Open Problems

In contrast to tasks, problems cannot be solved by simply reproducing some familiar procedure. At the simplest level, a problem demands from the learners that they *combine* known methods in a known domain to achieve some new goal. The challenge consists of dealing with a high number of potential combinations. An example of a *combination problem* is chess playing, where the player mastering the rules of the game has to deal with a sheer unlimited number of combinations to achieve the goal (chess mate to the opponent).

From the point of view of learning methodology, teaching how to solve combination problems or how to carry out tasks is much the same. The crucial point is the *closed* nature of the topic, which allows the learner to concentrate on mastering available knowledge on facts and methods. In contrast to *closed problems* (i.e. tasks and combination problems), *open problems* demand creative activities from the learner.

The characteristics of open problems are as follows:

- Only partial knowledge of the topic exists or is available.
- More often than not the existing knowledge is dispersed among people or institutions. A crucial part of learning at this level is finding out and accessing sources of know-how.

The characteristics given above imply that complete methods do not exist. At the simplest level, factual knowledge is complete but learners do not have full knowledge of or full access to problem solving methods. At higher levels both knowledge of facts and heuristic methods is incomplete. At even higher levels one has both incomplete and uncertain knowledge. This implies that the effect of actions can be uncertain or ambiguous. Such characteristics complicate problem solving enormously. Few people seem to be aware that most of the complex problems society has to deal with *necessarily* have to be confronted with incomplete knowledge of our part. As Hayek [6] puts it, successful solving of complex problems require from man that humans "...are adapted both to the particular facts which he knows and to a great many other facts he does not and cannot know."

5.3 Levels of Automation of Instructional Design for Closed

The passing of how-to procedures to the learner can be automated as *linear sequences*, *dialogue sequences*, through *interactive manipulation* and via *text and picture sequences (hyper link)*. The list is not intended to be exhaustive. Closed problems can in principle be fully automated through text, picture, video and audio instruction.

5.3.1 Linear Sequences

Linear sequences are typically video sequences (Figure 5.1). The learner being passive they are of limited use.

Videosequences

Fig. 5.1. Example of a linear sequence.

5.3.2 Dialogue Sequences

Dialogue sequences are one step more sophisticated (Figure 5.2). They allow communication with and feedback from an electronic tutor.

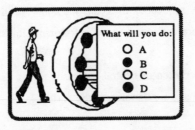

Fig. 5.2. Example of a dialogue sequence.

5.3.3 Interactive Manipulation

With interactive manipulation the trainee is asked to "carry out" some task using a set of tools. The electronic tutor provides feedback on the choice of tools including whether the operational

Fig. 5.3. Example of an interactive manipulation.

Hyperlink (text and picture sequence) uses the metaphor of the textbook (Figure 5.4). Textbook, pictures and sound are connected through following links:

- In the way of (pictorial) illustration of central topics.
- The audio/visual sequences have a reference to the textbook.

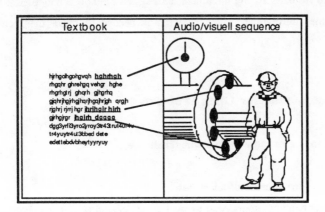

Fig. 5.4. Example of a Hyperlink screen display.

The textbooks can be illustrated with pictures, video sequences or graphical animation (Figure 5.5). Concepts are linked to pictorial representations, elements in the pictures refer to the electronic textbook, to the system manual, etc.

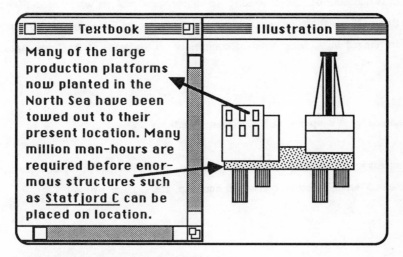

Fig. 5.5. Example of an electronic textbook.

We have abstained from discussing intelligent tutor systems although they probably will play a major role at some future time. Much research is needed to make them cost-effective throughout.

5.4 Levels of Automation for Open Problems

Open problems lead to one or more of following challenges:

- Localizing and accessing sources of know-how.
- Extending factual or heuristic knowledge to meet some demand (i.e. to achieve some desired goal).
- Developing methods to cope with incomplete and uncertain knowledge (decision making under uncertainty).
- Developing methods to estimate future developments making allowance for unforeseen events.

To discuss questions of general validity we outline some projects where ModellData AS is involved (in partial collaboration with the Norwegian Ministry of Education and Research). The projects are ranged in growing order of complexity (in the sense of the "challenges" listed above).

5.4.1 Time-delayed Response to Unforeseen Questions

At the simplest level, automated instructional design could allow for unforeseen questions that can be resolved through electronic mail, on-line help, etc. (Figure 5.6).

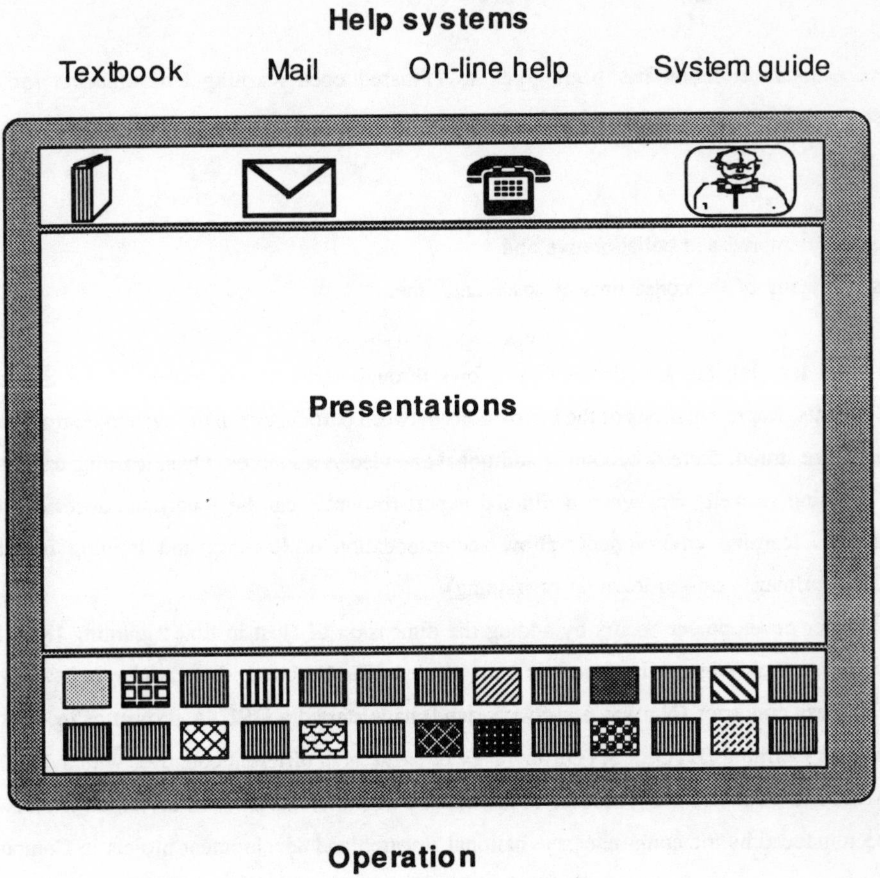

Fig. 5.6. Electronic mail and on-line help provide answers to unforeseen questions that textbook and system guide (electronic tutor) do not deal with.

The system offers help through several channels, such as an electronic tutor, on-line help, question box (mail), textbook or manual, etc. Presentations may occur as video sequences, graphics, animated pictures, etc. The system can be operated through peripheral pointing devices or pointing at sensitive areas on the screen.

5.4.2 Open Learning, On-job Training, JITOL

Recently, much attention has been given to IT-based open learning environments for the professional development of individuals [7]. The attribute "open" denominates forms of learning that are:

- Learner centered and collaborative and
- Escape many of the constraints of space and time.

In open learning the knowledge base grows through constant integration of the learners' requirements. Representations of the interactions between participants in the system (learners and teachers) are stored, thereby becoming additional knowledge resources. Open learning can mean open teaching as well, viz. when additional expert resources can be found and accessed. IT-based open learning environments allow accommodation of learning and training in other activities (primarily on-job learning or training).

A further development occurs by adding the dimension of "just in time" learning [8]. That is, acquiring knowledge at the time it is most needed. The European Community and two non-EC European countries (Norway and Switzerland) have started a DELTA-project called Just In Time Open Learning (JITOL). JITOL involves 12 partners in different countries with a duration of 3 years and estimated total resource of around 500 man-months. The EC invitation to Norway has been induced by the comprehensive national research and development project in Computer Assisted Learning and Computer Based Training. An important part of the Norwegian project has been dedicated to research, development and use of advanced tools for automation of instructional design and the network system for open learning--Winix. Winix takes care of e-mail, conference calls, transfer of files, including executable files, graphics and digitized pictures/video, design toolkit, network database, etc. Among the Norwegian users of Winix one finds universities, colleges, the Norwegian Navy, etc.

JITOL contains seven partial projects (Work Packages – WP), Norway participating in WP1 "System development," WP2 "Evaluation, testing and validation" and WP3 "pilot testing." For this chapter, the pilot project, Advanced Learning Technology Professionals (ALTP), is of special interest. The Norwegian ALTP sub projects aim at target learners who are graduate students, teachers and other professionals taking part in formalized, graduate studies. The two topics are (a) designing, developing and producing IT-based learning materials, (b) pedagogical applications of system dynamics/simulation. Around 50% of the participants will be located near the delivery centers in Western Norway, while most of the remaining participants will be spread all over Norway. Among the participants one founds personnel from the Norwegian Navy. The project admits participants from other European members of the JITOL project. The tutors are primarily university and college staff from at least 4 institutions in Norway. This JITOL-project should contain most of the challenges pertaining to open problems.

The ALTP courses must be designed within September 1992 and they will be tried at target learners in the academic year 1992/93. With all the caveats appropriate at this early stage, we intend to design the courses according to following principles:

- Taking advantage of the advanced professional level of the target learners, participants get as starting point a carefully defined structure of the course in terms of (a) aims to be met in ordered temporal progression, and (b) information about resources. The meat of the course is provided in joint effort by counsellors and participants in the just-in-time spirit.
- After the theoretical foundation has been established through short and localized courses, participants work in a project basis to meet the specified aims.
- Participants use a dynamic expanding database of resources to overcome the limitations of dispersed knowledge. That is, the resource database provides well-structured information about *available* expert knowledge in relation to topics; literature; programming tools; etc.

Accordingly, the course develops according to following stages: (a) Outline of the temporally ordered aims; (b) Construction of the resource database; (c) Providing a foundation as the starting point; (d) Course management (monitoring the database, supervising progress, etc.).

5.5 Learning and Decision-making in Complex Dynamic Systems

Most chronic problems faced by society range in this category: ecological issues, environmental problems, overpopulation, drug abuse, AIDS, etc. Although such problems remain conspicuously unsolved, steadily growing in magnitude and complexity, very few people attribute our lack of success to the challenges the problems present to cognition and problem solving abilities. We give here a short introduction to some aspects of this huge issue, focussing only on how complex dynamics systems "deceive" candid subjects (i.e., most people). The plain implication is that misjudgments and misunderstandings of crucial aspects promote wrong approaches, thus impeding solutions and even worsening the situation. To illustrate these points we use the burning problem of AIDS. Further details and references are found in Gonzalez [4 & 5].

Without exception, chronic problems develop along time scales in the order of tens or even hundreds of years, long time lags separating causes and effects. The slow nature of chronic problems let them grow insidiously, most people are passive spectators or even disaffected. Humanity never played down traditional epidemics such as Black Death, tuberculosis, etc. simply because the visible effects (i.e., the gravely ill people, the dead) gave a basically correct view of the magnitude of the epidemic. Traditional epidemics are WYSIWYG: what you see (the victims) is what you get soon: the infected, symptomless carriers on the way to illness. The simulation model in our computer program AIDS Information, Modification and Simulation – **AIMS** illustrates this point.

Compared with AIDS, which is definitely non-WYSIWYG. Few people realize that the 5,000 AIDS cases of Washington D.C. (nearly 1% of the population) reflect the number of symptomless carriers around 1980--i.e., two years before anybody had heard the word AIDS. Society's concern about fighting HIV-spread would be quite different if all the would-be victims already condemned by HIV to the death penalty were visible today.

Obviously, the time lag of around 12 years between cause (infection) and effect (AIDS outbreak) gives a long moratorium to wrong doctrines and makes it easy for those in charge of fighting the spread of AIDS to escape responsibility.

For a different example, consider the so-called safer sex strategy. Originally launched as safe sex, this strategy of using condoms allowed highly promiscuous people to keep practicing high promiscuity while believing to be out of danger. *Actual* condom use among those at risk has been found to be as low as 10-20 %. Simulating HIV-spread in populations using condoms in 20% of all sexual intercourse gives counterintuitive result: There is no fundamental difference in HIV-spread in comparison to no condom use at all.

Simulation models are an excellent tool to disclose the counterintuitive nature of complex dynamic systems. Candid linear thinking is completely inappropriate because it focuses on one action to achieve one goal, ignoring that most actions lead to unexpected consequences [1]. The recommendation of universal condom use as main means to combat HIV-spread is a case in point. Some of the important points one ought to have considered:

- Long experience with contraception has shown that condom use is among the least effective methods to prevent pregnancies (humans are not consistent and they are unreliable).
- Using condoms only in 1 out of 5 risky intercourse is much the same as having 20% less risky sex *without* condoms. The preventive effect of such a reduction in high-risk intercourse is negligible in the long term for high-risk groups, where many sexual encounters are potential sources of HIV-transmission.
- Youngsters believing in the tale of safe(r) sex probably increase their high-risk activity if they use condoms when they feel they are at risk. However, since you cannot see who is infected the ultimate effect is probably a general increase of HIV-transmission.

5.6 Conclusion

We have argued that an important parameter determining the extent of automation of instructional design is whether the issue is a closed or an open problem. Closed problems deal with topics where facts and heuristics are known and accessible. Open problems challenge the learner to localize, to find or even to discover crucial information concerning facts or heuristics.

Closed problems do not raise particularly interesting theoretical issues. Open problems are a formidable demand both because of their intrinsic importance and their challenge to instructional science, learning theory and technology.

References

1. Breuer, K., & Kummer, R.: Cognitive effects from process learning with computer-based simulations. Computers in Human Behavior, 6, 69-81 (1990)
2. Dörner, D.: Problemlösen als Informationsverarbeitung. Berlin: Kohlhammer 1976
3. Gonzalez, J.J.: Teaching problem solving in complex situations using simulation models. In K. Duncan, & D. Harris (Eds.), Computers in education (pp. 233-237). Amsterdam: Elsevier 1985
4. Gonzalez, J.J.: Coping with AIDS in the military: Computer-based education models to help prevent the spread of HIV, Part I. Medical Corps International, 5(1), 31-40 (1990)
5. Gonzalez, J.J.: Coping with AIDS in the military: Computer-based education models to help prevent the spread of HIV, Part II. Medical Corps International, 5(2), 38-44 (1990)
6. Hayek, F.: Law, legislation and liberty. Vol 1. Rules and order. London: Routledge & Kegan Paul 1973
7. Hodgson, V., et al. (Eds.): Beyond distance teaching towards open learning. Milton Keynes: SRHE/Open University Press 1987
8. Merrill, M. D., et al.: Limitations of first generation instructional design. Educational Technology, (1990)

6

Pedagogical Criteria for the Evaluation of the Automation of Instructional Design

Begoña Gros and José L. Rodríguez Illera

Department of Theory of Education, University of Barcelona, Baldiri Rexac, 08028 Barcelona, Spain

Abstract: The purpose of this chapter is to consider appropriate criteria for the evaluation of the automation of instructional design (ID). First, we review the current situation of ID advisors and their different perspectives. We simplify the different approaches used by various research groups to facilitate the discussion. Second, we analyze teaching and learning strategies from different positions, basically, the cognitive and constructivist approaches. And, finally, we point out some elements to think about with regard to the future perspectives of ID. In fact, we will center our reflections on three topics: knowledge format, instructional designer and forms of interaction.

Keywords: automated instructional design, evaluation, cognitive theories, constructivist theories, knowledge representation, instructional designers, interaction, interface design, pedagogical context

6.1 Introduction

Instructional design is a discipline that is concerned with understanding and improving the process of instruction. The purpose of any design activity is to improve the means of achieving desired goals, and the instructional designer has to know how to teach the content material in an effective manner. This means, obviously, using the best strategies to achieve student learning.

The decisions the instructional designer has to make are not simple. Problems appear for many different reasons. There are many theories about what learning is, and, consequently, about how to teach. Individual differences, content and context characteristics are also important to the process. Designing and creating instruction, especially for extensive or sophisticated courses, is a complex task.

To sum up, the designer must decide what content should be covered in a course, how it should be presented, and then produce the final course materials. Sometimes, the designer has good knowledge of the subject but does not know how to produce teaching and learning materials. To try to resolve this problem, the idea of automating instructional design (ID) has appeared to assist during the instructional design process.

Obviously, a solution to the problem would seem very interesting but this solution is not easy because the directions that we can choose are very extensive. In other words, the main question that we have to answer is, "how can automated ID work?" The answer to this question has many possible perspectives and should be studied in an interdisciplinary way, because it is not solely a psychological, pedagogical or computational problem. The main purpose of this chapter is to analyze how we should study the process and results of automated ID. To achieve this goal, first we will review the current situation of ID advisors and their different perspectives. Secondly, we will analyze the teaching and learning strategies from different approaches. Finally, we will point out some elements to think about with regard to the future developments of automation of ID.

6.2   A General View of Automated ID

The production of instructional software has a high cost and, often, the relationship between cost and effectiveness is not suitable. With the development of automated ID the cost should decrease but we also have to think about the quality of the final products. Recently, some tools to develop courseware, such as hypermedia authoring environments, have reduced the cost of producing courseware. For this reason, the contribution of an ID advisor has to be more ambitious. In other words, we think that automated ID has to assist in the instructional process, not only with the purpose of reducing cost, but also to increase the quality of current products. Obviously, economical aspects are important, but we are interested in education, so our main reflections are related to the idea that the result of our efforts in this area should provide better conditions for learning.

Although automation of ID has received a great deal of attention in the last few years, these products are not very widespread. Many systems have prototype status. Others are only for research purposes or still under development. This situation makes a general evaluation of the products more difficult. Another problem is to identify the final objective of the automation. We have detected two different positions on this question. First, some research groups want to develop expert programs for instructional designers who have only minimal training in instruction and learning strategies. Their purpose is to provide guidance in making instructional design decisions to produce the final courseware. This direction is more concerned with producing courses oriented, fundamentally, towards the area of the training of professionals in companies, industry, military , etc.

Another direction is adopted by some European groups. Their basic objective is the creation of open materials for distance education. That is, making tools which help produce programs that may be used by persons with differing levels of previous knowledge, or even with diverse objectives of training. The problem of specifying the way and the criteria in order to evaluate the process and results of automated ID is not only a question about the final objective. On the contrary, there are other variables that we have to consider because it is very difficult to establish a context free evaluation. Among the variables that we consider the most significant are (obviously, this is not an exhaustive list):

1. Final use: formal /non-formal education.

 It is not the same to produce a tool to automation of ID for the primary or secondary school as it is for distance learning or for military training, etc. Therefore, the context where the tool will be used is an important criteria to establish differences among instructional decisions relevant to evaluation.

2. Learner control: Open/Closed.

Another element to consider is the way that knowledge is organized and how the user should access to it. The freedom of the user to move through the system introduces important differences in the design, implementation and in the planning of the automation of ID.

3. External intervention.

When we talk about automation sometimes it is not clear if we are thinking of the automation of the whole process or if we are thinking to support specific design.

4. Level of users/students.

Different levels among the users are a function of development, cognition, skill, knowledge, etc, and these are all relevant to evaluation.

5. Level of instructional designers.

The process of automation ID changes a lot if we are thinking about a novice designer or in an expert. So, the degree of expertise is also one variable that we have to consider.

6. Presentation form.

The strategies of teaching can vary and this variable is also related with the previous variables because the ways to teach are influenced by the level of the students, external intervention, context, etc.

7. User interface.

Some automated ID products seems not to be very worried about the user interface and, sometimes these products are not very "friendly." We think that the user interface is very important from an educational point of view because an excellent tool would fail if the interface is not appropriate.

Besides these variables, when we think about the learning and teaching process, different pedagogical and psychological approaches arise. These perspectives must, necessarily, appear in a discussion about how automation of ID has to work. We want to center the discussion on two aspects: (a) how the knowledge is organized and (b) how the students have access to the content.

6.3 Approaches of Automated ID

Some automated ID products follow a specific theory of learning (see ID-Expert, SOCRATES, AIDA)[11,20], others are more eclectic and take ideas from different perspectives (e.g., IDE [19], IDIOM [7]). We think it would be better to establish a theoretical position, even if it doesn't have specific correspondence to the whole variety of products. For this reason, we are going to consider the main pedagogical problems of automated ID.

6.3.1 Cognitive Approach

The most widely applied instructional design theory is based on the work of Robert Gagné. This theory assumes an accumulative organization of learning events, based on the relationships among learned behaviors. Gagné's original work had an associationist approach: That is, different kinds of learning outcomes have their associated specific ways of teaching. Recent versions of the theory have incorporated ideas from cognitive psychology, but the essential characteristics of the original work remain.

Gagné's theory has provided an interesting approach, but has some problems that we must consider. One limitation involves the structure of the knowledge to be taught. The design of the content is made in an analytical way. First of all, we have to identify the components of the subject matter, and then use them to prescribe the course organization and the sequence of teaching. The elements of this analysis are individual content components such as facts, concepts, principles or procedures.

Using this approach it is difficult to achieve an integrated view because the course organization is made by a correspondence between content structure elements and instructional modules, from the bottom up, following the sequences suggested by Gagné's hierarchies. Gagné has recognized this limitation in a recent publication [3].

Another limitation of this theory is related to instructional strategies. In Gagné's theory the instructional strategies are independent of the content. He defines five phases of instructional development: analysis, design, development, implementation and evaluation. The outcome of each stage is the input to the next, and separate knowledge representations are used in each. His methodology provides no descriptions for how changes made in one stage should affect other stages.

Some of the first prototypes of automated ID which appeared in the 80's and followed Gagné's orientation. This work is often equated with the term, Instructional System Development (ISD), and some authors (e.g., Merrill) refers to early versions as ID1 (First Generation of Instructional Design, [11]).

Merrill points out several limitations when automating ID to the development of interactive technologies. Principal among these are [13, p.26]:

- Coherence: instructional analysis and design focuses on knowledge and skill components in isolation, and not on the integrated wholes, necessary for the understanding of complex and dynamic phenomena.
- Utility: prescriptions for pedagogical strategies are very superficial.
- Comprehensiveness: existing theory does not provide any means of incorporating expertise about teaching or learning gained from research and applying this in the design process.

Merrill's critical position seems to lead to a different perspective, more interested in producing flexible and re-usable instructional courseware, following a cognitive line.

In cognitive psychology, learning is viewed as much an individual as a social process. For this reason, instruction is the result of modeling individual processes. Merrill's theory is not an exception. This theory assumes learning is an internal and non-observable process.

The student's knowledge acquisition is based on several assumptions about [4, p.39]:

1. "There are different types of cognitive processes necessary to use each type of cognitive structure to achieve a given type of learned performance."

The cognitive conception started from the idea that there are different kinds of learning outcomes and each has a correspondence to a specific type of teaching process.   Content is independent of the general teaching strategies.

2. "The purpose of instruction is to promote the development of that cognitive structure which is most consistent with the desired learned performance."

The concept of "cognitive structure" attempts to overcome behaviorist conceptions about learning.   Here, learning is not an observable change; it is a deeper one.   After a learning process, the knowledge obtained results in changes in the cognitive structures of the student.

3. "The purpose of instruction is to promote incremental elaboration of the most appropriate cognitive structure to enable the student to achieve increased generality and complexity in the desired learned performance."

4. "The purpose of instruction is to promote that active cognitive processing which best enables the student to use the most appropriate cognitive structure in a way consistent with the desired learned performance."

5. Finally, Merrill proposes a practical principle, "The purpose of instruction is to provide the dynamic, ongoing opportunity for monitored practice that requires the student to demonstrate the desired learned performance, or a close approximation of it, while the instruction monitors the activity and intervenes with feedback both as to result and process."

The instructional models of Merrill and other cognitive positions (e.g., Anderson, Holland, Tennyson) overcome some limitations of behaviorism, but they also have some problems that are necessary to consider.

First of all, instruction is viewed as a correspondence between content and presentation form (following Merrill's terminology). In this way, the teacher has to adjust the content to the presentation. This adjustment is based on two kinds of activity: an exposition of the material and an inquisitorial process. The combination of showing what to learn, plus questions about the content, constitutes the teaching process.

The cognitive process of the student in getting the correct representation of the content, is evaluated through his/her answers. These answers have to show that the student has the same representation of the content as the expert on a specific topic. This perspective assumes that instructional knowledge should be well-structured, and that, after the learning process, the student will have the same knowledge representation.

The theory of Merrill, and its application in an expert system to assist in instructional design, called ID-Expert (corresponding to ID2 or second generation ID), offer important improvements in relation to previous cognitive theories. Among his contributions, maybe the most interesting is his idea of the transaction. Instructional transactions are "instructional algorithms or patterns of learner interactions which have been designed to enable the learner to acquire a certain kind of knowledge or skill" [13 p.50]. The main idea is that different kinds of knowledge and skill require different kinds of transactions. For instance, in ID-Expert, an instructional transaction shell selects those patterns of interactions that are more appropriate for a specific topic and presents the subject matter content to the knowledge base in a form that can be used by the transaction shell. The main advantages are, that once the transaction shells have been developed, they can be used again with another situation, and that the shell allows the separation of the subject matter content from the instructional strategies used to teach that content.

Currently, the cognitive model of learning is the most widely used in relation to the automation of ID. But it is not the only way to understand the instructional process. We are also going to consider the contributions of constructivist models.

6.3.2 Constructivist Approach

The application of constructivist theories of learning in education has a long and interesting history. However, when we talk about technology it seems that we have to forget or omit this history.

Recently, some authors have considered the importance of this position to the development of software (see, Educational Technology, May, 1991). We don't want to present constructivism in opposition to the cognitivist approach, because we think there are a lot of common aspects. Nevertheless, we want to point out some constructivist elements that we consider very important in the learning process, which the cognitive perspective might overlook.

(a) The constructivist process of learning

Cognitive and constructivist perspectives pointed out that the final objective of the instructional process is that the student obtains knowledge through a significant process, but the ways in which cognitivism and constructivism try to achieve this goal are quite different. For instance, in ID-Expert, different transaction shells allow the adaptation of the content to be taught for a specific learning purpose, but content is previously structured in a specific way. In other words, the outcomes of learning are associated with the structure of the content.

Constructivist instruction commonly confronts learners with some situations that make the inconsistencies in the learners' models plain, and challenges the learners either to construct better models or to build an alternative model suggested by the teacher. Conflict is always necessary to provoke learning. The main objective in this kind of conception is to get the students to become autonomous thinkers and learners. It is not only necessary to learn the specific content but also to be able to apply this content in different situations.

Spiro et al. [22] have developed an interesting constructivist theory that emphasizes the problem of oversimplifying the content. This theory shows the difficulty of finding out the structure of many instructional contents. However, the cognitivist position doesn't consider this idea very much. Usually, the content is viewed as something that is well-structured and has only one specific structure. In this sense, it is interesting to bear in mind the theory of Ausubel, who emphasizes the distinction between the logical structure of knowledge in a subject domain and the structure of the knowledge organized in the mind of the student and, as he said, there is no clear correspondence between them.

(b) Strategies of learning

The theories of Gagné and Merrill consider that learning goes from concrete ideas to general concepts, but when we receive information we need to find a relationship between this new information and previous knowledge. To get a significant relationship it is sometimes necessary to put examples, or concrete aspects, in contact with more general ideas. So, it is necessary to have general concepts (probably incomplete until that moment) with which to construct the association. In this way, Ausubel's model could be an alternative way to facilitate significant learning.

(c) Context

The role of context is very important in the constructivist approach. Learning should occur with realistic situations and reflect the real world in order to facilitate the transfer of learning. The constructivist emphasis on the social environment of instructional materials contrasts with the tendency in cognitive science to view the student-machine interaction as something independent or outside of the context. In the constructivist perspective, the machine is viewed as a mediator between the teacher and the student, or the teacher as a mediator between the student and the machine. Under this conception, the instructional designer should think about the specific context in which the program has to be used.

Another important idea that we have to consider is that the acquisition of knowledge is supported by learning in a social setting. Embedding instruction in a group has several advantages. According to Brown and Palincsar [1]: (a) cooperative learning provides a means of promoting the use of self-regulatory strategies in a group; (b) more complex problems can be tackled in a collaborative group than a single individual could accomplish; (c) the activities are modeled at different levels and become externalized through discussion; and finally, (d) the collaborative group provides support for learners at different levels of expertise, enabling them to use skills that are just emerging.

6.4 Some Elements for Reflection

To conclude, we would like to comment on some aspects which we think have still not been resolved, but which should, however, be taken into account in programs of automation of ID. Our perspective supposes a double analysis: (a) to support the effort which, from an educational point of view, is represented by the pragmatic establishment of an approach like ID2, which simplifies the type of problems which are pertinent to an ID project, thinking in real teaching terms and not exclusively from the theoretical approaches and (b) to question, for educational reasons, the logical space of the problem as construed in ID2.   The space of the problem may be informally defined thus:

If we had to summarize the general appreciation from a pedagogical point of view, it could be said that ID approaches, and specifically those called ID2, construct their problem as a case, or set of cases, of the general educational problem.   The special problem of the instructional designers usually reduces to deciding how to best transmit, faster and with the lowest cost, the educational content.   However, the general educational problem involves both the transmission of educational materials and their acquisition by students in various situations.   The training ideas which underlie ID approaches rest upon some important assumptions:

1. that the educative knowledge is (or may be) well structured;
2. that the principle decisions about training are made by the instructional designer, and
3. that the forms of interaction may be "encapsulated" in model-ramifications.

These three assumptions respond, in turn, to a certain "state-of-the-art" of current information technology knowledge, and to a pedagogical conception, about which we will now comment.

6.5 Knowledge Format

In the first place is the question of the format of educative knowledge.   The two principle tendencies start from opposing points of view.   For those who work in the field of instructional technology (IT), the question is how to model knowledge through rules and other forms of representation, which later may be re-used by the same system in such a way that the resulting reasoning resembles, as far as possible, human reasoning. On the other hand, approaches based on ID2 only consider the schematization of the knowledge necessary to achieve a specific function, that is, the teaching of a complex aspect which combines separable sub-domains.

The difference lies in that the second approach assumes that, in training, it is not necessary to take notice of the contradictory or unclear aspects of the structures of knowledge in general. However, various aspects seem to be, worthy of reflection:

- On one side, this difference only delays the more general problem, it does not resolve it. It is assumed that the objective of ID approaches, in the long term, includes the possibility of establishing "dialogues" between the system and the student, that will be developed in natural language, which as yet is not subject to automation.

- On the other side, as indicated in Spiro et al. [22], the problem of structuring very complex knowledge or knowledge which requires multiple perspectives also an unsolved problem.

- Furthermore, this difference does not resolve those cases of enterprises [3], which demand a type of knowledge about the world which is pre-supposed in the user - but which he or she may not have. Put another way, it does not attack the problem of the value of context to situate certain significances, nor that of the previous knowledge of the student.

- Finally, there is the question of relations within the knowledge of ID2. That is, the creation of materials to teach "enterprises" leaves out the teaching of general aspects about the organization of knowledge at higher levels.

If it is true that knowledge of the curriculum is constructed by way of a strong restriction on scientific knowledge which includes a simplification or schematization, it is also true that such forms of knowledge only respond to the most static educative knowledge, in which text books are included. The same formative dynamic leads to this framework being continually surpassed, as much in its aspects of content as in those aspects of the constant recontextualization of this same content. For this very reason, the four "models", which currently are used to format computer-based knowledge, reflect these variations:

- A specially constructed model, typical of traditional computer assisted instruction (CAI), which is not exhaustive and only contemplates those aspects of knowledge pertinent to the problem posed. The knowledge transmitted is the total knowledge of the system.

- A model can be constructed according to knowledge representation techniques derived from research into expert systems. This is the model proposed by ID2. The differences from the previous model are very important: the knowledge refers to the specific CAI project which is being constructed; without being exhaustive, it does model all those levels of representation which intervene in a hierarchical way; this "decomposition" of the project may be re-combined in its different levels and elements, to be taught in parts or in its totality; any change in, or addition to, any of the elements or levels is reflected in the instructional sequence. In general, it could be said that the knowledge, is made explicit according to a coherent system of modeling, and that this system is what generates the contents of the teaching.

- Attempts to represent the knowledge, in the field of intelligent tutoring systems (ITSs), constitute a third case. In these the representation does have to be exhaustive, in addition to other requirements not relevant to this discussion.

- Finally, hypertext information management systems contribute another point of view. In these, the representation is not exhaustive, due to the very conception of knowledge that tends to preside over them. The limits of the system are sometimes not well defined, in that the open-ended structure, which is at the base of the idea of hypertext, tends to make the very notion of limit, or of separation of knowledge, relative. However, hypertext specifics tend to be less ambitious and more pragmatic, supposing, in fact, a restriction on the general idea of knowledge.

At the moment, all the models involved seem to contribute important elements to the structuring of educative knowledge. None of them can offer a complete system of the multiple forms which knowledge adopts in the act of its transmission. For this very reason the forms of automation are far from being unique: not all educative knowledge responds always, in this act of transmission, to one sole strategy or representation, nor is all of it able to be transmitted. On the contrary, educative knowledge assumes a process of schematization and simplification, in relation to any (idealized) representation of scientific knowledge, which is not directly deducible from the structure of this knowledge.

6.6 Instructional Design

Another aspect of the question is that which emphasizes the fact that it is the instructional designer who, in some way, controls the instructional situation. Although this is usually the case, it is also true that it limits, to a great extent, the kind of teaching situations which may be created. The results of ID seem to be directed towards a very conventional type of CAI, in which students receive highly specific instructive packets and carry out a kind of individual teaching. Other alternatives are more difficult to manage. For example, if we were to think about the distinction between open and closed programs, the resulting programs would always be closed with regard to the type of content (even though they may have different levels and forms of treatment).

Another question which is also important is that which refers to the degree of automation that an instructional designer may reach, using this type of program. The prototypes reviewed until now only offer a kind of course which is not very motivating for the student, in which graphics hardly exist or are very schematic, and their integration with other multimedia technology is very limited. The development time of many CAI courses always includes the creation of graphical material, multimedia, as well as the final user interface. Having standardized the user interface, the result tends to be poorer than in the case of more crafted programs; for the same reason, only that which concerns the representation of knowledge is taken into account in the comparisons of development times.

But, in general, emphasizing the position of the designer responds to a conception of apprenticeship centered on teaching, rather than on the cognitive processes of the student. It concerns, on the other hand, an option which is congruent with current technical possibilities of the media and which depend, in part, on future developments in some of the previously mentioned areas. However, not all of the options depend on technological developments.

6.7 The Forms of Interaction

The supposition about being able to "encapsulate" interactions between the user and the program (present, for example, in Merrill's idea of "transaction shells") is, again, based on an image of the teaching process in which the computer takes the position of "instructor":

- This makes the results of ID apt for a very specific type of computer-based teaching, but not so appropriate for use in situations of teaching in person. The use of courses created with the ID approach in these situations is not anticipated in the majority of cases where something is lacking but, however, could be one of the most usual settings for its employment;

- Secondly, predefining the forms of interaction in discrete units (e.g, naming, whole-part relationships, etc.) assumes that the teaching takes place in a very specific way and that the student carries out the learning in a linear series of interactions: first, to name, then to relate, and after, to recompose parts, etc. However, although this is the ideal way prescribed by instructional designers, many students prefer a less restricted way of learning, in which the diverse procedures are more inter-related or, simply, in which it is possible to freely jump from one to another. This poses the more general question of knowing to what point the forms of interaction should not include an intelligent subsystem, capable of assuming that the user can change strategy without having to finish what he or she is doing, and without necessarily having to start again from the beginning.

Even so, the idea of the availability of predefined forms of interaction, relative to the cognitive procedures that the user employs, or should employ, seems a point of great interest, and an original idea for the automation of part of the design. In addition to the problem already indicated, the idea of the transaction shells, there is the more general question of knowing how these norms of interaction may be applied individually. That is, how is it possible to unite the appropriate contents for each subject with the form of interaction which is most suitable to produce teaching, suitable for the ZPD (Zone of Proximal Developing) [24] of a particular person? Human-based teaching has the unquestionable advantage of the flexibility which the teacher uses, according to the peculiarities of each person; these strategies are not solely a determination of content, but also a relation between adapted contents (to the specific case in question) and the chosen form of teaching.

On the other hand, human-based teaching strategies are always instantiated in dynamic learning and teaching strategies. The highly individualized relation between the user and the computer system means that these parameters do no exist.

6.8 Conclusion

To conclude this article, we will try to summarize the main ideas about the pedagogical criteria in order to evaluate the automation of instructional design:

- First of all, we must say that it is not possible to establish a general criteria to evaluate the automation of ID. For this reason, we have to determine a set of variables to study how we would know if automation is efficient. We pointed out some of them: context, open/closed system, external intervention, level of users, level of instructional designers, presentation form and user interface.

- After studying the current situation in the area of automation of ID we have found some common assumptions that are more or less shared by the experts in this area:

  1. The educative knowledge is (or may be) well structured.

  2. The principle decisions about training are made by the instructional designer.

  3. The forms of interaction may be encapsulated in models. Nevertheless, we think that it is important to review these ideas because they are not so clear as they seem.

- The main discussion about the quality of the automation is center to learning and instructional design. Which theories of learning and instruction are more appropriate for a particular situation? The answer to this question is not easy. We have referred to the cognitive and constructivist approaches. Both have interesting aspects and maybe the best thing to do is adopt an eclectic position, to try to specify the best of each approach in order to achieve the automation in a specific context. It is very easy to say but is very difficult to do. As a consequence this should be our main challenge.

References

1. Brown, A.L., & Palincsar, A.S.: Guided, cooperative learning and individual knowledge acquisition. In L.B. Resnick (Ed.), Knowing, learning, and instruction: Essays in honor of Robert Glaser. Hillsdale, NJ: Lawrence Erlbaum 1989
2. Gagné, R. (Ed.): Instructional technology: Foundations. Hillsdale, NJ: Lawrence Erlbaum 1987
3. Gagné, R., & Merrill, M.D.: Integrative goals for instructional design. Educational Technology: Research and Development, 38, 23-30 (1990)
4. Gagné, R., & Merrill, M.D.: Robert Gagné and M. David Merrill in conversation. Englewood Cliffs, NJ: Educational Technology Publications 1991
5. Gros, B.: La construcción de sistemas expertos aplicados a la enseÑanza. Nuevas Tecnologías y EnseÑanza, Graó/ICE, 137-154 (1989)
6. Gros, B., & Rodríguez Illera, J.L.: Inteligencia artificial y diseÑo de programas educativos. Revista EspaÑola de Pedagogía, 188, 39-57 (1991)
7. Gustafson, K., & Reeves, T.: IDiOM: A Platform for a course development expert system. Educational Technology, 31(3), 19-25 (1990)
8. Jonassen, D.H. (Ed.): Instructional design for microcomputer courseware. Hillsdale, NJ: Lawrence Erlbaum 1988
9. Jonassen, D.H., & Mandl, H. (Eds.): Designing hypermedia for learning. NATO ASI Series F, Vol. 67. Berlin: Springer-Verlag 1990
10. Mandl, H., Hron, A., & Tergan, S.: Computer-based systems for open learning. Report. Tübingen, Germany: University of Tübingen 1990
11. Merrill, M.D., Li, Z., & Jones, M.: Limitations of first generation instructional design. Educational Technology, 30 (1), 7-11 (1989)
12. Merrill, M.D., Li, Z., & Jones, M.: The second generation instructional design research program. Educational Technology, 31(3), 26-31 (1990)
13. Merrill, M.D.: Constructivism and instructional design. Educational Technology, 32(5), 45-52 (1991)
14. Perez, R., & Seidel, R.: Using artificial intelligence in education: Computer-based tools for instructional development. Educational Technology, 31(3), 51-58 (1990)
15. Ranker, R., & Doucet, R.: SOCRATES: A computer-based lesson development advisor. Educational Technology, 31(3), 46-50 (1990)
16. Reigeluth, C.M. (Ed.): Instructional design theories and models: An overviw of their current status. Hillsdale, NJ: Lawrence Erlbaum 1983
17. Reigeluth, C.M. (Ed): Instructional theories in action: Lessons illustrating selected theories and models. Hillsdale, NJ: Lawrence Erlbaum 1987
18. Rodriguez Illera, J.L.: Multimedia interactivos en educación. Nuevas Tecnologías y EnseÑanza. Graó/ICE, 155-168 (1989)
19. Russell, D. et al.: Creating instruction with IDE: Tools for instructional designers. Intelligent Tutoring Media, 1 (1), 3-16 (1990)

20. Spector, M., & Muraida, D. Designing and developing an advanced instructional design advisor. Final Report Research Projects. Brooks, TX: Armstrong Laboratories 1990
21. Spector, M., & Muraida, D.: Evaluating instructional transaction theory. Educational Technology, 32(10), 29-32 (1991)
22. Spiro, R. et al.: Cognitive flexibility, constructivism and hypertext. Educational Technology. 32(5), 24-33 (1991)
23. Tennyson, R.D., & Park, O.: Artificial intelligence and computer-based learning. In R. Gagné (Ed.). Instructional technology: Foundations. Hillsdale, NJ: Lawrence Erlbaum 1987

Part 1 Summary: Planning

Begoña Gros and Klaus Breuer

Three phases or stages constitute the development of instructional materials: planning, production and implementation. These three phases have special characteristic determined by different variables: specialists involved in each phase, duration of the activity, techniques required, etc. Nevertheless, these phases are not completely independent processes. Each phase assumes that special issues need to be considered but also that specification and development of each one determines and affects the rest.

This interaction arises clearly in the different chapters and discussions. The solution of most instructional development problems should integrate the total elaboration of the material. That is, it is not easy to talk about the evaluation of the production phase without thinking in the evaluation of the planning and implementation phases.

Although our goal in the part summaries is to summarize the main contributions of the presented papers, we will also make direct references to other issues: It is neither easy not desirable to avoid the interaction between them. To do so would give an unrealistic and simplistic idea of instructional development. This is an important point that the reader should keep in mind. Otherwise, you might feel a little lost in the middle of the discussions.

To talk about the planning process, we will divide the discussion into three steps: First, we will situate the problem of planning the automation of instructional design. Secondly, we will discuss the main controversial issues. Finally, we will make some suggestions about the kind of research that we will need to do in the future.

The Problem of Planning

Planning the automation of instructional design means to specify the final work of the system. In other words, planning involves, according to Peter Goodyear, the design of learning events, environments or resources, and the design of the activities involved in the system. In this phase the main decisions are the result of psychological and pedagogical designs. For this reason, the main questions arising during the planning phase are related to the application of educational principles into practice.

Much progress has been made in education during this century. Nevertheless, a lot of questions appear when we try to put educational theories into practice. It seems a paradox that the uses of artificial intelligence technology can improve knowledge about education but it is true that collaboration between both areas (education and technology) seems an interesting way to achieve the development of learning theories.

Changes in Education and Technology

When we talk about automation of instructional design it is necessary to center our attention in the words "instructional development." What does this expression mean?

It is not easy to find an answer to this question because each person considers the idea of instruction in different ways. Nevertheless, the idea has been changing during this century. For example, during the 1960s, instruction was based in a behaviorist paradigm. The teaching-learning process was affected by this model and the main emphasis was centered in the idea of instruction as the way to transmit knowledge.

Technology arrives to education under the influence of this educational model. So, as Tennyson (Chap. 3) points out, the first and second generations of Instructional System Development (ISD) have been a systematic approach to the development of instruction following the main ideas of the behavioral paradigm of learning. In other words, instruction was synonymous with declarative knowledge (knowing that). The main function of any teacher was to transmit knowledge and students had to learn this knowledge, mainly through a linear sequence of operant conditioning. Feedback is given in function of observable student answers.

The kind of technology that we need to facilitate learning of declarative knowledge is not very complicated. The objectives are clear and the way to produce learning and to evaluate it is also quite simple. However, due to cognitive and constructivist positions, we have learned that instruction is something more complex than knowing simple facts. Instruction also implies being able to acquire knowledge about how to do something, and why. When and where to apply knowledge is also an important aspect of the instructional process. In other words, instruction implies not only the acquisition of declarative knowledge but also the acquisition of procedural and contextual knowledge. That is, educators agree that it is as important to acquire a specific knowledge as to be able to transfer this knowledge in another context.

Current technology is more sophisticated, and for this reason when we talk about automation of instructional design we are thinking in the automation of a process that implies different levels of knowledge. For example, we need to consider how media may contribute to improvements in learning. To sum up, changes affect both basic instructional development procedures and highly sophisticated electronic delivery systems.

We agree that the alternative that Tennyson has proposed called, "Fourth Generation ISD," is a good description of the necessities that we have, for the automation of ID. The domains defined by this generation represent the use of the most sophisticated technology using advances from cognitive science, educational research and educational technology. Nevertheless, we have to be realistic and it is necessary to keep in mind that a lot of problems still remain in the production of this system. For example, problems in the design and production of computer-based instruction. As we said before, most specialists agree about the necessity of the use of the cognitive approach but when we try to define how to use these principles in practice, the agreement is extremely difficult. Developing concrete definitions for the processes of instructional development is one of the main challenges to automating ISD.

What Should be Automated?

An important question that we have to think about is what should or can be automated. According to Peter Goodyear, automation means to be "performed mechanically, without human intervention." This statement clarifies the definition of the problem, but it is still necessary to go ahead.

One possible agreement is to establish a difference between a strong version and a weak version of automation. In the first case, automation concerns the whole process of instructional development. In the second, automation is only a support for instructional designers. This is a relevant difference, because the knowledge involved in each case is quite different. However, in both cases there is another important variable that affects the specification of the problem: the difference between automation in the case of closed problems or open problems.

According to José Gonzalez, most efforts are made for closed problems. This kind of problem is defined by complete knowledge about the facts and methods, to arrive at a solution. On the opposite side, we find a lot of problems with incomplete knowledge in which it is necessary to use contextual or situated knowledge. The process of automation of both kinds of knowledge is quite different. The Fourth Generation ISD proposed by Tennyson also insists in this idea. We need flexible techniques to represent different levels of knowledge and abstraction.

In the same direction, other authors (Gros and Rodríguez, Chap. 6) emphasize the idea that knowledge used in the automation of ID is constructed by strong restrictions such as simplification or schematization of knowledge. Education knowledge assumes a process of simplification in relation a representation of scientific knowledge. In this context, some closed problems are not, in the real world, so restrictive. For this reason, it is necessary to review the taxonomies of learning used by instructional designers.

Theories of Learning and Theories of Instruction

During the planning phase it is necessary to establish a model of instruction. Almost all instructional systems are based on some specific theory of learning, or on some general assumptions about how to learn.

Through the discussion of these models it is possible to observe a high level of agreement. Most authors share a cognitive paradigm. The ideas about how to learn and how to teach are not very different. However, problems start when we try to define, or specify how instruction has to reflect these psychological principles. Different approaches appear and in the examples of the works presented by Gonzales and Vavik (Chap. 5) and Merriënboer, Krammer, and Maaswinkel (Chap. 4), we can see some of these differences.

As we mentioned, probably one of the main problems is the inadequacy of the taxonomies that have been used by instructional designers. We need an integration between instructional goals and learning outcomes. Maybe the way to achieve this integration is study what teachers really do in the classroom, and maybe this study will lead to a more integrated position of learning and teaching theories.

Evaluation

Evaluation is the activity that we need to be able to control the progress of our work. In relation to the evaluation of the planning process, we can consider two different perspectives; the economical and pedagogical types of evaluation.

One of the main purposes for automating of ISD is to decrease the cost of software development. So, the automation of ISD has to produce materials which are reliable and reusable and with a high level of generality. And, it is necessary to control and evaluate, with economical criteria, the effectiveness of the planning process.

Another side of the problem is the pedagogical evaluation. It is usual that the great efforts made in the development of technology have no clear correspondence to the uses made of them. So, it is very important to evaluate the planning process through the application of pedagogical criteria.

This is not a resolved question but some variables are proposed by Gros and Rodríguez to establish some criteria in order to evaluate the planning process of automation ID. Nevertheless, these criteria should also be applied in the production and implementation phases. According to Muraida (Chap. 8), evaluation is integral to each phase of planning, developing and implementation: It is not appropriate to completely separate evaluation of each phase.

Future Research

We have attempted to summarize the main issues presented in the workshop papers and the ensuing discussions about the planning phase. Many questions and problems have appeared and for this reason we would like to focus attention on the main issues that still present unanswered questions. From among these, we have selected the problem of the taxonomies of learning outcomes.

There is an important gap between learning and teaching theories. Taxonomies used by most systems are based in a simplification of knowledge, in an analytical exposition of content. It is necessary to review the way that knowledge has to be used and the strategies to access to specific knowledge. A possible methodology proposed is to study in more detail what teachers are doing in practice.

7

Issues Concerning the Development and Application of Educational Software

Juana Mª Sancho Gil

Dto. de Didáctica y Organización Escolar. University of Barcelona. Baldiri Reixac, s/n Torre D-4º 08028 Barcelona (Spain)

Abstract: This chapter addresses issues of educational software development taking into account the context nature of teaching and learning situations. Issues discussed include: (a) different social and cultural milieus; (b) school organizations; (c) age and background of students; (d) pedagogic demands of students and teachers; (e) curricula requirements; (f) multiplicity of learning tasks. Other indirect issues in the development and application of educational software are: (a) lack of a generalized consensus about the best teaching methods and the best learning strategies; (b) persistent lack of investment in educational resources and limited use of the existing ones; (c) institutional inertia to change.

Keywords: teaching devices, educational media, school context, educational innovation, computers in education, educational design, learning tasks

7.1 Introduction

When researchers from different backgrounds decide to pool their efforts together to develop educational software, they can do it from at least two different approaches. One of them can be to deepen, explore, and test hypotheses about the computer potential and the metaphors or theories which try to explain human learning. The other can be that their developments can be used in "real" teaching and learning contexts, for instance in schools. In fact, one could argue that both objectives should be closely related, if one wants to achieve the "ecological validation" proposed by psychologists [2]. However, it is not always possible to see a clear relationship between them.

My argument is that real teaching and learning situations are so complex and full of values and meaning, that it is difficult to take into account all of the issues which they raise. In this chapter, I am not going to speak about the internal issues and topics related to the automation of instructional design, as it will form the basis of the contribution of most of the other participants in this book. Instead, I am going to concentrate on a set of elements which constitute the essence of the school systems, and in doing so, are capable of influencing the processes of instructional development and application in real settings of any teaching device whose aim is to improve teaching and learning. I hope that by looking at this side of the question, I will help to explain the difficulties related to the automation of instructional system development.

7.2 Searching Dreams

Computer supported instructional design had its birth and its first developments in the confluence of at least three rising dreams: (a) the technological design of instruction provided by the application of the principles of behaviourism to training and teaching; (b) the computer revolution; and, (c) the cognitive revolution.

Behaviorists thought that teaching was a technological matter. For them it would consist in applying the principles of scientific findings in the laboratory to the design of technological devices to provide students with the best and most effective kind of teaching. The irruption of the computer gave an important boost to this teaching perspective. In a given moment, cognitive processes were seen as practicable computer programs. This view brought Newell and Simon to write in 1958 "there are now in the world machines that think, learn and create. Likewise their capacity to do these things is rapidly increasing to the point that -in a visible future - the range of problems which they will be able to undertake will be coextensive to the range to which the human brain has been applied" [17].

The over-optimistic appearance of the dream, has not prevented a bewildering awakening. Brunner, one of the promoters of the cognitive revolution, in one of his latest books makes a heavy critique of the development of this psychological approach to cognition. In his view, the cognitive revolution was about making a determined effort to restore meaning as a fundamental concept of psychology; not stimuli and responses, nor openly observable behavior, nor biological impulse and its transformations, but meaning. It was a deeper revolution. Its goal was to discover and formally describe meaning created by human beings according to their world experiences, to in turn propose hypotheses about the processes of meaning construction on which they were based [3].

From another view, looking at the development of educational technology and educational media, and at the problems faced by the educational system, I can argue that the first two have contributed little to the third. Because there are some formal teaching systems, it is possible to find educational or training devices designed to teach something to somebody as effectively and quickly as possible: for example, from the reading book by Caton to the most sophisticated ICAI, ICAL or interactive computer programmes. Especially after World War II, every technical innovation was seen as having fabulous opportunities for better education. According to Cohen [6],

> ...changes in publishing that made cheap books widely available was an early case: the paperback revolution was announced as a way to free students and teachers from the text, lectures and recitation...Educational television was another early hope, but prophecies of new freedom for teachers and students were quickly followed by stories about TV sets languishing in school closets...Computers-assisted instruction was much more exotic, though one remembers CAI more for its impact on large corporations than for its effects on school instruction.

However, as Cohen has pointed out, professional innovators and designers who are away from school often forget that educational systems and schools are very complex artefacts in which very different people interact.

7.3 School Teaching and Learning do not Happen in a Vacuum

When psychologists study learning processes, when educational designers plan instructional materials and even when educationists develop teaching methodologies, too often all of them seem to forget that teaching and learning are never done out of a context. This context, today more than ever, for most children between ages 4 and 18, and for about five hours per day, or course is school.

Schools are relatively new institutions with apparently very rooted behavior. In fact, the difficulty to introduce innovations in the school system has been the object of research and study for many years. Especially nowadays just due to the Information Technology Revolution, educational innovation is not only a technical problem, but a political and social one. For the authors of the last report by the Club of Rome [5], education has to face three great problems: (a) being able to choose, from the plethora of the accumulated knowledge in different fields, what should be transmitted; (b) the difficulty of updating teacher knowledge and skills; and (c) the inadequacy, as young people think that a feature of conventional education is, that it does not keep an adequate relationship with the world and does not prepare them to meet the market requirements.

The difficulty of introducing any innovation, new practice or device rest on the systemic character of the act of teaching when it is performed in school (or in any formal system). As I have shown in other writings [13], the basic features of the system in which school teaching and learning takes place can be seen in the Figure 7.1.

To this effect, the need is to move away from the simplistic approaches to change and innovation in education which were followed in the sixties and seventies with the development of "teachers proof" teaching materials and see that, as Brofenbrenner [2] has suggested, a way of understanding the complexity of a system educational software development is trying to intervene in it.

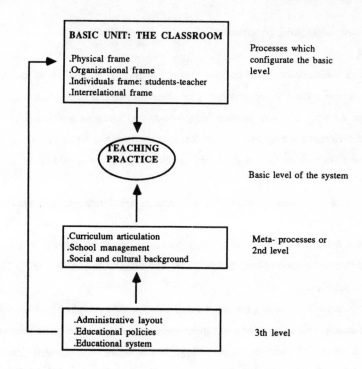

Fig. 7.1. Formalization of teaching practice as a system.

In the case of the school system, there is an apparent paradox. On the one hand, it is possible to find a behavioral pattern which can be explained by most institutional aspects of schooling. For example, Apple [1] writes about the hidden curricula in schools and Young [18] points out the existence of consistent patterns for school knowledge representation [18]. However, on the other hand, each classroom within each school makes up an entity, which can have many features in common with others, being at the same time singular (not unique) and unrepeatable.

7.4 Teaching and Learning Situations

Following the previous discussion, without being too exhaustive, it is possible to look at the different elements which influence the singularity of the classroom setting. Elements whose interaction can produce very different relationship contexts and teaching and learning ethos, which can result in different learning experiences for both students and teachers.

In a brief approach, in this interaction the following elements can be considered:

(a)   Different social and cultural milieus. School systems are implanted and also create different social and cultural milieus. These differences result in the shaping of diverse situations. In some places, social and cultural pressures can force schools to introduce educational or technical innovations, and in others any innovation can be seen as "losing the essence of schooling."

(b)   School organizations. Classrooms are not isolated entities, they are placed within a given school organization which can boost or inhibit educational innovation. The role of the headteacher or other staff members in providing, facilitating or obstructing the access to instructional media, has to be taken into account.

(c)   Age and background of student. Within a school system, even within a classroom, students coexist who not only have different chronological ages, but also with different out of school experiences, social backgrounds and cultural values. This, as cultural psychology has pointed out, can result in, not only different capabilities to undertake school knowledge, but different emotional positions and meaning facing it.

(d)   Pedagogic demands of students and teachers. When teachers and learners meet in the classroom setting, they both can be put under different kinds of pressure. Both usually have a quite clear view of what teaching should be about, and, at the same time, teachers have to answer social demands, through the curriculum and the school organization, and pupils need to give meaning to the world they are just discovering. Quite often both requirements are not easily found and negotiation becomes necessary.

(e)   Curricula requirements. As society becomes more and more complex, schools are more and more responsible for educating pupils to be able to respond to social challenges. So, in less than forty years, school curricula have been pushed to consider more and more diverse kinds of knowledge, skills and values.

(f)   Multiplicity of learning tasks. The development and implementation of school curriculum means the performance of many different learning tasks in a school day and for scholastic years. The different learning tasks proposed by teachers have different teaching demands and challenges for them, and different learning difficulties and challenges for students, and these activities result in a set of varied learning tasks. What is more, regarding the eventual use of instructional software in the classroom, at least if we refer to the existing one, teachers can find activities and tasks proposed that are too simple or too complex [15].

7.5 School Tasks and Computer Tasks

According to Kemmis et al. [10], in instructional programs as well as in classroom situations, students can face a set of different learning tasks:

(a)   Recognition. Students learn from a text. The "correctness" of their answer is judged in terms of the direct relationship between their response and the texts as the perfect version.

(b)   Recall. As in the previous situation, students learn from a text and the "correctness" of their answer is again judged in terms of direct relationship between their response and the texts as the perfect version.

(c)   Reconstructive understanding or comprehension. Answers can range from quite elementary types of comprehension to some fairly subtle ones. They are not text-dependent but discourse-dependent, that is to say, the correctness of the responses can be judged by reference to the semantic content of the information given.

(d)   Global reconstruction or intuitive understanding. These answers generally involve prolonged activity, and control over the interaction rests on the student more than on the program. They create the opportunity for students to "get a feel" for an idea, to develop a sense of applicability for problem solving or diagnosis strategies, or to learn subtle recognition skills.

(e)   Constructive understanding. These are extremely open-ended and involve the student in creating fields of knowledge.

In these two last kinds of tasks the arbitration of whether or not learning has occurred requires a far more complex judgment: the correctness or incorrectness of the response can not be decided in terms of a simple discrepancy between response and text. That is to say, the higher the cognitive level of the task set in a computer program, the more difficult and challenging it is to automate it.

7.6 Other Indirect Instructional Development Issues

In the previous sections I have given an overview of a set of issues related to teaching and learning in school contexts which are relevant to the problem of developing and implementing educational software. In the next sections I will refer to other issues which also play a part in this process.

7.6.1 Lack of Consensus about Teaching Methods

The educational field is full of books, reports, conferences and discussions trying to define and find what will be considered as "good" teaching. However, the answer to this important question is not easy. And it is not easy because it deals with individuals, and individuals cannot be understood out of their culture. As Geertz [8] points out, that without culture, individuals are incomplete animals which are complete and finished through culture. And culture is full of values and meanings. So to be able to determine what good teaching is, I have to be prepared to give also answers to questions such as: "good for what" and "good for whom."

In doing that, I have to refer, on the one hand, to educational goals, and educational goals are narrowly related to political, social and economical goals. And, on the other hand, to individuals idiosyncrasy, and that has to do not only with individual psychology but also with history, anthropology, sociology.

In fact, in order to improve people's capabilities to learn, in a world in which "learning to learn" is seen as one of the greatest values, the use of many different teaching methods and the diversification of learners' experiences and ways to access information and knowledge seem to be one of the challenges of education.

7.6.2 Are There Such Things as "Best" Learning Strategies?

Even in the case in which teaching is homogeneous, students use different strategies and ways to approach knowledge. Entwistle [7] has categorized three different approaches to learning: deep, superficial, and strategic. Apparently, students use one approach or another according to the kind of task and the kind of teacher. And Pask [12] distinguished two learning styles for tasks which involved comprehension: holistic and serialist, which represent logical preferences in the use of certain learning processes. In a research study, I presented instructional materials designed according to the holistic and serialist principles, and then gave students these materials according to their learning styles. Students were matched and unmatched: holistic with holistic materials, holistic with serialist materials and so on. The result was that the weakest students matched performed almost as well as the best students unmatched. So an instructional method can only be effective when students have comparable learning styles.

7.6.3 Persisting Lack of Investment in Educational Resources

Although there is a high rhetoric about the social benefit created by schooling, usually, this does not go along with the kind of investment needed, specially if we compare it to other fields. So traditionally, education has not received enough economic attention both in research and development and in school equipment and staff recognition.

In the late sixties and early seventies developed countries such as the United States, Great Britain, Sweden, and so on, gave an important impulse to research and development in education by dramatically increasing government funding. The idea being that coordinated and widely funded educational research and development will achieve these results already obtained by industry, that is to say, an increase of effectiveness and productivity. However, even in those days of noticeable and decided effort to invest in education matters, in 1971 John Brademas, the president of the Education Select Subcommittee of House of Representatives of the United States, pointed out that about 10% of the Department of Defense budget and 4.6% of the Public Health was spent in research and development. In contrast, less than a third of one per cent of the nations educational budget was used in planned research, innovation and renovation processes.

According to data provided by the National Center for Educational Statistics [11] between the fiscal years of 1980 and 1989, federal funds for elementary and secondary education declined 17%. From 1981, the Department of Education budget declined from 0.6% to 0.4% of the gross national product and from 2.5% to 1.8% of the federal budget [4]. Federally funded educational research also declined. Between 1980 and 1989 funds for educational research and development decreased by 33%. Although total funding for federal research and development increased by 24% during the Reagan years, that increase was in military defense area. In the fiscal year 1987, defense accounted for 64% of the total federal research and development funds, and education for 0.2% [16].

Though this situation could be generalized to other countries, during the eighties, many educational systems have developed special programs to make sure that most schools benefit from working with computers. Since the mid-seventies, almost all European countries started different kinds of projects to help schools and educational and training institutions to cope with the challenges of the Information Technology Age. Only in Spain, were there has been a decentralized administrative system for educational matters since the early eighties, there are six different plans to introduce Information Technology in the school curriculum at the moment.

In Catalonia (Spain), after several years of uncoordinated experiences at primary, secondary and vocational school level, since 1985, there has been a local government program to systematically and gradually introduce computers at every state school level. A special budget has been provided to this commitment which includes the provision of computer equipment (hardware and software) for all state schools in Catalonia. Until May 1991, the PIE had covered a total of 657 educational institutions. However, in spite of the important amount of money spent (sometimes at the expense of other needs) at the present moment the ratio teacher/computer is 1 to 3 and student/computer ratio is 5 to 8.

But the lack of educational resources is not the only problem faced at school level when it comes to the use of instructional materials, another one is the limited use of the existing ones. And this have very much to see with teacher education and school routine.

7.6.4 Institutional Inertia to Change

Finally, one of the most important issues which can prevent the introduction of any technology at school level is the institutional inertia to change. Teachers and administrator are very much influenced by their own learning experiences and it is extremely difficult for everybody to abstract him or herself from his or her own way of understanding and thinking about teaching and learning. In fact, as Shipman and Rainor [14] have suggested, professional identity is built by knowledge and experience accumulated through teachers experiences as students. So, if along with the use of a technology comes the suggestion that their knowledge is obsolete or their role inadequate, their professional identity will feel attacked and the technology will be resisted.

7.7 Conclusion

When we speak about learning automation, if we do not want to follow a very simplistic perspective, we need to take into account the nature of teaching and learning situations in a given context. The latter are characterized by their singularity. Features which could influence this are: (a) different social and cultural milieus; (b) school organization; (c) age and learning background of pupils; (d) psychopedagogic demands of students and teachers; (e) curricula requirements; and, (f) multiplicity of learning tasks. Other issues which can help to understand the problem of designing and using educational software are: (a) the lack of a generalized consensus about the best teaching methods and the best learning strategies; (b) the persistent lack of investment in educational resources and limited use of the existing ones; and, (c) the institutional inertia to change.

References

1. Apple, M.W.: Ideology and curriculum. London: Routledge & Kegan Paul 1979
2. Brofenbrenner, U.: The experimental ecology of education. Teacher College Record, 78, 157-203 (1976)
3. Brunner, J.: Acts of meaning. Cambridge, MA: Harvard University Press 1990
4. Clark, D. L., & Astuto, T. A.: The disjunction of federal education policy and educational needs in the 1990's. In D. Mitchell, & M.E. Goerzt (Eds.), Education politics for the new century. London: Falmer Press 1990
5. Club of Rome: La revolución global. Barcelona: Plaza y Janés 1992
6. Cohen, D. K.: Educational technology and school organization. In R. S. Nickerson, & P. P. Zodhiates (Eds.), Technology in education: Looking toward 2020. Hillsdale, NJ: Lawrence Erlbaum 1988
7. Entwistle, N.: Understanding classroom learning. London: Hodder & Stoughton 1987
8. Geertz, C.: Interpretation of cultures. New York: Basic Books 1973
9. Husén, T.: The learning society revisited. Oxford: Pergamon Press 1986
10. Kemmis, S. et al.: How do students learn? Norwich, UK: CARE, University of East Anglia 1977
11. National center for educational statistics: Federal support for education: Fiscal years 1980 to 1989 (NCES 90-662). Washington, DC: U.S. Department of Education 1990
12. Pask, G.: Styles and strategies of learning. British Journal of Educational Psychology, 46, 128-148 (1976)
13. Sancho, J. M.: Los profesores y el curriculum. Barcelona: Horsori 1990
14. Shipman, M., & Raynor, J.: Perspectives on the curriculum. Bletchley, UK: The Open University 1972
15. Straker, A.: A sorry state of affairs. The Times Educational Supplement, May 9, 1986
16. U.S. General Accounting Office.: R&D funding: The Department of Education in perspective (CAE/PEMD-88-18FS). Washington, DC: Author 1988
17. Weizenbaum, J.: Computer power and human reason. San Francisco: W. H. Freeman 1976
18. Young, M.F.D. (Ed.): Knowledge and control: New directions for the sociolgy of education. London: Collier-Macmillan 1971

8

Evaluating Automated Instructional System Development

Daniel J. Muraida

Instructional Design Branch, Armstrong Laboratory, Human Resources Directorate
(AL/HRTC), Brooks AFB, Texas 78235-5601 USA

Abstract: This chapter discusses the need to evaluate the automation of instructional system development. First, an accurate model of the ISD process is portrayed to provide a schema for its evaluation. ISD is an ill-formed problem-solving process and should be viewed in terms of cognitive tasks. In automated cases, the process of the system should be mapped onto the components of the ISD model. This would form the basis for an analysis of the contribution of each component to the development tasks. Evaluation will make developers sensitive to the influence of different contexts on the nature of instructional development.

Keywords: evaluation, automated instructional design, instructional design, expert systems, assessment

8.1 Introduction

The high front end costs of computer-assisted instruction (CAI) have generally been attacked in two general ways. Instructional delivery strategies have been implemented in an attempt to increase student performance indices to levels which justify the initial investment. Secondly, authoring tools have been developed to streamline and expedite instructional design work [11]. Evaluation of CAI, however, has given more emphasis to instructional delivery and its supporting knowledge bases and architectures. As a result it appears that the evaluation of automated instructional development has been given short shrift [20].

8.2 Evaluation of Automated Instructional System Development

What does this phrase mean? If one were to guess that it refers to the formative evaluation of products of automated development environments that would be partially correct. However, for the purposes of this chapter evaluation of automated instructional development refers to the assessment of the congruency between user characteristics, the requirements of the instructional development goals, and the nature of the instructional material. Why should developers and evaluators be concerned about calibrating automated development assistance so finely?   To answer this question it is necessary to examine the instructional development process and its automation more closely.

8.3 Instructional System Development

Instructional technologists are often guilty of using the terms instructional design and instructional development as synonyms for the entire process of creating instruction, or using them to refer to separate phases of that process.   We will refer to the entire process as "Instructional Development" using design and development to refer to individual phases. The purpose of the instructional development process is to implement decisions for structuring the environment with conditions which will foster learning [5]. Like the instructional design process, instructional development is typically described at the task level, albeit in terms of developing test items, implementing instructional strategies, and producing instructional materials. While these procedures are part and parcel of instructional development, many fledgling practitioners tend to implement them at a superficial level or in a rigidly linear fashion.

The reason for this situation is that Instructional Development is often a highly complex and ill-formed problem solving process [4; 16]. Designing, developing and delivering successful instruction requires that the designer possess specific knowledge about what works for the learners in question as well as what works across contexts. At the expert level these skills have been characterized as high level thinking processes which employ heuristics more frequently than algorithms [15]. Nelson et al. [15] assert that Instructional Development encompasses a range of approaches and prescriptions of which heuristics and algorithms are the endpoints. Given the potential for complexity in instructional design and development, and the experience-based differences among practitioners, it is obvious that automated guidance must take those differences into account. Providing guidance at levels inappropriate to the background of the designer will likely result in inefficient and ineffective use of the tool.

Evaluating the instructional products that emerge from the use of automated instructional development system does nothing to correct deficiencies in the system itself. In those cases where something is wrong we definitely want to know why. Without knowing how well the guidance fits the needs of the designers one is not in a position to take corrective action. But the nature of Instructional Development and the background of the designer probably account for only part of the problem of adaptive guidance. Automation itself is a factor.

8.4 Authoring Environments and Instructional System Development

Automation of instructional development may actually compound the difficulty of the process. Goel and Pirolli [6] report cases of increased difficulties for instructional designers when the process is automated. They contend that this is a general phenomenon in the automation of design and development processes (e.g., in architecture and mechanics). Automating instructional development means that the designer has to be at least minimally competent in the use of the computer as a rapid prototyping tool. Coupled with the development decisions that are required of any instructional designer, courseware authoring adds additional complexity.

More specifically, the problem engendered by introducing authoring environments is their potential to cause breakdowns in what might otherwise be a minimally acceptable level of designer productivity. In the ideal situation, of course, the authoring environment remains in the background, supporting the designer in his/her tasks. This allows the designer to focus on the development task at hand without having to deal explicitly with the intricacies of Instructional Development or computer operation.   In Bodker's [2] terms the authoring environment is an artifact which should allow the user to operate directly on an object (instructional design and development).

As an example of how the nature of authoring environments may affect the process of development, consider word processing applications. The early word processors were line-oriented, restricted to manipulating single lines of text. Moving large sections of texts was a line-by-line process. As screen editors became available and more sophisticated it became possible to manipulate progressively larger units of text. Users could take whole blocks of text, move them, and copy them as desired. With the primitive word processors it was possible for the user to create rather elegant documents at the cost of dealing a large number of complex commands. The population capable of using this type of tool efficiently was probably rather narrow. By contrast, current word processors can be used by a much broader populace. The end products of these two types of systems might appear quite similar, but the costs and level of effort involved in their development would contrast sharply [20].

In the case of courseware authoring systems a much broader range of tasks confronts the designer. It is very likely that designer experience may be high in some areas and minimal in others. The implication is that authors with different experience profiles may encounter situations where they must deal explicitly with the artifact they are using at different points in the development process [2]. Realizing cost savings and economy of effort is extremely difficult if one cannot identify the points at which authoring environments breakdown for the designer.

Data supporting the relationship between the quality of adaptive instructional design and development guidance and the instructional impact of the ensuing courseware do not exist in abundance. The available data are essentially the products of pilot studies which provide suggestive support for the hypothesis that good automated guidance begets good CAI [2]. There is evidence, however, in the human-machine system design literature to suggest that "adaptive aiding" can improve human performance [17]. This line of research suggests a number of basic principles of adaptation suggesting when and where to provide guidance or "aiding" and how to foster user acceptance of the aiding (e.g., "Ensure the users feel they are in charge..."). These principles appear to be quite germane to automated instructional development. Moreover, Rouse [17] has set forth a number of issues which should be investigated if the adaptive guidance hypothesis is to receive a thorough test. It is proposed that this test would yield information of direct importance for CAI production. One of Rouse's [17] major contentions is that the data base on adaptive aiding needs to be extended to a broader array of task domains so that the implications of aiding can be understood for situation assessment, planning, and monitoring functions. This implies that the Instructional Development domain should be given close scrutiny so as to accurately determine the roles for automated guidance.

8.5 The Nature of Instructional System Development

The traditional Instructional System Development model was based on a series of modifications to an engineering approach to curriculum development [13; 3; 1]. Virtually all the models include the familiar phases of analysis, design, development, implementation, and maintenance, or some closely linked variation. They differ in the amount of detail they provide in each phase, and some of them differ, depending on their age, in the degree to which they interpret Instructional Development as a linear process, and in the degree to which they incorporate cognitive approaches to instruction [12]. Almost all models, however make some overture to cognitively-based instruction.

As mentioned earlier, Nelson et al.[15] have portrayed Instructional Development as a predominately ill-structured problem solving process. Their paper contends that Instructional Development problems and models, lie on a continuum from ill-structured to well-structured. Furthermore they assert that instructional designers vary along the same dimension from novices to experts, with corresponding cognitive differences in the way they approach their tasks. Nelson [14] substantiated this in a study of novice and expert instructional designers' thought processes. What Nelson et al. [15] have done to the domain of Instructional Development is to subject it the cognitive analysis of its most current instructional strategies. This implies that instructional designers may use the same type of problem-solving techniques and tools (e.g., schemata, metacognitive processes) to accomplish their work. Furthermore, this implies that communicating with the designer, as in communicating with the learner, requires a message tailored to his/her level of expertise.

Tennyson's model [12] emphasizes the use of cognitively-based instructional strategies, as do other models. What sets his model apart, however, is its emphasis on human activities (what instructional designers do) as opposed to instructional development milestones. This model attempts to specify what actions the designer must take to create conditions conducive to learning. Instructional Development is viewed as being an inherently iterative process in which the designer may go from design to development, to implementation and back to design or development. This view ties in closely with Nelson's assertion [15] that instructional designers often go from level to level of a problem rather than working in a "top-down" fashion. In line with this notion, one of the major issues which Tennyson addresses is the need for the designer to trace the effects of instructional needs, goals, and actions across Instructional Development phases. In essence this suggests that automated instructional development cannot be modeled apart from the phases of the process.

Coupling Tennyson's model with Nelson's characterization of Instructional Development would appear to yield a model which explicitly describes how the designer organizes his/her thoughts about Instructional Development, in terms of planning, schemata use, and metacognition during the evolution of a courseware design.

8.6 Modeling and Evaluating System Development

As was suggested in the previous section, it is unrealistic to say that one is modeling or evaluating one particular phase of Instructional Development, given that the designers often recycle from phase to phase. It would appear that Tennyson's and Nelson's work provide a reasonably accurate description of the entire enterprise. What is needed now is a systematic approach for capturing the designer variables in a way that permit evaluators and researchers to establish their impact on the resulting courseware.

In the absence of viable alternatives it appears that an observational approach offers the greatest potential for generating valid data. Observational studies of complex problem solving [9; 7] appear to offer a reasonably close analogue to Instructional Development problem solving.

Hammond et al. [9] and Hamm [7] have presented evidence to support the notion that complex problem solving often requires a shift between analytic and intuitive thinking. Analytical thinking, according Hamm, is characterized as slow and deliberate, and usually highly accurate and consistent. Intuitive thinking is, by contrast, rapid, unconscious data processing, characterized by moderate levels of accuracy. Until recently however, claims about shifts along a continuum between intuition and analysis during task performance could not be studied directly [10; 19]. Hamm's [7] efforts to study the effects of task characteristics on a moment by moment basis appear to provide a molecular level of analysis which would enable observers to pinpoint the components of the instructional design task which require differing levels of intuitive or analytical thinking.

Using two observational instruments, which focus respectively, on observer assessments and task performer perceptions, Hamm [7] has attempted to capture the continuum of cognitive modes between intuition and analysis by scaling general features of cognitive modes common to a broad range of problem solving activities. Data are collected using protocols obtained as subjects "think aloud" [18]. Hamm's methodology has demonstrated the capacity to identify intuitive and analytical components of complex task performance in content areas where a fair amount of agreement exists on the manner in which cognitive modes are distributed (e.g, clinical diagnosis) [8]; and engineering [9; 7].

The cognitive continuum dimension appears to be useful in that it provides an abstract, meta-language to describe the real-time process of Instructional Development that is not tied to the peculiarities of a particular authoring environment. By relating the cognitive mode of the designer to his/her activities at a particular juncture in an Instructional Development task it should be possible, in principle, to determine which aspects of a design task could benefit from algorithms, and conversely, which might benefit from some other form of support (e.g., coaching, critiquing, etc.).

At a more molar level, the use of the cognitive continuum approach incorporates the variable types alluded to above: Designer experience and ability; and the design environment, in conjunction with the nature of the design task. It is expected that these variables will be related to the type of cognitive mode a designer applies to a development task, as well as the ensuing product.

This approach is an attempt to combine variables related to the designer, the Instructional Development tasks, and the Instructional Development environment into a model which is representative of most automated design and development situations. This can be accomplished by identifying the most representative variables in the above categories, rather than attempting to create an overspecified (in the regression sense) model. This approach could provide an evaluator with the means to pinpoint problems in Instructional Development guidance. It is intended to provide the evaluator with a source of systematic formative evalution data. It will not, however, attribute those problems to components of the authoring environment's architecture.

Establishing the connection between flaws in guidance and the operation of the functional architecture could be accomplished through automatic data collection. This would involve recording user inputs as well as information on the operative functional components during each user-computer exchange. The more difficult problem is sorting out what type and sequence of guidance and which functional components are making substantial contributions to the resulting CAI. If Instructional Design was truly a linear process then the analysis and attribution of causality to particular variables would be rather straightforward. The iterative nature of the process, however, makes for a knotty methodological problem. This is a puzzle which instructional technology researchers will have to wrestle with as investigators and evaluators attempt to collect systematic data on the design guidance hypothesis.

Assuming that a satisfactory solution can be developed it remains for evaluators to identify important instructional guidance parameters to manipulate (e.g., content areas, knowledge types, explanation levels, etc.) across different cohorts of designers, so as to produce a complete profile of automated guidance during pilot and field tests.

8.7 Conclusion

A call has been issued for empirical analysis of adaptive designer guidance. It has been suggested that evaluating automated instructional development systems without a valid taxonomy of the underlying competence they represent is futile. In assembling that taxonomy it is critical to include the role of automation as a factor contributing to the complexity of Instructional Development. Equally important is the recognition that Instructional Development is a complex problem solving activity with all that that implies for communicating with designers. It appears that an observational approach to the collection of formative evaluation data is feasible, however, the analysis and interpretation of that data may be problematic. If Instructional Development is treated as a domain for aiding (and perhaps training) it seems that we should employ what we know about learners and problem solvers to make adaptive guidance a reality.

References

1. Andrews, D.H., Goodson, L.A.: A comparative analysis of models of instructional design. Journal of Instructional Development, 3 (4), 2-16 (1980)
2. Bodker, S.: A human activity approach to user interfaces. Human-Computer Interactions, 4, 171-195 (1989)
3. Branson, R.K.: Applications research in instructional systems development. Journal of Instructional Development, 4(4), 14-16, 27-31 (1981)
4. Duchastel, P.C.: Cognitive designs for instructional design. Instructional Science, 19(6), 437-444 (1990)
5. Gagné, R.M., Briggs, L.J., & Wager, W.W.: Principles of instructional design (4th ed.). Ft. Worth, TX: Harcourt, Brace, Jovanovich 1992
6. Goel, V., & Pirolli, P.: Motivating the notion of generic design within information processing: The Design space problem. AI Magazine, 10(1), 18-36 (1989)
7. Hamm, R.M.: Moment by moment variation in experts'analytic and intuitive cognitive activity. IEEE Transactions on Systems, Man, and Cybernetics, 18,5, Sept-Oct (1988a)
8. Hamm, R.M.: Clinical intuition and clinical analysis: Expertise and the cognitive continuum. In J. Dowie, & A. Elstein (Eds.), Professional judgment: A reader in clinical decision-making. Cambridge, UK: Cambridge University Press 1988b
9. Hammond, K.R., Hamm, R.M., Grassia, J., & Pearson, T.: Direct comparison of the efficacy of intuitive and analytical cognition in expert judgment. IEEE Transactions on Systems, Man, and Cybernetics, Vol. SMC-17 (1987)
10. Howell, W.C.: Task influences in the analytic-intuitive approach to decision-making. Houston, TX: Rice University, Department of Psychology 1984
11. Hickey, A.E., Spector, J.M., & Muraida, D.J.: Specifications for an advanced instructional design advisor (AIDA) for computer-based training. Brooks Air Force Base, TX: AL-TP-1991-0014 Air Force Systems Command 1991

12. Kintsch, E., Tennyson, R.D., Gagne, R.M., & Muraida, D.J.:Designing an advanced instructional design advisor: Principles of instructional design, Vol. 2. Brooks Air Force Base, TX: AL-TP-1991-0017 Human Resources Directorate, Technical Training Research Division 1991

13. Miller, R.B.: Some working concepts of systems analysis. Pittsburgh, PA: American Institutes for Research 1954

14. Nelson, W.A.: Procedural differences and knowledge organization in expert and novice instructional designers. Paper presented at meeting of American Educational Research Association. Washington, DC (1987)

15. Nelson, W.A., Magliaro, S., & Sherman, T.M.: The intellectual content of instructional design. Journal of Instructional Development, 11(1) (1988)

16. Pirolli, P.: On the art of building: Putting a new instructional design into practice. In H. Burns, & J. Barlett (Eds.), Proceedings of the 2nd Intelligent Tutoring Systems Research Forum, San Antonio, Tx, April, 1989

17. Rouse, W.B.: Adaptive aiding for human/computer control. Human Factors, 30(4), 431-443 (1988)

18. Rowe, H.A.H.: Problem solving and intelligence. Hillsdale NJ: Lawrence Erlbaum 1985

19. Schwartz, D.R., & Howell, W.C.: Optional stopping performance under graphic and numeric CBT formatting. Human Factors, 27, 433-444 (1985)

20. Spector, J.M., Muraida, D.J., & Marlino, M.R.: Cognitively-based models of courseware development. Educational Technology: Research and Development, 40, 45-49 (1992)

9

ISD EXPERT: An Automated Approach to Instructional Design

Robert D. Tennyson[1] and Klaus Breuer[2]

[1]Learning and Cognition, Department of Educational Psychology, University of Minnesota, Minneapolis, MN 55455, USA
[2]Disce, Schledebrückstr. 23, D-33332 Gütersloh, Germany

Abstract: This chapter presents specifications for an automated instructional system development (ISD) system. The goal is to improve the means by which authors design, produce, and evaluate instructional development. Research and theory developments in the fields of instructional technology and cognitive science have advanced the knowledge base for instructional design such that learning can be significantly improved by direct instructional intervention. Unfortunately, these advancements have increased the complexity of employing instructional design, making instructional development both costly and time consuming. Proposed is a computer-based ISD system that will assist both competent and inexperienced instructional developers in applying advanced instructional design.

Keywords: instructional design, automated systems, intelligent systems, authors, computer software

9.1 Introduction

In this chapter I will present specifications for the development of an automated instructional system development (ISD) computer program to help authors employ the most advanced knowledge in the field of instructional theory when designing and producing curriculum and instruction. There are in the current literature several examples of computer-based tools intended to improve the productivity of the ISD process. Hermanns (1990) describes Computer-Aided Analysis (CAA), a computer program which aids in job task analysis. Based on a hierarchically-organized list of job tasks entered by the instructional designer, CAA produces as output a set of preliminary terminal learning objectives that can be further reviewed and edited by the developer. Ranker and Doucet [14] describe SOCRATES, which allows the user to fill in information that is used by SOCRATES to create an instructor's lesson outline including objectives, events of instruction, samples of student behavior and test questions. Perez and Seidel [13] present an overview of their specifications for an automated training development environment that will be based on the Army Systems Approach to Training (SAT) model of instructional design. The main features of the environment are a set of tools for developing the components of instruction and an expert design guide for assisting the designer in using the tools. Merrill and Li [10] propose ID Expert, a prototype rule-based expert system for instructional development that makes recommendations about content structure, course organization, and instructional transactions (tutor/student interactions) based on information supplied by the designer.

These systems differ greatly in function and scope and in the degrees to which each makes use of automated methods to reduce the level of competence required of instructional designers. This chapter proposes framework specifications for an automated ISD system that would employ intelligent interface techniques to allow even the most inexperienced author to immediately begin to develop quality instruction. Labeled ISD Expert, the proposed system would make expert knowledge about the most sophisticated ISD methods readily available to all potential authors, thus minimizing or eliminating the need for formal instructional system development training.

The ISD model proposed for ISD Expert (see Chapter 3) was developed to reflect an application model rather than a teaching model. That is, most ISD models are based on learning ISD, thus they resemble a linear process that attempts to include all possible variables and conditions of ISD. The result is that they do not take into account any other ISD situations other than complete start to finish instructional development. The assumption is that in all ISD situations, ISD starts at the analysis phase and proceeds step-by-step to the final completion of the implementation phase. ISD Expert, in contrast, views the author's situation as the beginning point of any possible ISD activities. For ISD Expert, the ISD is an associative network of variables and conditions, that can be addressed at any point in instructional development depending on the given situation.

This chapter does not provide complete specifications for ISD Expert: instead, it provides a framework from which specifications can be designed and developed. The content of this chapter includes both the philosophy of ISD Expert and the framework specifications. Given the complexity of ISD and the effort necessary to develop an automated system, hopefully, this chapter will also serve as a means for extending the dialogue on the concept of automated ISD systems and tools.

9.2 Philosophy of ISD Expert

Given the range of experience and training in ISD among instructional developers, I am proposing an automated system that will be designed for authors who are content domain experts but not necessarily ISD domain experts. This is a reflection of the fact that the user of ISD Expert will not be an ISD expert initially; rather, the proposed ISD Expert would take into account a range of expertise and experience in instructional design theory and practice.

To accomplish this goal, I am further proposing an automated system that would employ intelligent human-computer interface techniques. The intelligent ISD Expert would operate at two basic levels: First, a coaching expert that would direct inexperienced authors through the acquisition of ISD skills while helping them deal with their specific situation; and, second, an advising expert that would assist competent authors by making recommendations for their specific situation. For example, for an inexperienced author, the coaching function would deal with basic ISD skills and direct the development effort. In contrast, for the competent author, ISD Expert would function as an advisor, making recommendations while the author controlled the actual ISD decision making. In this environment, both inexperienced and competent authors will be exposed to opportunities to increase their individual expertise through a process of learning ISD while using the system [16].

The importance of the distinction between the coaching and advisement functions is based on a review of research findings in expert systems. An example from this body of research is Clancey's [4;5] work with MYCIN, a medical diagnosis consultant program, and GUIDON, a tutorial program designed to make use of MYCIN's rule base for teaching purposes. Clancey found that the rules encoded in MYCIN were inadequate for teaching because the knowledge required for justifying a rule and explaining an approach was lacking. He found it necessary to add additional components to GUIDON to help organize and explain the rules [6]. In a similar fashion, ISD Expert will have the ability to support and explain its recommendations and prescriptions in the language of ISD, not merely by enumerating the rules applied to make a recommendation. An example of one approach to providing this ability can be found in Swartout [18]. Swartout combined declarative and procedural knowledge, in the form of domain principles, to create the knowledge base for XPLAIN, a drug prescription consultant which provides detailed justification of its prescriptions.

Although ISD Expert can not be considered a means for teaching ISD, the very nature of the system's philosophy which assumes that authors will gain knowledge with experience, will result in continuing improvements in ISD applications. That is, as authors gain competence in ISD, the system would exhibit the characteristics of a conventional automated system. Therefore, it should increase the efficiency of instructional development and help in those areas where even experienced ISD authors initially lack specific expertise.

9.2.1 ISD Expert Intelligent Author-Computer Interface

ISD Expert, as proposed, would operate as an automated system employing intelligent author-computer interface (ACI) methods between the author and the system [1]. The ISD Expert intelligent ACI model (see Figure 9.2) would consist of four modules: the author's model of instruction, an ISD tutor (with both coach and advisor capabilities), an ISD knowledge base, and an instructional content knowledge base. Both knowledge bases would have knowledge acquisition capabilities. The ISD Expert tutor would be responsible for the interface between the individual authors and specific activities associated with developing their respective instructional needs.

9.2.2 ISD Expert System Functions

In addition to the intelligent ACI component, the ISD Expert system would have three functions (see Figure 9.1).   The first function would be to aid in the diagnosis of a given author's situation.   This diagnostic function would evaluate the current situational condition(s) of the author (e.g., does the author want to prepare a computer-based graphic program for use in a lecture; does the author want to design a new course?). Following the situational evaluation, the second function would recommend prescription(s) along the lines associated with the level of author experience.   That is, instead of trying to force all situations into a single solution, the prescription(s) would be individualized, based on situational differences and ISD experiences of the author.   And with the third function, ISD Expert, through the system's tutor, would help the authors in accomplishing the prescriptions.   As authors become increasingly more sophisticated in using ISD Expert, they will be ready to accept increasingly more advanced variables and conditions of instructional design theory and practice.

9.2.3 ISD Knowledge Base

The knowledge base for ISD Expert is the fourth generation ISD model (see Chap. 3).

9.2.4 Cognitive Theory

With growth of research and theory in cognitive psychology [2], ISD Expert will exhibit a strong cognitive learning theory basis in both its ISD knowledge base and its approach to author-computer interaction. The effects of cognitive theory can be seen in such things as the importance of macro (i.e., curricular) level activities in ISD, contextual analysis of the information to be learned, evaluation of the learners, employment of interactive media, instructional strategies for higher order thinking, employment of structured and discovery instructional methods, effect of the affective domain on the cognitive, influences of group interactions on learning, and context and situational variables on knowledge acquisition [19]. The result has been the development of fourth generation ISD models that resemble a self-organizing structure (see Chap. 3) and have a cognitive learning paradigm foundation for the various procedures of instructional development.

Along with a cognitive learning foundation for the ISD content, I am proposing that the human-computer interface of ISD Expert exhibit a cognitive approach as opposed to a behavioral one.   The contrast between the two approaches is the assumption made in regard to the interaction between the author and ISD Expert. In a behavioral approach the interaction between the author and the ISD expert system would be made at a reductionist level, that is, small incremental steps in linear sequence of instructional development in which the author is simply, and constantly, filling in requests for information without understanding the individual ISD tasks in relationship to the given situation.   This is a common approach employed in automated systems for novices where the task is relatively concrete and the user is simply filling in information. However, it must be assumed that the ISD task is complex and requires an author who can intelligently use the system more productively as he/she gains competence. Therefore, a cognitive approach assumes, even initially, that the author can connect the individual ISD tasks with his/her given situation.

To summarize, from a cognitive psychology perspective, ISD Expert is an automated system that assumes that the author can from the start function in the role as an instructional designer. This implies that even at an initial level of ISD, the author will have a real instructional problem/need and that he/she will be able to solve the situation with the prescription(s) offered by the ISD Expert system. And, as the author becomes more experienced with ISD Expert, he/she will be able to make increasingly sophisticated use of the system.   ISD is a complex process, but the complexity is in part due to the given situation. Thus, for the initial, inexperienced author, the potential employment of ISD Expert will focus on noncomplex situations, but with the author feeling that he/she is participating in real ISD decision making. This approach to the author should limit training for ISD Expert to a set of basic software functions and activities. Instead of viewing training on ISD Expert in the conventional linear fashion where the author works through a set of meaningless practice situations, the training will be embedded in the initial individualized ISD situation. For example, if the author wants to develop a test, his/her initial entry into ISD Expert will deal with test construction. In other words, training and gaining experience will be driven by the individual author's situation. Rather than a two year graduate program as prerequisite to being an instructional designer, the author will be an instructional designer with ISD Expert beginning with his/her first time situation. Because ISD is a complex environment and the needs of individual authors will vary at any given time, over an extended period of time, the individual authors will acquire more ISD knowledge as situational needs occur.

9.2.5 Computer Technology

Because ISD Expert is intended to improve the performance of instructional designers, rather than to advance the state of the art in automated systems techniques and methods, it is most productive to make use of existing, standard computer hardware and software architecture whenever possible in the development of ISD Expert.

Certain restraints are imposed on the hardware and software choices by the requirements of the environment in which ISD Expert will most often be applied. These requirements are summarized as follows:

- Support for several simultaneous authors at both local and remote sites;
- Large data storage capacity for knowledge bases and programs;
- Sophisticated graphics capability
- Provision for incorporating special-purpose programs (for example, to support research projects) into ISD Expert on an ad hoc basis;
- Employment of interactive media.

Where hardware is concerned, a basic decision is whether to implement ISD Expert on a central mainframe or minicomputer, or on microcomputers (i.e., PCs). Simons [17] and Harmon, Maus, and Morrissey [8] address the expanding role of the microcomputer in AI development, citing growing hardware capacity, wider availability of sophisticated software tools and increasing user familiarity with microcomputers as the forces contributing to the growth in expert system development for microcomputers.

I am proposing that ISD Expert be implemented in a network of PC's connected to a central network and file server with one or more large-capacity (perhaps 300 megabytes) hard disk drives for program and knowledge base storage. While there are a number of physical network topologies that could be used to implement ISD Expert, Figure 9.2 represents the general concept. There are some tradeoffs involved in using this configuration as contrasted with a network of "dumb" terminals connected to a single, central mainframe and data storage. For example, transmitting large quantities of data to/from the central file server to the PC's does require system overhead. However, the advantages outweigh the drawbacks. Given the local processing power of PC's, the intelligence of the system will be distributed throughout the system, minimizing the demands on the central unit. There is a large and growing quantity of AI software available for microcomputers at relatively low prices in contrast to mainframes. PC graphics are superior to all but the most sophisticated and expensive mainframe graphics systems.

The software used to create ISD Expert must provide an open architecture. That is, it must be practical to write local programs for special purpose functions (e.g., as research projects) and link them into the standard software with a minimum of effort. Also, the knowledge bases must be accessible to local programs as well as to the standard software. Automated system development is done either by using expert systems shells, which are commercially-available skeleton systems that can be instantiated with the specific domain knowledge required for an application, or by writing the automated system from scratch in a general or special purpose programming language. Harmon et. al. [8] report that of 115 expert systems surveyed by them in actual use in the United States in 1986, 92 were produced using shells while 23 were written using programming languages (chiefly LISP).

Proposed is that ISD Expert be implemented using commercially-available expert system shells. However, in view of the fact that ISD Expert must also support customization, the shells that are chosen must support what are termed "own-code exits" to facilitate the linking in of custom programs. These custom programs must be written in a high-level computer language, preferably one with extensive AI features (e.g., LISP; PROLOG).

9.2.6 Summary

To establish a framework for ISD Expert, it is important to clearly specify the philosophy of the system (Morgan, 1989). A well specified philosophy will help keep the system under control during development and later when doing revisions. Proposed in this section is that ISD Expert have a foundation in cognitive psychology [11]. And, that this foundation specifies for the system both the content and the author-computer interface [12]. Specific areas of the proposed philosophy are as follows:

- An expert system that has both diagnostic and prescriptive functions
- An expert system that will serve both competent and inexperienced authors
- An intelligent ACI system with both advising and coaching capabilities
- Knowledge base will employ the fourth generation ISD model authoring activities
- Employment of interactive media
- Cognitive learning theory as the foundation of the ISD procedures
- Cognitive paradigm approach to ACI
- Entry to system based on individual author situation
- Training as a concurrent activity with ISD activities
- A computer-based network system with remote capabilities
- Software tools that provide an open architecture
- Employment of a high-level language (e.g., an AI language)
- Commercial shells that include access to own-code programs
- Data dictionaries for knowledge acquisition components

The above discussion on a proposed philosophy for ISD Expert provides the foundation for the following section on framework specifications. The next section presents a basic framework for ISD Expert.

9.3 ISD Expert: System Framework

The purpose of this section is to propose framework specifications employing the above described philosophy of an automated system for instructional system development. Because of the range ISD knowledge of authors, I am proposing that ISD Expert be designed according to the methodology of intelligent human-computer interface systems. That is, rather than either attempting to teach ISD to the author or to develop a system around one linear approach that restricts and narrows the richness of ISD, my proposal is the design of a system that begins with the individual author's given situation. In this proposal, the intelligent ACI method will be concerned with improving both the authors application of ISD and their own models of instruction. As such, it will employ coaching and advising methods of human-computer interaction.

Furthermore, the proposed system will encourage the growth of the authors knowledge of ISD, but with the complexity of ISD being transparent. The purpose of ISD Expert will be to diagnosis the given situation of the author and then prescribe recommendations for dealing with his/her individual situation. It is assumed that each author will present a different situation and, therefore, will require a unique prescription. To accomplish this goal, the employment of heuristics is proposed for programming ISD Expert (see 3; Waterman, 1986). Two important features of the heuristic method, as contrasted, for example, with production rules, are (a) the flexibility needed to implement prescriptions in conditions of uncertainty or novelty (i.e., prescriptions are established in real time by integrating best available information from the system's knowledge base) and (b) the elimination of the need for an exhaustive reduction of ISD content knowledge to production rules.

One of the serious problems in expert systems design for nonstatistical areas has been the attempt to reduce complex and abstract concepts to production rules. Even though I am proposing the use of a network and file server (with large capacity disk storage) system for the operation of ISD Expert, it is the programming time involved in trying to apply the reductionist approach to an environment as complex as ISD that rules out the exclusive use of the production rules programming methodology. The software architecture of ISD Expert must be open to allow for future extensions. The production rule method is not suitable for this type of complex situation [5]. So much of the ISD process is situation bound; therefore, the system must be adaptable, allowing for prescriptions to be finalized by the author.

Proposed for ISD Expert is an expert system with four main components: an intelligent author-computer interface component, a diagnosis function component, a prescriptive function component, and an instructional production guide component (Figure 9.1). The intelligent ACI component will be the means by which authors will interact with ISD Expert. Rather than use a menu driven system, I am proposing a tutorial interaction between the author and ISD Expert. The diagnostic component will function as the evaluator of each author's situation and provide an evaluation report [7]. This report will serve as the guidelines in preparing the prescription. Additionally, the prescription will be based on the author's ISD model as well as the diagnostic report. The fourth component will provide the author with assistance in the production of materials from the prescription(s). The level of assistance will again be influenced by the author's ISD model.

9.3.1 Intelligent Author-Computer Interface Component

The intelligent ACI component for the ISD Expert is illustrated in Figure 9.2. The main modules are as follows: (a) an author's model of ISD; (b) the ISD tutor (coach/advisor); (c) the ISD knowledge base model; and (d) the content knowledge base. I will now discuss the role of each component of the ISD Expert tutor.

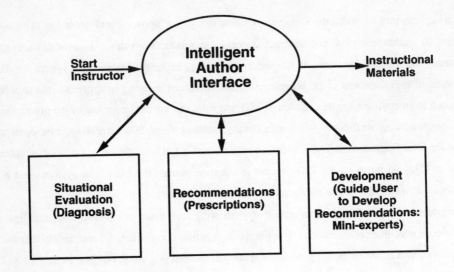

Fig. 9.1. ISD Expert Components

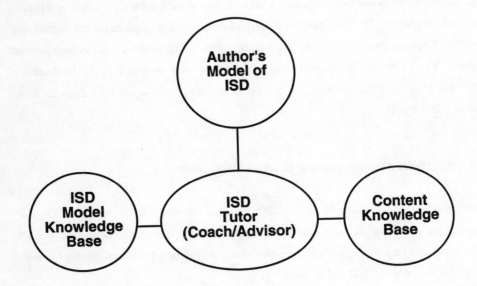

Fig. 9.2. Intelligent Author-Computer Interface Model

Author's Model of ISD

The purpose of this module is twofold: (a) to establish the level of ISD expertise of the author and (b) to help the author improve his/her own model of instruction. This is necessary because no formal attempt is to be made to directly train the authors in ISD. The individual author's model will be updated with each use of the system. This profile of the author will help the system in its prescriptive recommendations. For example, inexperienced authors will have a narrow and limited knowledge of ISD and, also, of the ways in which their instruction could be improved; thus, prescriptions would be at their level of understanding. On the other hand, more experienced authors would be able to use more advanced prescriptions. It is important to keep the ISD prescriptions at the level of the author's competence and also to provide an opportunity for creativity and the possible use of different ideas generating from the author [15]. A key feature of the proposed ISD Expert is the power of the author to disagree with a given prescription and still to be able to continue with the ISD process.

ISD Tutor

Intelligent ACI systems work on the premise that a meaningful dialogue must be established between the user and the system. An important feature of the dialogue is the mixed initiative, where the user has an opportunity to query the system as well as being controlled by the direction of the system. The ISD Expert tutor will approach the diagnostic function from the situation of the author. Personalizing the diagnostic activity will provide the opportunity for the tutor to search the content knowledge base to include specific references in the prescription to available existing materials and resources.

Because of the range of knowledge and experience in ISD of potential authors, two basic modes of interface are proposed. At one extreme will be authors who are completely inexperienced in ISD. For these individuals, a coaching mode is proposed. The coaching mode is a well established method of instruction used in intelligent computer-assisted instruction (ICAI). This mode assumes that the author will need direct and controlled assistance in dealing with his/her given situation. The function of the tutor as coach is to approach the ISD activity in a disciplined way while helping the author develop ISD skills. Prescriptions for the situation are specific and the coach is responsible for the decision making. In contrast is the advising interface. For the experienced author, the tutor as advisor would offer alternative prescriptions, with the final decision(s) in the hands of the author.

The tutor, as part of the intelligent ACI component, is the point of contact between the author and the other ISD Expert components (see Figure 9.1). In the proposed design, the tutor gathers information about the author's specific situation and, by interaction with the Situational Evaluation component, prepares a report of the given problem/need. This evaluation report is sent to the Recommendations component where a prescription(s) is prepared. When the prescription(s) is prepared, the tutor presents it to the author; at that point, depending on the mode of the tutorial interaction (i.e., coaching or advising), there may occur a dialogue between the author and the tutor to finalize the prescription. Once a final prescription is prepared, the tutor interacts with the ISD model knowledge base to set up the authoring activities. The tutor also assists the author in certain aspects of materials production through the fourth component of the ISD Expert system. Updating of the author's model will be the continuing role of the tutor in ISD Expert.

ISD Model Knowledge Base

The knowledge base of ISD Expert will reside in the ISD model knowledge base module. Once the prescription(s) is decided upon, the necessary authoring activities are compiled by the tutor from the ISD model knowledge base and presented to the author. (Authoring activities of the knowledge base are presented in Chap. 3.) Information within this module will be stored as structured data files, organized as an associative network. The purpose here is to efficiently locate information without the restrictions of rigid production rules. That is, the ISD model knowledge base should exhibit the heuristic search characteristics of an information retrieval system.

Content Knowledge Base

The fourth module of the proposed intelligent ACI system for ISD Expert, the content knowledge base, is a source from which curricular and instructional materials resources may be obtained. These materials may be included in the implementation of prescriptions developed by ISD Expert or they may stand alone. For example, if an author wants a simulation for a given lecture, he/she could query the content knowledge base to see what might be available. In another situation, ISD Expert may develop a prescription and obtain the necessary materials from the content knowledge base without the author explicitly requesting the action. Access to the content knowledge base may be either by direct author query via the tutor or indirectly as a result of the implementation of prescriptions.

The content knowledge base will help eliminate duplication of effort in instructional development by providing a catalog of available materials. Information in the content knowledge base would come from two sources. Material that is developed on ISD Expert as a result of instructional development can be added to the content knowledge base. Material may also be input from sources external to ISD Expert. For example, many materials and resources that are developed in R & D efforts independently of ISD Expert would be useful in course applications if authors had access to them. General information manuals and other media-based resources (e.g., video disk materials) are another example of materials from external.

9.3.2 Situational Evaluation Component

The first activity in the proposed ISD Expert system is the evaluation of the given author's situation. The assumption is that each author will have a different need or problem, depending on his/her given situation. As the ISD Expert tutor establishes the author's model of instruction (see Figure 9.2), the Situational Evaluation Component will diagnosis the situation employing AI techniques. Again, it is assumed that the tutor will determine the competence level of the author and in turn adjust the report of the evaluation. For example, if the tutor determines that the author is competent in ISD and the situation is to develop a lesson on trouble shooting, the report would indicate those two conditions, which would influence the type of prescription(s) recommended. By focusing on the given situation, ISD Expert can employ the complexity and richness of the fourth generation ISD model without directly training the author about the entire model.

9.3.3 Recommendations Component

The purpose of ISD Expert is to help authors improve their instructional product development by applying the most advanced variables and conditions of instructional design theory. This is made possible by the recommendations component, which interacts with the ISD knowledge base to interpret the situational evaluation diagnosis and recommend a prescription to deal with the given instructional situation. Also, the prescription is adjusted to the author's level of experience. This is an important feature of the proposed ISD Expert because it prescribes an effort of development that can be efficiently accomplished by the author. For example, if an inexperienced author is presented with a prescription that would fit an experienced author's profile, the novice author would not be able to adequately follow the production activities (Component 4). The result would be that the prescription is implemented inefficiently or not at all. Presentation of the prescription will likewise be based on the competence of the author. The competence level of the author will determine the program control (i.e., coaching or advisement) employed in the production component.

9.3.4 Production Component

The term production is used here to reflect a variety of different types of instructional situations that might occur. ISD includes, in addition to instructional development, test development, computer-based management development, print materials development, instructional aids, visual aids, etc. The function of this component is to guide the author in the production process. As such, this part of the expert system directly interacts with the tutor. Because of the range of ISD activities, this component would be composed of mini-experts, each reflecting a different authoring activity. That is, the mini-experts would be the various activities within the ISD model. For example, if the situation is to develop a test for trouble shooting, the author's model indicates an experienced author, and the prescription recommends a simulation, a mini-expert on design of simulations within component 4 would guide the author in the production of an appropriate simulation. An important feature of ISD Expert will be to facilitate the employment of advanced interactive technology for instructional delivery. For example, for computer-based instruction, this component would directly produce the courseware [20].

Once the production effort is completed, component 4 would send a report back to the tutor to update the author's model and to reference the effort in the content knowledge base. To further improve the efficiency of ISD Expert, instructional strategy (IS) shells will be accessible by the mini-experts to do the actual product development: IS shells would only require that the author enter into the system content information and the system would develop the product.

The above four components of the proposed ISD Expert system would be designed and programmed as independent expert systems so as to allow for future additions and elaborations. This is necessary because of the continuing growth in the instructional design theory field. That is, most expert systems are designed for specific, contemporary applications; when changes occur, a new expert system is designed and implemented.

9.4 Central Network System

In this section, I propose for the computer-based environment a configuration for a centrally-based network and file server for both local and remote PC workstations. Because of the proposal for a content knowledge base (see Figure 9.2) with acquisition capabilities and an author's instructional model within ISD Expert, a large capacity disk storage should be an integral part of the system. Also, given the computing power of PCs, much of the intelligent interfacing would take place at the workstation.

Although there are a large number of commercially-available shells for program development (e.g., HYPERcard), most do not allow for "own-code" exits. With such software, the development effort becomes constrained by the closed architecture of the given shell; the shell becomes a methodology in itself rather than a tool to be used in implementing multiple methodologies. I am proposing that ISD Expert be programmed in a high-level language with artificial intelligence features, but that commercially-available shells be used when feasible to augment the system features.

9.5 Development Plan

The framework specifications presented in this chapter offer a complete expert system for automating instructional development. To produce such a system, there are two possible approaches. The first would be to develop the ISD Expert system as presented. The second would be to follow an incremental approach in which an initial prototype is developed that only has a minimal set of features and is aimed at a competent author. That is, an ISD Expert that would only have an advisor level tutor and the situational evaluation and recommendations components. The content knowledge base and acquisition features of the intelligent interface tutor and the production component would be added in subsequent elaborations.

Although the first approach seems possible, there are a number of problems that need to be considered that might favor the second approach. An initial problem is the cost factor. As stated earlier the majority of expert systems are developed using commercial shells. Cost in terms of software is the time required to produce a product that will be timely and profitable. That is, the proposed ISD Expert would most likely be a software product that would need to generate income within a reasonable timeframe. Rapid prototyping is a procedure to develop software employing shells that are linked by some general language [9]. Thus, instead of five years to produce a complete version of ISD Expert, an initial prototype could be developed in much less time.

A second major problem in producing a complete ISD Expert in the first approach is the necessary research needed for the new system. There has been minimal empirical research to date on instructional variables and conditions associated with the extension of cognitive learning theory to instructional design theory. Even though it is possible to develop an initial prototype, research in cognitive instructional design theory needs to be done as well as the interaction of media within this theoretical framework. A third problem area relates to the specification of the human-computer interaction variables and conditions necessary to run and manage the complex environment of ISD Expert.

Within the constraints defined above for approach one, I recommend the following incremental approach to ISD Expert development.

1. Framework specifications. This step conceptualizes the idea or vision of the expert system. This chapter serves as an example of the first activity in producing an automated instructional development system.
2. Functional specifications. From the initial outline of the basic system, the specific functions provided by the system need to be defined. From this step a rapid prototype can be developed as follows:
   - Write functional specifications;
   - Summarize what is known/not known about the functions;
   - Estimate the complexity of the functions;
   - Based on the summary and estimates, group the functions into ISD Expert 1 (i.e., a prototype), and then prioritize the functions for successive implementations for versions ISD Expert 2, ISD Expert 3, etc. Each version would add layers of functions and increased use of a high-level computer language.
3. Logical design. Starting with the prototype, define the logical components that provide the specified functions.
4. Physical design. Define the software modules which implement the logical design of the system.

5. Programming. With the prototype, rapid software development is recommended while with the successive versions, the software procedures defined in this chapter would be followed.

6. Testing. Once the prototype is developed, it should be tested following standard computer software benchmark criteria.

7. Implementation. Complete the remaining tasks to implement ISD Expert 1 while simultaneously accumulating the experience and research findings needed to produce ISD Expert 2.

8. Incremental development. Basically starting with number 3 above, iteratively build ISD Expert towards a system that includes all of the functions defined in numbers one and two.

Cycling through an incremental approach to development of ISD Expert would produce an initial product for employment and research within the constraints of costs and system knowledge. The initial prototype (or ISD Expert 1) would exhibit many standard characteristics of the third generation ISD model (see Chap. 3) with successive versions taking on more of the ideas associated with the fourth generation ISD model (see Chap. 3).

9.6 Conclusion

The purpose of ISD Expert is to improve learning by aiding authors in the employment of contemporary instructional design theory. This chapter presents framework specifications for an expert system to implement the concept of ISD Expert. Because of the experience range of authors for ISD Expert in terms of instructional design theory and practice, I am proposing an expert system that employs an intelligent human-computer interface system. That is, ISD Expert will interact with authors on an individual basis according to their respective competence with principles and variables of instructional design theory. ISD Expert will dialogue with authors along a continuum of decision control ranging from system control (coaching function) to complete author control (advising function). Inexperienced authors will be coached to develop basic ISD skills while the more competent authors will be advised on the employment of advanced instructional design variables and conditions.

An author's instructional design model is a necessary module for an intelligent human-computer interface component because it replaces the need for a separate training program for authors.   The sophistication of ISD Expert's prescriptions will be directly influenced by the author's instructional design model.   Therefore, both ISD novices and experts will be able immediately to use ISD Expert.   That is, the proposed system would take into account experience in instructional design theory and practice.

Proposed for the ISD knowledge base is the fourth generation ISD model (see Chap. 3).   The content knowledge base is proposed as a data base for instructional materials within subject matter areas.   Both knowledge bases will have acquisition capabilities.

The basic proposed ISD Expert system will have four interactive components: (a) an intelligent author-computer interface component; (b) a situational evaluation component (diagnosis), (c) a recommendations component (prescriptions), and (d) a production component. Proposed is that ISD Expert be designed for a computer-based network system using a high level AI type language and expert system shells.   The system will also employ a large capacity disk storage for the two knowledge bases (i.e., ISD model and instructional content and materials); both knowledge bases will employ acquisition capabilities.

To implement the concept of the fourth generation ISD model, the situational evaluation component of ISD Expert will diagnose each author's given problem and/or need.   This will make the system application orientated rather than the conventional lock-step system that is most suited for the teaching of ISD.   From the diagnosis, ISD Expert will generate a prescription. For those authors who seek assistance in implementing the prescription, especially those requiring the development of instructional materials, the fourth component will guide the production effort.   This production component will be composed of mini-expert systems that have specific functions (e.g., instructional strategy shells).

Because of both development costs and gaps in instructional design theory, I recommend an incremental approach to the development of ISD Expert.   Initially, the project should begin with rapid prototyping techniques to produce a version one of ISD Expert.   Subsequent versions would be elaborated according to the functional specifications as outlined in this chapter and from on-going research findings.

In conclusion, we are proposing an expert system that will bring the power of instructional design theory and practice to authors who would not normally have the opportunity to employ such knowledge in their instructional efforts. The proposed ISD Expert will improve learning by making instructional development both effective (i.e., by employing the most advanced principles and variables of learning and instructional theories) and efficient (i.e., by reducing the time and cost of conventional methods of instructional development).

References

1. Anderson, J.R.: The expert module. In M.C. Polson, & J.J. Richardson (Eds.), Intelligent tutoring systems (pp. 21-53). Hillsdale, NJ: Lawrence Erlbaum 1988
2. Bonner, J.: Implications of cognitive theory for instructional design: Revisited. Educational Communication and Technology Journal, 36, 3-14 (1988)
3. Bonnet, A., Haton, J.P., & Truong-Ngoc, J.M.: Expert systems: Principles and practice. Englewood Cliffs, NJ: Prentice Hall 1988
4. Clancey, W.J.: Tutoring rules for guiding a case method dialogue. International Journal of Man-Machine Studies, 11, 25-49 (1979)
5. Clancey, W.J.: The epistemology of a rule-based expert system: A framework for explanation. Artificial Intelligence, 20, 215-251 (1983)
6. Clancey, W.J.: The knowledge level reinterpreted: Modeling how systems interact. Machine Learning, 4, 287-293 (1989)
7. Guba, E.G., & Lincoln, Y.S.: The countenances of fourth-generation evaluation: Description, judgment, and negotiation. Evaluation studies review annual, 11, 70-88 (1986)
8. Harmon, P., Maus, R., & Morrissey, W.: Expert system tools and applications. New York: Wiley 1988
9. Hewett, T.T.: Towards a rapid prototyping environment for interface design: Desirable features suggested by the electronic spreadsheet. In A. Sutcliffe, & L. Macaulay (Eds.), People and computers V (pp. 305-314). Cambridge, UK: Cambridge University Press 1989
10. Merrill, M.D., & Li, Z.: An instructional design expert system. In S. Dijkstra, B. van Hout Wolters, & P. C. van der Sijde (Eds.), Research on instruction: Design and effects (pp. 21-44). Englewood Cliffs, NJ: Educational Technology 1990
11. Newell, A., & Card, S.: Prospects for psychological science in human computer interaction. Human Computer Interaction, 1, 209-242 (1985)
12. Norman, D.A.: Cognitive engineering. In User-centered system design (pp.31-62). Hillsdale, NJ: Lawrence Erlbaum 1986
13. Perez, R.S., & Seidel, R.J.: Using artificial intelligence in education: Computer-based tools for instructional development. Educational Technology, 30(3), 51-58 (1990)

14. Ranker, R.A., & Doucet, R.M.: SOCRATES: A computer-based lesson development advisor. Computers in Human Behavior, 6, 162-171 (1990)
15. Russell, D., Moran, T., & Jordan, D.: The instructional design environment. In J. Psotka, L. Massey, & S. Mutter (Eds.), Intelligent tutoring systems: Lessons Learned (pp. 96-137). Hillsdale, NJ: Lawrence Erlbaum 1988
16. Schiele, F., & Green, T. HCI formalisms and cognitive psychology: The case of Task-Action Grammar. In M. Harrison, & H. Thimbleby (Eds.), Formal methods in human-computer interaction (pp. 9-62). Cambridge, UK: Cambridge University Press 1990
17. Simons, G.L.: Expert systems and micros. Manchester, UK: NCC Publications 1985
18. Swartout, W.R.: XPLAIN: A system for creating and explaining expert consulting programs. Artifical Intelligence, 21, 285-325 1983
19. Tennyson, R.D.: Cognitive learning theory linked to instructional theory. Journal of Structural Learning, 13, 362-371 (1990)
20. Tennyson, R.D. Computer-based enhancements for the improvement of learning. In S. Dijkstra, B.H.A.M. van Hout Wolters, & P. C. van der Sijde (Eds.), Research on instruction: Design and effects. Englewood Cliffs, NJ: Educational Technology 1990

10

Automating the Development of Intelligent Learning Environments: A Perspective on Implementation Issues

Barbara Wasson

NORUT Information Technology, N-9005, Tromsø, Norway

Abstract: Intelligent Learning Environments (ILEs) facilitate student learning by providing the optimal learning conditions. An ILE should possess the ability to dynamically configure instruction based on the subject domain, the student, and the pedagogical knowledge that prescribes how to transform the domain knowledge into pedagogically valid content for each student. Automating the development of ILEs adds another level of complexity. This chapter investigates aspects of the automation process in terms of how a system's behavior and authoring capabilities facilitate automation. Four systems that illustrate the automation process are examined and a summary of how they address the implementation issues is given.

Keywords: intelligent learning environments, authoring tools, automated processes

10.1 Introduction

The development of intelligent learning environments (ILEs) is a difficult and complex endeavor. The goal is to develop an ILE that will facilitate learning by providing the optimal learning conditions for a given student at a given time. ITS research has shown that such a goal requires that an ILE posses the ability to dynamically configure instruction based on the subject domain, the particular student and the pedagogical knowledge that prescribes how to transform the subject domain knowledge into pedagogically valid content for each particular student. Automating the development of ILEs adds another level of complexity. The goal shifts. Not only must the ILE developer deal with the intricacies of building an effective ILE, but also with the additional task of providing tools and automated processes which enable an author to customize the underlying ILE for classroom use.

This is an organizing chapter that puts dimensions on the question of how to automate the development of ILEs. More questions are asked than answers given. ITS research is presented as a source of technology useful in the automation of the development of ILEs. Implementation issues such as the representation of knowledge, reasoning about knowledge, functional or cognitive architectures, generation of instructional plans, and providing authoring tools are identified in light of contemporary ITS research projects. First, however, a characterization of ILEs is presented in order to illustrate the complexity of developing an ILE. Second, a discussion on automation issues is given at a general level. Third, several perspectives on implementation issues are presented for later use in highlighting how the individual ITS research projects contribute to the automation process. Fourth, four systems that illustrate aspects of the automation process are briefly examined and a summary of how they address the implementation issues is given. The chapter concludes with a summary and conclusions.

10.2 Characteristics of ILEs

The complexity of an ILE is demonstrated by identifying characteristics that can be used to delineate the range or scope of possible ILEs. This section is included because it is important to understand the plethora of issues that the ILE developer must consider at the conceptual level before dealing with the actual implementation (i.e., writing the program) of a system. Dillenbourg, Hilario, Mendelshon and Schneider [5] distinguish between a *cognitive architecture* (or the conceptualization) which translates an instructional, psychological, or cognitive theory into computational terms, and a *computational architecture* which specifies particular AI techniques (such as blackboards, simulations, case-based reasoning etc.) that will be used to realize the cognitive architecture.

10.2.1 A Characterization

Figure 10.1 presents a characterization of ILEs that is useful for illustrating the complexity of the cognitive architecture. Given this space of characteristics, a wide range of ILEs can be specified. Although some of the terminology was originally used to describe on-line assistance, it can be applied to ILEs as well.

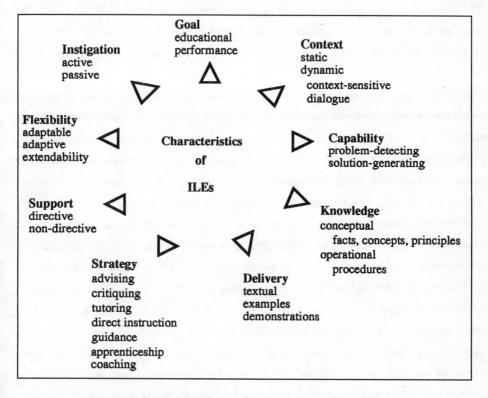

Fig. 10.1. Characteristics of Intelligent Learning Environments.

Systems can be analyzed according to their goal [8]. *Educational* ILEs have the main objective of supporting learning in general (e.g., learn about physics, geometry, or programming), and *performance* oriented ILEs focus is on training the student to perform (e.g., monitor a plant or fly an aeroplane). The type of knowledge to be learned can be *conceptual* or *operational* [2]. *Conceptual* knowledge comprises knowledge of *facts* (e.g., Tromsø is in north Norway), *concepts* (e.g., the concept of recursion) and *principles* (e.g., Kirkoff's law), while *operational* knowledge is knowledge about *procedures* (e.g., how to handle a nuclear power plant emergency).

Two approaches to providing instructional support are referred to as *directive* or *non-directive* [10]. With *directive* support, the ILE decides what instructional actions will be used (e.g., presenting the student with increasingly complex domain models, or giving corrective feedback). ILE facilities (e.g., a notebook, scratchpad, or goal-map) that do not contain any suggestion about the way in which a student should proceed, but are helpful to the student, are *non-directive* supports. To distinguish between systems that take the context of the situation (e.g., issues such as what the student is trying to accomplish, what menus or options have recently been displayed, and how long it has been since the last feedback) in which the interaction is taking place into account when providing feedback or support and those that do not, the characteristics *static* or *dynamic* are used [12]. *Static* feedback is given independent of the context in which it is invoked. For example, the same feedback is provided whether the student is a novice or expert, or the student is trying to perform a legal or illegal move. *Dynamic* feedback is dependent on the situation and can be divided further into *context-sensitive* feedback and *dialogues*. In *context-sensitive* feedback, the ILE has an understanding of the current context and this influences the feedback that will be provided. In *dialogues*, the ILE provides an answer to an explicit student question. A system can be characterized according to whether the user or the system instigates the interaction [9]. In *passive* feedback, the student must explicitly request an interaction (e.g., through a help menu, by asking a question, or asking for a critique), whereas in an *active* feedback, the ILE interrupts the student when it determines that the student requires feedback (e.g., sub-optimal behavior is recognized, or remediation is necessary).

Systems can also be differentiated based on their *problem detection* and *solution generation* capabilities [8]. Many ILEs are concerned with detecting sub-optimal behavior and informing the student of this (e.g., recognize a buggy program and inform the student pointing out the bugs), thus they are *problem detecting*. Some ILEs, however, have the capability to go beyond the mere detection of problems, and are able to suggest better alternatives, hence are *solution generating* (e.g., recognize the bugs in a program and remediate by helping the student overcome the bugs). The flexibility of systems can be described as *adaptable, adaptive* and *extendable*. In order to accommodate to the various levels of students and individual student preferences, the ILE should be *adaptable* — changeable by the student (e.g., the student can select the level of help to be received) — and *adaptive* — the ILE changes its own behavior based on observations of the student or inferences about the student (e.g., the ILE observes that the student is becoming more experienced and decides to provide less explicit help messages). Furthermore, *extendable* ILEs allow the student to add functionality to the system (e.g. defining a new patient case in a medical ILE).

Delivery mechanisms, described according to they way information is conveyed to the user, include *textual descriptions, examples* or *demonstrations* [17]. *Textual descriptions* consist of written messages that must be read and understood by the user; *examples* are actual or simplified pieces of the application used to illustrate some condition; and *demonstrations* lead the user through steps that illustrate how to accomplish some task. During demonstrations the system may either just animate the task, or may engage the user in interacting with the demonstration.

There are many instructional strategies that can be incorporated into an ILE. These include — and this is not meant to be an exhaustive list — *advising, critiquing, tutoring, direct instruction, guidance, apprenticeship, Socratic tutoring,* and *coaching*. The functionality of each of these strategies varies placing different requirements on the ILE and resulting in different instructional behaviors.

10.2.2 Interaction of the Characteristics

The characterization presented above is important for illustrating the range of possible ILEs that can be developed, or produced. For example, before an ILE's cognitive and computational architectures are specified, a detailed evaluation of the subject domain and the educational philosophy on which the ILE is to be built, is to be undertaken. This might lead to a decision to develop an ILE that can be characterized as a *performance* ILE that focuses on *operational knowledge* using a *cognitive apprenticeship* strategy that gives *dynamic* and *active advice* and *guidance* to the student. Or, the decision might prompt the development of an *educational* ILE that is capable of giving *dynamic context-sensitive adaptable advice* and *guidance* in finding the correct *solution* to problems given to the student. Or, the decision might result in an ILE that provides on-line assistance though *passive* instigation in the form of *critiquing* and on-line *textual documentation* with the facility to allow the user to *adapt* and *extend* the on-line assistance as desired.

10.3 Automation Issues

There are several questions that arise and need to be addressed when discussing the *automation of the development of an ILE*. This section poses some of these questions and offers thoughts that provoke more questions instead of giving answers. In order to facilitate the discussion, the following terms are used to distinguish the actual participants in the development process. The *system designer* refers to the person who designs and implements the system to be used by an ILE author. The *author* is the person who actually produces an ILE for a particular educational use (i.e., the ILE to be used by the student). And, the *ILE itself*, by automatically generating aspects of the instructional process, is involved in the development process. In this way the development of an ILE can be thought of as a collaboration between the system designer, the author and the ILE itself.

What does it mean to automate the development of ILEs?

A distinction can be made in the final objective of automation. *Is the goal to develop a system that guides instructional designers in making instructional design decisions to produce a final ILE?* This presupposes that a particular instructional design methodology has been chosen and an expert system that guides the author through the instructional design process has been implemented by a system designer. In fact, the system could be used as a training system for instructional designers. *Or, is the goal to develop an authoring system that provides a set of tools and automated processes with which an author can develop an ILE?* There are two approaches to automation that fall under this second goal. In the first approach the system designer builds a set of tools designed to acquire (and the ILE itself use) the knowledge required for a pre-defined ILE shell (see the section on SIMULATE), or for a pre-defined ILE based on a particular instructional design model (see Baker, Chap.11). The second approach is for the system designer to provide a set of generic tools (see Gonzales this volume) and generic processes that enable an author to develop a wide variety of ILEs without pre-defining a particular instructional strategy or philosophy. That is, the system has generality and flexibility. For example, the ILE might be flexible enough to represent a number of instructional strategies as opposed to being intended for use in a particular pedagogical situation. Also, these generic tools and processes may not necessarily have been designed or built for educational purposes. For example, distance education ILEs might use telenetworking facilities, on-line databases, simulation packages, etc.

What can be Automated?

An alternative way to view automation is to ask what can be automated. Three aspects of the development can be identified: *input of knowledge, behavior of the system,* and *output of information.* The input of knowledge, or *knowledge acquisition,* refers to the knowledge that an author must provide for an ILE. The behavior of the system, or the *generativeness,* refers to the automated underlying processes, or the dynamic pedagogical decision making that the ILE itself provides "for free." The generativeness has been built into the ILE by the system designer. The output of information refers to the automation of what is *delivered* (or seen) by the student — how a video is shown, a simulation carried out, or the where menus appear on the screen, for example.

Facilitating the Automation

The three aspects of automation — *knowledge acquisition, generativeness* and *delivery* — must be facilitated. Acquisition of knowledge can be facilitated by authoring tools that are built by the system designer for use by an author. Several questions that need to be addressed by research arise. *Who is the author?* Is the author a teacher who will use the ILE in their classroom? An authoring specialist versed in using a particular set of authoring tools who cooperates with the teacher who will use the ILE? A professional working for a business (e.g., a publishing company) that will produce ILE courseware, thus might have a stronger computer science background than the classroom teacher?, etc. The target author will have an impact into the design of the tools as illustrated by the next questions. *How can tools be developed at an abstract enough level to enable easy use?* Will the author require special training to use the tools easily and effectively? Is it possible to present the underlying computational system in an understandable way that does not require deep computer science knowledge in order to use the authoring tools? That reflects the way that the author thinks about instruction? Or, is it possible to build tools that reflect the way that author's think about the instructional process and have the ILE itself translate that into the needed computational knowledge. *What are the kinds of tools that are required?* Tools for the author to enter the knowledge that is required by the ILE itself and tools for enabling the author to monitor the system's behavior in order to understand what is going on and confirm that the system is behaving in the intended manner. Also, if the author is not the teacher who is going to use the ILE, then tools that enable the teacher to understand what is going on in the system are required. Such tools might provide the teacher with answers to questions such as: What is the model of the student that is being created? What is the system curriculum?

There are two aspects to the behavior of the system: *representation of knowledge* (i.e., knowledge representation), and the *processes for reasoning* about this knowledge (e.g., inference engine). What is the knowledge that needs to be represented and the reasoning process that will use this knowledge to automate aspects of the development of ILEs? Furthermore, these aspects can be discussed at a functional level such as the use instructional planning, having a student model, and domain knowledge sources, etc., or can be discussed according to actual computational techniques such as production rules, frames, forward-chaining, etc. that will be used to actually build the system. Focusing on discussing system behavior at a functional level, questions such as the following can be asked: How is *dynamic* system behavior (made at the time it is needed according to the current state of the system) obtained? How does this dynamic behavior contribute to the automation? Systems can dynamically generate instructional goals, instructional plans, exercises for the student, etc. The author need only provide high level information such as topics to be learned and the relationships between them and an instructional strategy, and the system will automatically generate instruction for a particular student. Also, the automatic generation of advice, diagnosing student errors and misconceptions, recognizing a student's mental model, natural language dialogue between the system and the student are also aspects of system behavior that contribute to automation of the development of ILEs. Many of these issues are the focus of on-going ITS research projects.

What is the division of the instructional decision making between the ILE system designer, the ILE author, and the ILE system itself?

The final issue to discuss deals with the interaction among the participants in the development process. Issues to think about are concerned with the division of instructional decision making. For example, *where does the decision about the instructional philosophy or instructional theory that the ILE reflects lie?* If the ILE system designer takes an instructional theory "off the shelf," then it is the system designer that has made a choice and the ILE author is "stuck" with the decision. For example, a system designer might decide to build a set of authoring tools for a system whose behavior supports simulation-based learning — the author that uses these tools, is then confined to authoring a simulation-based ILE (see the section on SIMULATE). On the other hand, if the ILE system designer provides a set of tools with which an author can build a system based on whatever instructional approach desired, then more power lies in the hand of the author.

10.4 A Perspective on Implementation Issues

In this chapter implementation issues are viewed from the perspective of an ILE's *generality, flexibility, generativeness, reusability, authorability* and *evaluability*. These aspects of the implementation are described as follows:

Generality is the applicability of the ILE for use in different pedagogical situations such as simulation-based learning, guided-discovery tutoring, critiquing, etc.

Flexibility refers to the ability of the ILE to represent a variety of instructional strategies, different curriculums, types of knowledge, granularity in diagnosis, amount of system and student control, etc.

Generativeness pertains to the ability of the ILE to automatically and dynamically generate aspects of the instructional process - instructional goals, instructional plans, exercises, dialogue content, etc.

Reusability relates to aspects of the ILE, such as the conceptual design, the architecture, instructional strategies, domain representation, planning rules, etc., that can be reused.

Authorability applies to the ease with which the required knowledge can be entered into the system and understood - the availability of tools for knowledge acquisition, for visualization of knowledge representations at an understandable level, for monitoring system behavior, etc.

Evaluability refers to the ease by which the system can be evaluated for its support of authoring (including formative evaluation), for the degree to which computational model reflects the conceptual model of the designer, for its pedagogical effectiveness, etc.

The first 5 issues are used to focus the discussion of four systems that address the behavior of the system and authoring aspects of the automation process.

10.5 Behavior of the System

Two systems are chosen to illustrate how the behavior of an underlying system contributes to the automation of the development of intelligent learning environments. Through the explicit representation of pedagogical knowledge the two systems are able to dynamically react to the current instructional situation and tailor instruction for a particular student. PEPE [22,23,24] is a framework for content planning that automates aspects such as the generation of instructional content goals and a content plan. GTE [18,19] is a framework for representing instructional expertise that is used to generate the instructional process.

10.5.1 PEPE: An approach to content planning

PEPE [22] is a computational framework that explicitly represents the pedagogical knowledge required to make pedagogical content decisions. Content planning, in PEPE's terms, entails dynamically generating a content plan for a concept to be learned, tailored to the current instructional situation. Three levels of knowledge achievement, *fact*, *analysis*, and *synthesis* (adapted from Bloom's [3] taxonomy of cognitive objectives) are recognized for each concept to be learned. A content plan specifies, the concept, the knowledge achievement level and the learning situation to be created (akin to Shuell's [15] learning functions). Learning situations such as *focusing attention, acquisition of new knowledge, remediation of a misconception, review of a known concept*, etc. have been identified.

Figure 10.2 presents the PEPE architecture where it can be seen that content planning has three facets: goal generation, plan generation, and plan monitoring. The content planning rules — goal generation rules (GGR), plan generation rules (PGR), and plan monitoring rules(PMR) — synthesize information from the concept knowledge base (CKB), student model (SM), misconception knowledge base (MKB), student history (SH), and plan history (PH) knowledge sources. A cyclic algorithm selects an instructional point by generating (using the GGR) a content goal relevant to the student's current knowledge state (SM) and the concepts to be learned (CKB). A content plan is created (using the PGR) to achieve the goal (consulting the PH and SH). The content planner then monitors (using PMR) the execution of the content plan in order to determine when the current instructional plan has been carried out successfully, needs to be interrupted, or has failed and replanning must take place.

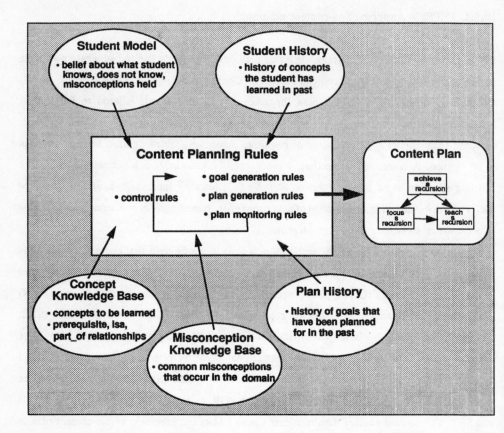

Fig. 10.2. The PEPE Architecture

PEPE is given as an example of an instructional planner that automates aspects of the production of instruction through dynamic system behavior. According to the perspective on implementation issues given earlier, it has *generality*, *flexibility*, *generativeness*, and *reusability* which are described in more detail as follows:

> *Generality* of PEPE, as was argued in Wasson [23, 24], is the ability to be used in various pedagogical situations such as *one-on-one tutoring* and *negotiated tutoring*, or in a *cognitive apprenticeship* environment.

Flexibility arises from (a) its representation of the concepts to be learned at various levels of granularity and levels of knowledge achievement, (b) the representation of various curriculums and viewpoints on a domain (as illustrated in [23]), and (c) the ability to represent various instructional strategies (cognitive apprenticeship, one-on-one tutoring, and socratic dialogue were illustrated in [23]) through the content planning rules.

Generativeness in the ability to dynamically generate a content goal and content plan relevant to the current knowledge state of the learner and the representation of the concepts to be learned.

Reusability of an instructional strategy with a different curriculum, of a curriculum with different instructional strategies (by changing the planning rules) as demonstrated in [23].

10.5.2 GTE: Generic Tutoring Environment

GTE (Generic Tutoring Environment) [18,19] is an architecture for the representation of instructional expertise. The GTE formalism, which views instruction as a *generic knowledge-based task*, is based on a framework for modelling problem-solving expertise [16] in terms of problem-solving tasks, problem-solving methods and domain models. Thus, GTE captures instructional knowledge as *instructional tasks* (e.g., give-example, give-exercise, select-topic, etc.), *instructional methods* (e.g., give-exercise task by make-exercise&verify&remedy), *knowledge sources* (e.g., models of the domain, student, and case) and *instructional primitives* (e.g., examples, topics, concepts, exercises). The instructional process is generated by instantiating those entities in a given context or teaching situation [18]. A generic task structure, see Figure 10.3 for an example, is a repetitive decomposition of a task into subtasks by applying task-decomposition methods [18]. Instructional primitives are used to support instructional methods' decision making and link to the domain to be taught with the knowledge sources providing the content of the instructional primitives.

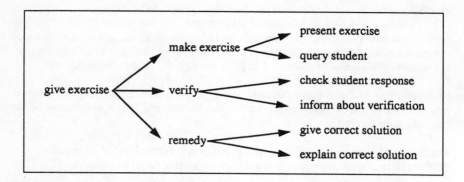

Fig. 10.3. A generic task-structure for the task "give exercise" (from [17]).

GTE offers courseware authors a library of generic instructional expertise from which they can select or reject particular pieces of expertise and tailor it for their own use. GTE has been extensively tested in a variety of different projects and applications including:

- dialogue management in Nobile [4]

- as an advice system for curriculum design in the Epos project [6]

- implementation of the instructional strategies in Capra [7,21]

- maintenance support for the hydraulic system of a Boeing 737 [20]

GTE offers *generality, flexibility, generativeness, reusability* and *authorability* as described below:

Generality of the generic tutoring environment has been demonstrated by its applicability to dialogue management, advice-giving, maintenance support through mixed-initiative dialogues.

Flexibility of representation of instructional expertise by instructional tasks, instructional methods and instructional primitives offers various levels of abstraction — generic expertise is constrained by appropriateness to a particular domain.

Generativeness through dynamic generation of the instructional process — dynamically generating instruction using an instructional method to decompose an instructional task, implement it through appropriate instructional primitives, and the ability to dynamically generate a dialogue with a student.

Reusability of instructional tasks, methods and primitives from a generic library of instructional expertise as demonstrated by its application to a variety of pedagogical situations and applications (i.e., different domains and contexts).

Authorability is currently a programming activity to be carried out by an experienced programmer. There is a recognition, however, of the need to have the authoring activity become an activity of defining elements of a course at an instructionally appropriate level of abstraction [17] by finding a level of abstraction at which authors will be able to work.

10.6 Authoring Issues

The two research projects discussed in this section have been selected because they have explicitly addressed authoring issues in addition to careful specification of underlying architectures. SIMULATE [10] focuses on authoring issues and is one aspect of a larger project, the DELTA SAFE project [11], investigating computer simulations in an instructional context. KAFITS [13, 14] is a knowledge acquisition framework for ITSs which builds on about 8 years of research in ITSs carried out by Beverly Woolf and her colleagues at the University of Massachusetts, Amherst.

10.6.1 SIMULATE

A European DELTA project (the SAFE project [11]) has investigated the use of computer simulations in an instructional context and has produced a functional architecture for intelligent simulation learning environments (ISLEs). This architecture, shown in Figure 10.4, comprises an ISLE shell and the SIMULATE authoring tools. The ISLE shell has the simulation itself predominant with all instructional support organized around it to foster exploratory learning [10]. The ISLE shell is to be generic enough to cover a wide range of subject-matter domains,

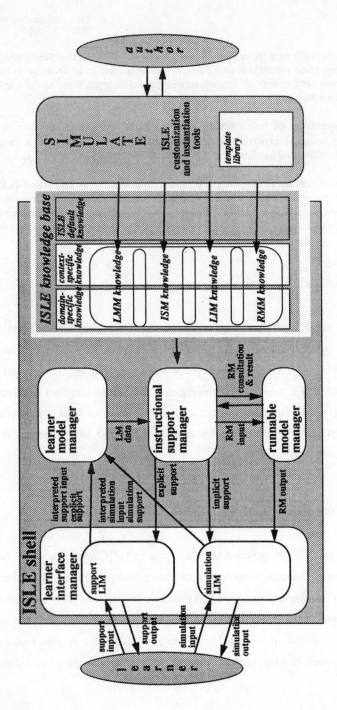

Fig. 10.4. The functional architecture for an ISLE (from [17])

learning goals, simulation models, instructional approaches, interface styles etc. This coverage is to be provided by specifying a minimal default architecture that is invariant for all ISLEs and the ISLE knowledge base which is created anew for every new domain and instructional context.

SIMULATE [10] is a set of ISLE customization and instantiation tools which operate on the ISLE knowledge bases to provide domain-specific and context-specific knowledge. The SIMULATE workbench is used for developing many different kinds of ISLEs and is designed to provide experienced authors power and less experienced authors (i.e., minimal authors) with a generic shell where they need only enter the simulation model. Using the SIMULATE tools, the generic ISLE shell is customized by specifying information on an instructional context (e.g., specifying the ISM and LMM knowledge), and the ISLE shell is instantiated by providing information on the simulation domain (i.e., providing LIM and RMM knowledge).

Although an ISLE has not been built to date, the functional architecture is grounded in strong theoretical research into simulation-based learning environments. A comprehensive investigation into the combination of simulations and ITS-environments has lead to a detailed report on the information relevant for the different components that will constitute an ISLE [11]. Out of this detailed investigation into issues such as learner characteristics, instructional strategies, learning goals, learning processes, learner activity, etc., came the functional architecture. Thus, it is research that cannot be ignored.

The ISLE shell and the SIMULATE tools offers *generality*, *flexibility*, *generativeness*, *reusability* and *authorability* as described below:

> *Generality* of the architecture is in its ability to cover a variety of instructional approaches for different pedagogical situations (e.g., of a Socratic flavor). The architecture is based on an explicit cognitive apprenticeship perspective on computer-based simulations.

> *Flexibility* is obtained through the ability to provide learner control or system control, directive or non-directive support by the specification of the instructional knowledge. Also, the ability to cover a wide range of subject-matter domains, instructional strategies, learning goals, simulation models and interface styles.

> *Generativeness* comes from having a runnable simulation *dynamically* supported by instructional assistance for the user. The system generates the instructional support and the simulation interface based on the information provided by the author and stored in the ISLE knowledge base.

Reusability is provided through a generic shell which provides instructional support that can be applied to an instantiated simulation knowledge base. The author of the system can specify the information for the knowledge sources that he or she chooses, or can use the defaults given by the shell. The domain can be changed and use the same instructional context, or vice versa.

Authorability is a major consideration of the project. The goal is to provide authoring tools to *customize* the instructional strategies and to *instantiate* the simulation.

10.6.2 KAFITS

KAFITS (Knowledge Acquisition Framework for Intelligent Tutoring Systems) is a set of intelligent tutoring system (ITS) knowledge acquisition tools tailored for usability by teachers [13,14]. Using a user-participatory design process, where those who are actually going to use the final tools are involved in the design and development process from the beginning, has resulted in a set of tools that facilitate the rapid prototyping and testing of a curriculum and multiple tutorial strategies. The envisage several uses of KAFITS [13]:

- by teachers who want to customize a tutor for a particular class or student (e.g., make a teaching strategy more verbose);
- by teachers who do not want to customize a tutor, but want to better understand what is going on inside the tutor;
- by publishers who want to update a curriculum to reflect changing perspectives on the content or pedagogy of a subject area (for installation by a teacher);
- by a school district employee, capable of using the tools, who works with teachers to modify the tutor to their satisfaction; and,
- by instructional designers and educational theorists to rapidly prototype tutors for experimentation with alternative curricula and instructional methods.

6.2.1 The KAFITS Tools

KAFITS comprises *editing tools* for entering, inspecting and modifying knowledge structures, and *monitoring tools* which trace the dynamic behavior of the system during a tutoring session. Some tools can serve as both.

The *Domain Knowledge Browser*, shown in Figure 10.5, is the most sophisticated and most used editing tool that was used to create, test, and modify a knowledge base for a static tutor. In Figure 10.5 it is being used to view the slot Hints of the presentation LE-Intuition-Easy-1 (for the Linear Equilibrium topic). The domain expert, or a knowledge engineer, can use the domain knowledge browser to go back and forth between testing the knowledge base by running the tutor, and inspecting or editing components of the knowledge base. The running of the tutor can be interrupted at any time in order to make a change to the knowledge base and resumed where it left off.

The *Topic Net Editor* is an editing tool for creating a topic network for a domain. Figure 10.6 gives a topic network developed for the static tutor. The nodes and arcs can be created, moved, deleted and edited. To inspect the contents of a node (or to start running the tutoring session with a particular topic), the editor just clicks on a node. Double clicking on a node invokes the domain knowledge browser on that exact topic. The topic net editor serves as a monitoring tool as well by having the nodes highlight as they are traversed by the running tutor.

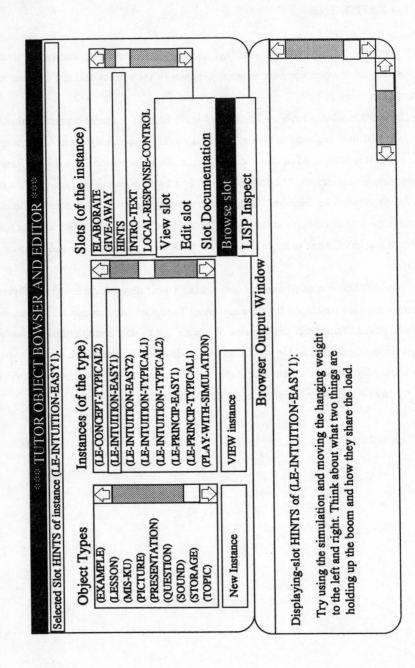

Fig. 10.5. The Domain Knowledge Browser (from[14]).

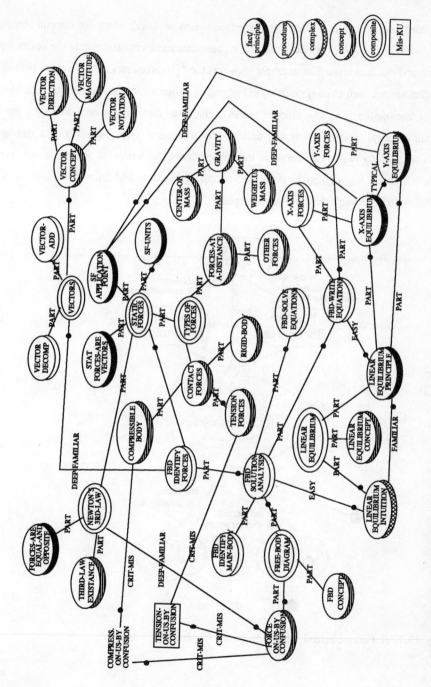

Fig. 10.6. Topic Net Editor (from [14]).

A third editing tool is a *PAN* (parameterized action network) editor for tutorial strategies. A PAN, see Figure 10.7 for an example, is a representational formalism where the nodes represent actions and the arcs tests. The example shown is the "give-feedback" PAN where the editor has specified actions such as congratulate, tell-wrong or tell-correct to be carried out depending upon student knowledge (i.e., the student model), characteristics of the domain (e.g., the task is difficult or easy), and a switch that defines a characteristic (e.g., helpful) of a strategy. The PANs are also tools that can serve as monitoring tools. As a tutorial session is run, the nodes of the PANs are highlighted to show the current action state and allow the editor to trace the flow of control through the tutorial strategies.

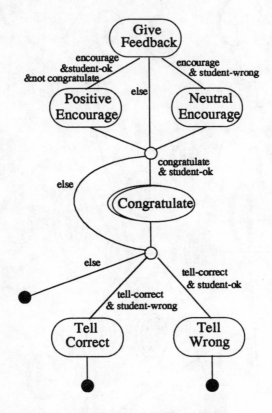

Fig. 10.7. A Parameterized Action Network (from [14]).

Two other session monitoring tools include an *Event Log* that gives a detailed trace of decisions and inferences, and a *Topic Level Display*, see Figure 10.8, that details the current topic with its levels, student model values, and the pending topics.

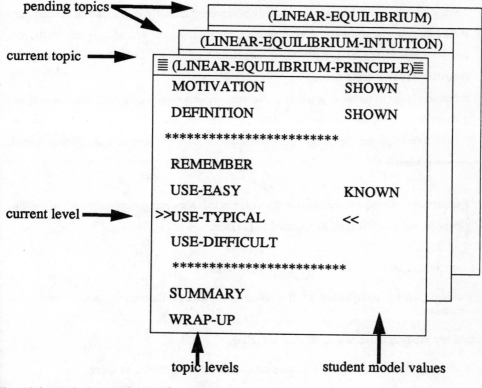

Fig. 10.8. Topic Level Display (from [14]).

5.2.2 Observations from Experience

One major focus of the KAFITS project was to investigate the representational adequacy — what types of objects, attributes, and relationships are adequate for a domain independent tutoring system with multiple teaching strategies. Experience in using the tools with teachers in developing actual tutors led to several interesting observations which can be summarized as:

- *procedural specification versus declarative representation:* some teachers had difficulty envisioning the topic network as a declarative representation of topics and the relationships between them — they wanted to view the topic net as a procedural representation of what comes next in a course.
- *curriculum representation:* what granularity of representation of a course should be used, how should the knowledge be chunked, how big should a topic be, and what is the overlapping and interdependence of topics? These questions lead to the use of *parts* attribute and *composite* type for topic nodes.
- *spiral teaching:* using topic levels (e.g., remember, easy-use, use-typical, use-difficult) and prerequisites (e.g., familiarity, deep-familiarity) between them, the effect of spiral teaching — where concepts are first taught at an introductory level and later at more advanced levels — was achieved.

Furthermore, the experience in using the tools has led to several principles critical to building ITS construction tools. These, as reported in [13] are:

- do not force users to make decisions in a rigid order,

- provide graphic, rectification of the content, knowledge framework, and dynamic data structures,

- facilitate rapid iterative test/modification cycling,

- where, possible, anticipate the cognitive capabilities and limitations of users.

KAFITS offers generality, flexibility, generativeness, reusability and authorability as described below:

> **Generality** of the tools and knowledge representational framework was designed for quasi-domain independence where most of the tutorial strategies are intended for any instructional domain (i.e., any domain knowledge base) and others are for particular curricula. The ability to represent multiple tutorial strategies gives applicability to a variety of pedagogical situations.

Flexibility through the representation of knowledge objects, attributes and relationships, gives the ability to represent multiple tutorial strategies and topic networks at various levels of granularity. Topics to be learned are represented according to the knowledge levels to be achieved. PANs enable tutorial strategies to behave dynamically.

Generativeness is provided by having the tutorial strategies applied to a topic network according to a student model, thus creating an individualized course for the student.

Reusability of the multiple tutorial strategies seems possible, although it has not been tested to date. There are plans, however, to test the development of tutors for diverse domains thus testing the reusability of the topic network representation and the tutorial strategies.

Authorability has been a major focus as described above. Editing and session monitoring tools for entering knowledge and visualizing the tutor's behavior have been provided.

10.7 Conclusion

Intelligent Learning Environments have been characterized (see Figure 10.1) according to their goal, the type of knowledge to be learned, and the type of instructional support and instructional strategies provided. The development of an ILE is dependent upon the underlying characteristics and the demands they place on the specified system. Thus, the development can be seen as a complex and intricate process. As a result of this complexity, the majority of ILEs developed to date have been research vehicles built by computer scientists or cognitive psychologists knowledgeable in artificial intelligence (AI) programming techniques. To facilitate practical use of ILEs by the educational community (and take ILEs out of the research lab), ways to enable non-AI programming specialists to develop ILEs must be found. Automating the process of development is an attempt to bridge this gap between theory and application.

This chapter has discussed issues involved in the automation of the development of ILEs. Questions about what is meant by automation have been raised. For example, the goal of automation needs to be clear, and the roles of the participants — the ILE system designer, the ILE author, and the ILE itself — need to be understood. The *input of knowledge* (knowledge acquisition), the *behavior of the system* (generativeness), and the *output of information* (delivery) have been identified as aspects of development that can be automated. The provision of authoring tools for knowledge acquisition and, visualization and monitoring of system behavior facilitate the input of knowledge. The representation of knowledge (e.g., domain, pedagogical and student) and, processes for reasoning about the knowledge (e.g., instructional planning rules for generating instructional goals) enable dynamic system behavior.

Implementation issues have been presented from the perspective of an ILEs *generality*, *flexibility*, *generativeness*, *reusability*, *authorability* and *evaluability*. These perspectives have been used to focus the discussion of four systems that address how knowledge acquisition and dynamic system behavior can contribute to the automation process. The four contemporary systems, PEPE, GTE, SIMULATE and KAFITS have been briefly examined with key issues in the automation process being identified.

Finally, this chapter has attempted to organize the issues around which the automation of the development of ILEs can be discussed. This is a field in its infancy and one of the first steps is to delineate the terminology, the techniques, and the technologies that will serve to bind the research community together. This chapter presents a foundation for further discussions.

Acknowledgements

I would like to thank Svein-Ivar Lillehaug for his helpful comments on an earlier version of this chapter.

References

1. Berkum, J.A. van: Functional requirements for an intelligent simulation learning environment. DELTA-Project SAFE Report No. SIM/42B (1991)
2. Berkum, J.A. van: Learning goals for simulations. In: T. de Jong (Ed.), Computer simulations in an instructional context (T. de Jong, Ed.). DELTA-project P7061 (D1012) SAFE Report No. SAFE/SIM/WPI/EUT-rep/comp.final (Final Report) October 1991
3. Bloom, B.: Taxonomy of educational objectives, Handbook I: Cognitive domain. New York: David McKay 1956

4. Cerri, S.A., Cheli, E., & McIntyre A.: Nobile: User model acquisition in a natural laboratory. In M. Jones, & P. Winne (Eds.), Foundations and frontiers of adaptive learning environments. NATO ASI Series F, Vol. 85. Berlin: Springer Verlag 1992

5. Dillenbourg, P., Hilario, M., Mendelsohn, P., & Schneider, D.: The MEMOLAB project: Current status. TECFA Document 91-5, University of Geneva 1991

6. Erol, N.: ECOLE: Epos collaborative learning environment. DELTA Project EPOS D7002, Dida*El srl. IC 90-02-02, Milan 1990

7. Fernandez, I., Diaz de Ilarraza, A., & Verdejo, F.: Building a programming tutor by dynamic planning: Case studies and a proposal. In Proceedings of the 1st International Conference on Intelligent Tutoring Systems (ITS-88). Montreal 1988

8. Fischer, G., Lemke, A.C., & Mastaglio, T.: Using critics to empower users. In CHI-90 Conference Proceedings (pp. 337-347). New York: ACM 1990

9. Fischer, G., Lemke, A., & Schwab, T.: Knowledge-based help systems. In CHI-85 Conference Proceedings (pp. 161-167). New York: ACM 1985

10. Hijne, H., & Berkum, J. van: A functional architecture for intelligent simulation learning environments. In Proceedings of DELTA & beyond. The Hague, The Netherlands October 1990

11. de Jong, T. (ed.): Computer simulations in an instructional context. DELTA-project P7061 (D1012) SAFE Report No. SAFE/SIM/WPI/EUT-rep/comp.final (Final Report) October 1990

12. Kearsley, G.: Online help systems: Design and implementation. Norwood, NJ: Ablex 1988

13. Murray, T., & Woolf, B.P.: Tools for teacher participation in ITS design. In Proceedings of the 2nd International Conference on Intelligent Tutoring Systems (ITS-92), Montreal. Lecture Notes in Computer Science, Vol. 608. Berlin: Springer-Verlag 1992

14. Murray, T., & Woolf, B.P.: A knowledge acquisition tool for intelligent computer tutors. SIGART Bulletin, 2, 9-21. New York: ACM 1991

15. Shuell, T.J.: Designing instructional computing systems for meaningful learning. In M. Jones, & P. Winne (Eds.), Foundations and frontiers of adaptive learning environments. NATO ASI Series F, Vol. 85. Berlin: Springer-Verlag 1992

16. Steels, L.: Components of expertise. AI Magazine, 11, 2 (1990)

17. Tuck, R., & Olsen, D R.: Help by guided tasks; Utilizing UIMS knowledge. In CHI-90 Conference Proceedings (pp. 71-78). New York: ACM 1990

18. Van Marckle, K.: A generic task model for instruction. In S. Dijkstra, H.P.M. Krammer, & J.J.G. van Merriënboer (Eds.), Instructional models in computer-based instructional systems. NATO ASI Series F, Vol. 104. Berlin: Springer-Verlag 1992

19. Van Marckle, K.: A Generic tutoring environment. In Proceedings of the 9th European Conference on Artificial Intelligence: 655-660 (1990)

20. Van Marckle, K.: KRS: An object-oriented representation language. Revue d'Intelligence Artificielle, 1, 4 (1987)

21. Verdejo, M.F., & Mayorga, I.: Rewriting Capra in GTE. Report de Recerca Universitat Politecnica de Catalunya, Barcelona 1991

22. Wasson, B.J.: PEPE: A computational framework for a content planner. In S. Dijkstra, H.P.M. Krammer, & J.J.G. van Merriënboer (Eds.), Instructional models in computer-based instructional systems. NATO ASI Series F, Vol. 104. Berlin: Springer-Verlag 1992

23. Wasson (Brecht), B J.: Determining the focus of instruction: content planning for intelligent tutoring systems. Ph.D Thesis, Department of Computational Science, University of Saskatchewan, Saskatoon, Saskatchewan, Canada. (Research report 90-5) 1990
24. Wasson, B.J., & McCalla, G.I.: Negotiated tutoring needs student modelling and instructional planning. In R. Moyse, & M. Elsom-Cook (Eds.), Negotiated learning. London: Chapman 1991

Part 2 Summary: Production

Begoña Gros

After specification of the learning environment that we want to automatize, we will summarize the main problems concerned with the production phase.

The production phase is related to the transformation of the model built in the planning phase, to an adequate execution of the delivery process. The main problem in this phase is to specify the production processes necessary to create different courseware types.

In order to automate instructional development, it is necessary to build programs to permit an automatic transformation of the specifications of the system. Tools such as authoring languages, shells, etc. have been developed for this purpose.

Different approaches have been developing to automate production, and the main discussion between the experts of this area is centered in this question. For this reason, in this summary I am going to show the main issues in relation to the following questions:
- Which instructional production functions can and should be automated?
- Which ways are more valuable for the automation of production?
- Which specialists should to participate in the production process?
- How is it possible to evaluate the production process?
  Finally, I will propose some research topics necessary to make progress in this area.

Theoretical Issues Involved in the Production Process

The main purpose in the automation of ISD is to create tools that permit the easy transfer of our specific instructional content into a courseware. This idea introduces an important question that has appeared in many discussions: which instructional development functions can or should be automated?

The answer is not simple. According to Wasson (Chap. 10), it is possible to automate the input of knowledge (i.e., knowledge acquisition), using authoring tools, the behavior of the system (the representation of knowledge and reasoning about the knowledge) and the final interface. The problem is how to achieve a correct automation of each component. Different technical approaches exist and there is some agreement among the experts about the kind of tools that must be developed. It seems necessary to produce tools with high levels of generality, flexibility, re-usability and authorability.

Seemingly, the discussion about the development of automation ID is more concerned with technical issues that pedagogical and psychological aspects. Nevertheless, during the production of the system we can not forget the specifications made in the planning phase.

According to Sancho (Chap. 7) it is necessary to think that the real situation of learning is very complex and so full of values and meaning that is very difficult to contemplate all the variables. This remark introduces an interesting discussion about the gap between the development of technology and the real application of the tools in practice.

While we are involved in the production of technology, it is necessary to emphasize the support of teachers in the use of these materials. As Krammer and Dijkstra (Chap. 12) point out, dissemination and diffusion of technology, in education, is always difficult. Changes in education are gradually and, as Spector (Chap. 13) said, we have to distinguish between educational innovation and the improvement of education technology.

To sum up, it is necessary to develop tools to facilitate the main instructional processes used by teachers, and we have to try to avoid an elitist point of view. We have to create technology according to the real world, with real needs. This idea connects with one of the ideas proposed during the workshop discussion about the planning process: the necessity to analyze the classroom and look at the teaching-learning processes in real situations.

Main Controversial Issues

Different ways to automate ID.   As we said previously, it is possible to select different technical approaches to produce the automation of ID. During previous chapters the reader has had the opportunity to look at some of these approaches.   Basically, proposals have been centered in three areas: simulations, intelligent tutoring systems (ITS), and expert systems. Tennyson and Breuer (Chap. 9) agree with Gonzalez on the idea that it is necessary to deal with ill-structured problems and they propose an automated ISD system (ISD Expert) as a way that can help in the solving of ill-structured instructional development problems. For example, instructional development is related to the acquisition of a contextual level of knowledge. For this reason, ISD Expert can be used to work with complex and dynamic instructional development environments and it is especially effective for ill-structured ISD problem tasks.

Currently, there are no effective tools to deal with ill-structured instructional development problems. So, I think that it is necessary to create tools to permit the automation of production in such areas. Especially in regards to automating instruction for higher order learning activities.

Other approaches introduce the use of artificial intelligence, basically through the production of intelligent tutoring systems (ITS). ITSs have become widespread during the last few years but they are also very controversial. As Merriënboer et al. suggest, the main effort must be made in the modelling and diagnosis processes. Both are very important for the correct working of the system but, very often, the simplification made by the developer does not have a clear correspondence to the designer's specifications. One example is the student model, that is sometimes a simplification of the remedial interaction between the teacher and the student, without taking into account variables about context, ways of learning, previous history of the student, etc.

Two other alternatives to produce the automation of ISD are mentioned by Tennyson and Breuer: expert systems and neural networks.

Expert systems are used in a lot of prototypes. The main difference between expert systems and neural networks is the way the program arrives to the solution. Expert systems methods are basically linear, beginning with the problem and proceeding to the solution following a procedural sequence (i.e., If...Then decisions). With the use of neural networks, as suggested by Tennyson and Breuer for ISD Expert, the program starts with a diagnosis of the situation and then proposes a prescription. After the solution, the system validates it and then stores the prescription as contextual knowledge. This alternative seems very interesting because it emphases the heuristic representation of the problem, which is an important aspect that we must consider, because most programs only follow an algorithmic process.

Which specialist should participate during the production process? It seems clear that the software engineer or computer scientist have most responsibility in this phase. However, the work done by these specialists should be controlled by the rest of the team, because it is the only way to establish a correspondence between the specifications of the planning phase and the production of the program. For this reason, I agree that the cooperative work between different specialist during those processes is very important. Nevertheless, problems very often appear because practitioners, instructional designers, teachers, etc. do not have enough information to evaluate the work in process carried out during this phase. But, the ideal model should be an integrated activity preference being given in each phase to the main expert.

Evaluation. When we spoke about evaluation of the planning process, we mentioned that it is very difficult to establish a separation between the evaluation of planning and development. For this reason, Muraida suggests the use of the expression "instructional development" to refer to the entire process: design and development.

According to Muraida (Chap. 8), the evaluation of automated instructional development refers to an assessment of the congruency between users' characteristics, the requirements of instructional development goals, and the nature of the instructional material.

What is needed is a systematic approach of evaluation of the designer variables, to facilitate the study of their impact on courseware development.

Most of the methods used in evaluation of software are quantitative. But, if instructional development is viewed as an ill-formed problem solving process, it will be necessary to think about the use of observational methodologies. According to this idea, I suggest the necessity to create an evaluation method that integrates intuitive and analytical components. To achieve this goal, Muraida proposes the production of a complete profile of automated guidance, during pilot and field tests.

To sum up, until now, evaluation has been made through a final approach. Nevertheless, what is necessary is to elaborate systematic formative evaluation data that permits comparison of differences between the request of the users and the instructional development.

Future Research

I can summarize the necessary future research in two areas: (a) development of tools of automation; and (b) evaluation methods.

(a).   It is necessary to improve the tools of automation of ISD. The authors have suggested four different areas: simulation, intelligent tutoring system, expert systems and neural networks.

(b).   It is necessary to study real and valid measures of evaluation, that permit us to include quantitative and qualitative data. The main purpose is to find a way of creating a formative evaluation to facilitate the comparison between requirements made during the planning phase and the development of the system.

11

Adapting Instructional Design Methods to Intelligent Multimedia Authoring Systems

Michael Baker

Centre National de la Recherche Scientifique, Laboratoire IRPEACS, 93, chemin des Mouilles, BP 167, 69131 Ecully Cedex, France

Abstract: Given the recent development of Intelligent Multimedia Authoring systems, there are few well-developed methodologies for authoring courseware. This chapter describes one case of automating an instructional design model - the "SHIVA" system. On the basis of a conceptual structure of the courseware, and a set of multi-media Units of Learning Material, the system automatically decides the teaching presentation sequence, whilst adapting to the students' responses. An integrated formative evaluation program provides findings which contribute to understanding of how to adapt existing instructional design models to the specificities of interactive intelligent multimedia.

Keywords: authoring, instructional design, multimedia, artificial intelligence, training

11.1 Introduction

Given the recent development of Intelligent Multimedia Authoring (IMA) systems, there are few well-developed associated methodologies for authoring courseware. System designers have therefore turned to the adaptation and partial automation of instructional design models that were originally developed for traditional "face-to-face" teaching. However, course design processes presuppose specific *media* for the materials to be presented, and a specific *delivery system* for presenting them. The question therefore arises as to the extent to which one instructional design method, developed for given media and delivery systems (such as face to face teaching, and/or texts) needs to be modified in transferring the method to others (such as automated computer-based pedagogical decision-making and multimedia). Even in the case where this transference may reasonably be made, IMA systems may present special problems for courseware designers in understanding potentialities of new interactive media and complex pedagogical decision-making processes in AI systems.

In this chaper I describe one specific attempt to incorporate a "traditional" instructional-design method in an IMA. The system concerned is called "SHIVA", developed within the framework of the EEC DELTA Program ("Advanced Authoring Tools" project, No. D1010), and the instructional design method which it incorporates is that of Posner and Rudnitsky [21]. SHIVA allows authors to design graphically the high-level conceptual structure of courseware, and to instantiate these conceptual pedagogical objectives in multi-media units of learning material. The system dynamically determines the teaching sequence presentation as a function of the authors' decisions, the student's responses, and instructional knowledge represented in the system, using well-understood techniques in AI and Education.

The design of SHIVA thus assumes that the instructional design task may be *divided* between the authors' decisions concerning high-level course structure and the system's dynamic decisions concerning presentation order. We describe results of an integrated formative evaluation program, designed to test this and a number of other important assumptions incorporated in the design of SHIVA. The evaluation involved case-studies of teams producing pilot courseware for specific domains (geography and business English), and of experts using SHIVA to perform simple authoring tasks. Results obtained contribute to our understanding of how to adapt existing instructional design models to the specificities of interactive multimedia and different teaching domains.

The chapter is structured as follows. Firstly, I describe the Posner and Rudnitsky [21] instructional design method. Secondly, I describe SHIVA, and how it was developed in order to incorporate the instructional design method. Thirdly, I describe results of the formative evaluation programme, designed to establish the extent to which authors are able to achieve their goals with the system. Finally, I attempt to draw some general conclusions concerning automation of instructional design in IMA systems.

11.2 The Instructional Design Method

The "course design" method of Posner & Rudnitsky [21] aims to bridge the gap between theory and practice in curriculum development, and is intended for secondary school teachers and teachers in training. The method needs to be described in some detail here in order to describe which parts of it were automated and which were not.

P&R make two fundamental distinctions : between curriculum and instruction, and between processes and products of planning. The curriculum (product) represents *what* is to be taught. Its development (process) involves selecting and organising *intended learning outcomes* (ILOs), guided by educational goals and values. The process of instruction is guided by an *instructional plan* (product), which defines the specific materials and instructional activities designed to achieve the ILOs of the curriculum. Once instruction is put into effect, actual learning outcomes may be assessed, and a plan for *evaluating* the course design may be defined. A simplified version of the P&R course design method is shown in Figure 11.1.

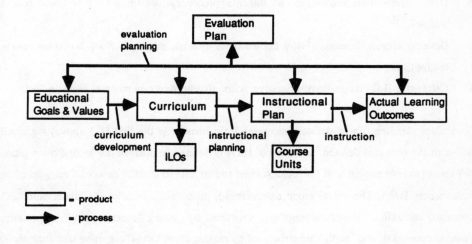

Fig. 11.1. The Posner & Rudnitsky course design method.

Here I shall concentrate on the two main processes and products: planning the curriculum planning and planning instruction. It should be noted that although the method is presented in linear form, each new step involves revising the previous ones in the light of new information. Course design is therefore an *iterative process*.

11.2.1 Curriculum Planning

The process of defining "what is to be learned" is one of successive refinement, from a general course outline to specific categorised ILOs. The basic steps involved are summarised below.

1.   Define *course outline* (theoretical framework, initial ideas, course title),
2.   Select ILOs from course outline (exclude materials, activities),
3.   Define central questions, expand list of ILOs,
4.   Categorise ILOs into skills and understandings,
5.   Make conceptual maps (understandings), cognitive task flowcharts (skills),
6.   Analyse terminology in skills and understandings,
7.   Arrange list of ideas and make lines between them,
8.   Define prerequisite knowledge and students' preconceptions for ILOs [-> revise course outline],
9.   Develop course rationale ("why do we have to learn this stuff ?") [-> revise course outline], and
10. Categorise ILOs (cognitions, cognitive skills, psycho-motor-perceptual skills, affects).

Curriculum planning can be divided into three main phases. In the first [1-3 above] a general outline of the course is defined, and a set of ILOs is defined from it. In the second main phase [4-7 above] the current list of ILOs is categorised and structured initially (a second categorisation phase occurs later). The initial broad categorisation to be made is between "understandings" (concepts) and skills. "Understandings" are structured by making "concept maps" (essentially, semantic networks), and "skills" are structured by making flowcharts ("cognitive task analysis"). In the third phase [8-10] the course outline and a (partially) structured set of ILOs is further refined in the light of different perspectives : the pre-existing knowledge of the target student population, the course rationale, and further more-detailed structuring of the ILOs. I shall briefly discuss each of these phases in turn, concentrating on the specific practical directions given to course designers ("how to do it").

In the first phase the general problem is to identify possible ILOs. Advice given to course designers as to how to produce a tentative outline is as follows: "The best way to produce a tentative course outline is to consult several good resource books on the topic [21, p. 16]. " Once a draft outline is produced, the criterion for selecting ILOs from it is as follows: "An ILO comes into being because you think an item in your list of initial ideas or course outline is something to be learned" [21, p. 17]. "

For example, in a course on cooking specific *materials* (eg., Rombauer's *"Joy of Cooking"*) and *activities* (eg., "trip to local restaurant") are therefore not ILOs. Finally, identifying "central questions" helps to give the outline *focus*: "In order to develop central questions, formulate the most important questions addressed in the course" [21, pp. 20-21].

In the second main phase, the list of ILOs is to be refined, structured and categorised. As to how this is to be done, P&R rely mainly on giving examples of different types of conceptual maps and skill flowcharts; but general injunctions towards clarity, "balance," and avoidance of ambiguity and redundancy are given. In general, maps may be hierarchical or heterarchical, they may be specified in greater or lesser detail (for which several related maps may be made), and they may employ several different kinds of relationship. Once ILOs have been classified into skills and understandings, and a draft set of maps has been successively refined, ILOs may be further classified, as shown in Figure 11.2.

In effect, this step requires categorisation of ILOs in terms of the type of *learning* involved.

In the third phase of curriculum planning, the categorised and structured ILOs are to be refined by considering the extent to which they may be pedagogically realised and justified, by considering the student population's prior knowledge, and the pedagogical rationale of the objectives. Given that students try to make sense of their learning experience based on what they already know or believe, P&R suggest two main practical ways in which this prior knowledge may be taken into account. Firstly, the designer should review existing courses which the students have taken. This will not, however, determine what students *know*, rather what has been *presented* to them. P&R therefore make the following suggestion:

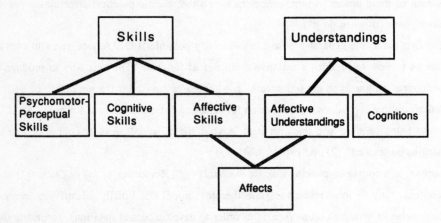

Fig. 11.2. Classification of ILOs.

> The best way to find out this crucial information is to talk with them [the students] in open-ended interviews and group discussions asking them for their explanations or descriptions while listening to them very carefully. In these diagnostic settings, we can find out the extent to which their views are idiosyncratic or common to the other learners; whether their ideas derive from prior instruction, mass media, life experience or their own "spontaneous reasoning"; and possibly how deeply held their beliefs are and, thus, how difficult they will be to change [21, p. 36].

This extract is worth quoting in full since it highlights the extent to which current automatic diagnosis in intelligent tutoring systems does not take into account the *context* of prior learning. Finally, the course rationale is "...a statement that makes explicit the values and educational goals underlying the course" [21, p. 42]. These serve to facilitate acceptance of the goals by students ("Why do we have to learn this stuff ?"), to refine ILOs (those for which a justification cannot be found should be rejected) and to guide the instruction itself (to what extent are general goals being achieved?). It may seem surprising that the rationale is defined *after* ILOs have been defined, since "logically" the rationale should come first. However, P&R adopt the view that the rationale is best incorporated into a course design method with the function of refining an initial outline of the specific content of the course.

11.2.2 Instructional Planning

"Instructional planning consists in planning a series of events around a particular activity, stimulus, or vehicle for communicating ideas" [21, p. 83]. The main phases are summarised below.

1.   Cluster ILOs into coherent and manageable course units
2.   Design instructional foci for each course unit
3.   Give a title to each unit
4.   Develop general teaching strategies
5.   Elaborate instructional foci into description of general teaching strategies
6.   Write rationale for each of units
7.   Reconsider total instructional plan

The two main stages of instructional planning involve: forming course units [1-3] and defining teaching strategies [4-7]. There is clearly a relationship between the two stages since one way in which ILOs may be 'clustered' is in terms of the ILOs relevant to a specific instructional activity (such as a visit to a museum):

> Instead of forming units around clusters of ILOs, units can be designed around themes and problems; around instructional activities such as projects, debates, field trips, papers, around stimuli for thinking such as case studies and photographs; or around vehicles for communicating what we know or feel, such as books or poems [21, p. 89].

In the first stage, the ILOs which are clustered together should form a coherent whole, and should thus be closely related in a concept map (in the case of understandings). Two main questions arise here: "how big should units be ?" (how many ILOs clustered together ?), and "should ILOs of different types be clustered together ? (eg., skills and understandings clustered together for a specific activity). P&R give no unequivocal answers: in general the students should be able to view the unit as coherent and manageable, and the size of such units may depend on the subject of the course. In addition to defining the units themselves, the course designer must also organise them into coherent *sequences*. For P&R, this is carried out on the same bases as those for organising the units themselves. The following are a set of different bases for clustering ILOs into units, and for organising units into sequences.

Alternative principles for organising and sequencing units:

1.   World-related sequences. Sequences in which there is consistency between the ordering of units and empirical relationships between events, people and objects as they exist or occur in the world (eg. sequencing of history content based on chronological sequence of events).

2.   Concept-related sequences. Reflect organisation of the conceptual world ; consistent with way in which ideas relate to one another (eg. geometry taught deductively).

3.   Inquiry-related sequences. Derive from the nature of the process of generating, discovering or verifying knowledge (eg., logic or methodology of physics).

4.   Learning-related sequences. Draw on knowledge of the psychology of learning (eg., empirical prerequisites; difficulty of material, etc.).

5.   Utilization-related sequences. Knowledge and skills organised in social, personal or career contexts; frequency of utilization.

Clustering ILOs into coherent sequenced units may thus be viewed as a *top-down* process. However, in practical situations, teachers rarely begin "from scratch": they usually have some specific teaching materials, and pre-programmed activities, into which the ILOs must fit, at least to some extent, in a *bottom-up* way. They may even not be designing a course, but rather *re-designing* one. Units may therefore also be designed around themes, problems, and instructional activities such as debates, field trips, experiments, or case-studies. P&R term these "vehicles for communicating" *instructional foci*.

The second main stage of instructional planning is to design *instructional strategies*:

> Instruction…is made up of all the purposeful activities of a teacher aimed at producing, stimulating, or facilitating learning in students. Instruction deals with how - what methods, materials, strategies, tasks, incentives, and the like can be employed to encourage learning [21, p. 127].

"Instructional strategies" are described as specific interaction patterns between teacher and students. Choice of appropriate instructional strategy depends on the categories of ILOs taught in the unit. P&R provide an exhaustive table thus linking cognitions, cognitive skills, psychomotor skills and affects to instructional strategies. For example, in teaching cognitions, teachers should "emphasise the attributes of the concept," "ask students to find instances of the concept," "ask students to relate the concept to other concepts," "explain the implications of the assertion," etc. In teaching cognitive skills the teacher should "stimulate recall of relevant prerequisites," "furnish external prompts," "provide practice of the skill," "provide feedback," and so on. In fact, although P&R state that instructional strategies describe interaction patterns, most of their directions specify what the *teacher* should do, not the students. They do, however, briefly mention the use of simulations and role playing.

After the course design is finished, the course may be *evaluated* and possibily *modified*. This involves defining observable behaviours that will count as evidence that student has acquired ILOs. Information gathered in evaluation may be used to modify the course en-route. Although this stage is presented as the end of the course design process, it in fact imposes a "backward constraint," in that the course should be designed to be *evaluable*.

11.3 The SHIVA Intelligent Multi-media Authoring System

I now describe the intelligent multi-media authoring system which was based on a partial automation of the Posner and Rudnitsky course design method. Amongst those available, this method was chosen because of its relative simplicity and explicitness, which thus facilitated implementation.

11.3.1 Origins and Development Strategy

SHIVA was produced as the result of the integration of two pre-existing systems - ECAL and ORGUE - to produce an integrated prototype, which was further developed in conjunction with a formative evaluation programme. ECAL ("Extended Computer-Assisted Learning") was a system produced at the Open University [10], within the perspective of "bridging the gap" between AI prototype ITSs and existing CAL systems used in training. The ORGUE "Courseware Engineering Tools" were produced at CNRS-IRPEACS. They comprise graphical editing tools for the production of multimedia CAL courseware. SHIVA was produced by a European consortium within the EEC DELTA programme. The partners were CNRS-IRPEACS (France), Open University (UK), Apigraph (France), SEL (Germany) and DATAMAT (Italy). To simplify somewhat, ORGUE and ECAL were combined in SHIVA by replacing the ECAL text-based editor with ORGUE, adding new editors, and refining the composite system during formative evaluation. Evaluation work was conducted in collaboration with the University of Nottingham, Department of Psychology (UK). I will briefly describe ECAL and ORGUE before describing how they were integrated in SHIVA.

11.3.2 ECAL

ECAL was based on a simplified version of the Posner and Rudnitsky course design model. The system was limited to teaching "cognitive skills" and "conceptual knowledge" (in P&R's terms), the only "teaching situations" incorporated are simple text presentation screens (a WYSIWYG wordprocessor is provided), and it is assumed that a curriculum has already been created. ECAL contains two main components: an authoring environment and a presentation environment. In the authoring environment, the author creates a set of frames (screens), and indexes each of them to the concept ILOs of the curriculum. This corresponds to 'clustering' the ILOs into teaching materials. The author does not explicitly represent relations between ILOs, these being calculated automatically by the system on the general basis that if ILOs are linked to the same frame, they are *related*. A simple knowledge representation is thus derived, forming one of the bases upon which the presentation system automatically determines the presentation sequence of frames. In addition to calculating the "relatedness" between ILOs, each ILO is assigned a value for its "generality" and "importance" based on the range of frames in which it occurs, and the number of frames in which it occurs. The frame presentation algorithm is also based on a simple student and dialogue model. The "numeric overlay" student model records a confidence factor (0-1) for the degree to which the student 'understands' each ILO. Thus confidence is increased after presentation of frames, and decreased or increased in the case where the student gives the correct or incorrect response to frames which pose questions to the student. The dialogue model contains a record of the current ILO on which the interaction is focussed, and a "dialogue history" (a record of which frames have already been presented, and which ILOs remain to be satisfied). At the highest level, the frame presentation algorithm selects an ILO focus (if not already determined) based on importance and generality of the ILO, or its relatedness to the previous focus. The system then attempts to choose a frame which maintains the focus from those which are linked to it. One teaching strategy used is that of "general to specific", i.e. choosing a frame with a high relevance which is more specific than the current frame, and which introduces a minimal amount of new material (student model). Since the basic presentation algorithm was retained in SHIVA I discuss it in more detail later.

11.3.3 ORGUE

ORGUE forms part of a general system termed a "Courseware Engineering Tool," consisting of a set of graphic editors for creating multimedia presentation materials and for linking them into flowcharts which determine their pedagogical sequencing. The set of editors is specially designed to allow the author to run the courseware, in whole or in part, and thus to anticipate the learner's activity. An appropriate editor with specific funtionalities, is dedicated to each particular audiovisual task, but each editor is designed with a view to incorporating materials from others (eg., bitmap photos in graphics, sound with graphics). The editors incorporated include the following:

MINIGR - a vectorial graphical colour editor, based on the metaphor of the overhead projector.

DIESE - an editor for retrieving and inserting text into a graphical context.

PICCOLO - a tool for modifying digitised still photographs, rather than for creating them.

SAXO - a numerical sound editor, allowing the recording, retrieval and graphical editing of natural sound at several quality levels, in a mode compatible with the ISDN.

DIGITISED VIDEO EDITOR - an editor for high resolution digitised video images (from a videodisc). The editor allows the insertion of video sequences into courseware, windows which are resizable during real-time playback.

SIMENU - an editor which allows the interfaces of all the editors to be customised to authors' preferences, including the student environment.

The pedagogical flowchart interface allows the author to describe graphically the progressive succession of courseware. The contents of flowchart boxes may be either specific multimedia scenes, or hierarchically embedded sub-flowcharts. Links between boxes may incorporate counters (the number of times the learner has traversed that path) and boxes may also include the execution of any other Pascal program. The screen is divided into three parts. On the left, the flowcharts are created by the author, on the upper right a tree-like representation allows the author to navigate within the course structure, and on the lower right the author selects multimedia scenes to be linked into flowchart boxes from a reduced-size display. The author may run the whole or part of the course at any time (automatic compilation), and execution errors are indicated graphically on the flowchart.

11.3.4 SHIVA

ECAL and ORGUE were integrated in SHIVA by retaining the strongest aspects of each, and by developing new tools for authors in response to the requirements of multimedia systems and general homogeneity of the combined authoring tools. The elements of ECAL retained were the underlying conceptual knowledge representation for the curriculum (ILOs), and its attendant pedagogical decision-making program. The simple text frames of ECAL were replaced by the multimedia frames of ORGUE, with the appropriate media editors. A "Unit of Learning Material" (ULM) in SHIVA can thus contain an arbitrarily large hierarchical flowchart linking multimedia frames. The method of attaching keywords (ILOs) to text frames in ECAL was replaced by a new editor called PSAUME.

PSAUME allows authors to graphically create ILOs, and to . to ULMs. Since ULM-ILO maps may become very complex for course, parts of the initial map may be represented in subviews. Although SHIVA automatically calculates relational networks between ILOs on the basis of this map, these are no longer hidden from the author, but rather may be viewed in separate CONCEPT and FRAME windows. Whilst these windows are "read only", some degree of control is given to the author over concept maps, since "pre-requisite" relations between concepts may be specified (see the right-hand window in Figure 11.4). Just as in ORGUE, the author can inspect the contents of ULMs as represented in PSAUME.

In the development of PSAUME we began to address the problem of deciding how pedagogical decisions could reasonably be *shared* between the author and the system (in ECAL the author had nly very indirect control over pedagogical sequencing, in terms of which keywords were linked to which frames). In addition to allowing authors to specify pre-requisite relations between ILOs, we therefore also attempted to allow authors to provide information on *student modelling*, within the flowchart structure of ULMs. In part this problem arises from the fact that if ULMs are very large - and there is nothing in the system which prevents this - student modelling will necessarily be very 'coarse-grained', and in the case where students give incorrect responses within flowcharts, it will be difficult to assign 'blame' to the concept misunderstood, amonst those linked to the ULM. Authors can therefore inspect the flowchart structure of an ULM in PSAUME, and link ILOs graphically to parts of it, thus indicating "if the student passes by this route in the flowchart, decrement the confidence value of this ILO in the student model".

Although the ECAL pedagogical decision-making program was retained in SHIVA, it was adapted to include new rules relating to new activities provided for the author - for example, rules relating to concept pre-requisites. The algorithm is summarised in Figure 11.3.

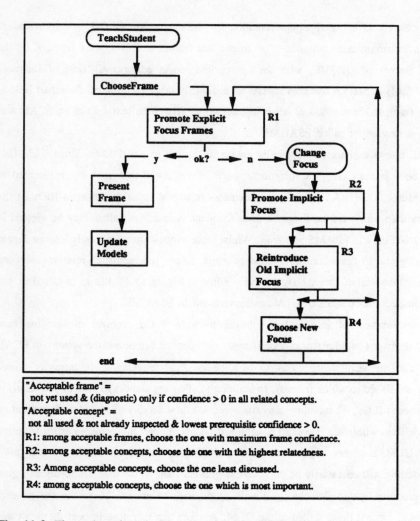

Fig. 11.3. The pedagogical decision algorithm in SHIVA.

In order to determine whether the course meets their training goals, authors need to anticipate the eventual pedagogical sequence as a function of the learners' activity. In ORGUE they could do this by running the course, reacting as a hypothetical learner, and modifying the flowchart accordingly. However, since SHIVA makes automatic pedagogical decisions, authors using this system also need to understand the bases upon which these decisions are made. A set of "pedagogical debugging tools" has therefore been developed, available either from PSAUME or in the student environment. In PSAUME authors can *simulate* the course, by hypothesing students' responses to frames (either all correct, or all incorrect). The frame presentation order is displayed, together with ILO focus for each frame taught, the pedagogical rules invoked, and changes in the student model. In the student environment, changes in the student model and pedagogical rules fired may be traced as the author steps through the course.

In addition to creating new editors for ILOs, in response to the demands of ECAL, a new editor was also produced to facilitate the creation of ULMs which integrated different media. In order to facilitate "horizontal" links between different media editors, and the creation of multimedia "scenes," a new *multimedia editor* has therefore been developed. The editor contains a screen where windows containing scenes from each editor (video, graphics, sound, etc.) can be composed into multiple-media scenes, and provides a central point of access to each separate media editing tool.

11.4 A Formative Evaluation Program

As the name suggests, a formative evaluation is one which is carried out in order to influence the form of a system whilst it is "taking shape." Given the nature of the project, evaluation was concerned principally with the *authors'* point of view, rather than that of learners (although the production of a course which teaches effectively is of course the principal goal of authors). The project therefore contained an initial cycle of formative evaluation of the prototype at an early stage of development. The evaluation has had a formative role in influencing the implementation. For example, the difficulty of predicting decisions of the system gave rise to the development of simulation functionalities for authors, and results of a detailed task analysis [1], using videos of expert authors performing an experimental task, led to a number of recommendations for interface re-design.

At the outset, it was immediately apparent that two main problems needed to be addressed:

1.   The degree of homogeneity and coherence of the set of interfaces in the hybrid system;
2.   the coherence and user-acceptance of the functional model of authoring incorporated explicitly or implicitly in the system.

These two issues are of course related since specific interfaces are provided to support authors for a large part of the authoring model. We addressed the first problem mostly using Human-Computer Interaction evaluation techniques, and the second by studies of Pilot Courseware production for specific domains. Given the aims of this paper, we describe the evaluation and its results very briefly (see DELTA D1010 Final Report for further details), in order to assess issues arising in the automation of instructional design.

11.4.1 Human-Computer Interaction

We used a variety of methods to assess the usability of the interfaces incorporated in SHIVA. In order to assess the consistency of the author-machine dialogue we have conducted an analysis using a modification of Task-Action Grammar (TAG) [17] known as D-TAG (Display-oriented TAG) [14]. D-TAG is more suitable for evaluating the interface to SHIVA since it captures the display-based nature of the interaction. Whilst it has some limitations in, for example, allowing the prediction of errors and in assessing the learnability of the interface, it has proved useful in identifying inconsistencies in task-action syntax, for example. Such methods previously been applied single interfaces, which are already largely consistent (for example, to Macdraw™). Since SHIVA is a prototype system, originating from two previous programs, it contains a large number of different interfaces, so these methods are difficult and time-consuming to apply. We therefore used more informal methods in order to focus on more restricted problems which posed genuine difficulties for authors, and within constraints of the programming effort required to modify the system. These methods for included "walkthroughs" with the system a series of prespecified tasks, by HCI-experts who were members of the SHIVA design team but who had not been involved in interface implementation.

We also conducted detailed observational studies of experienced authors using SHIVA to create and modify a small course (student contact time, approximately 30 minutes). This study enabled us to explore the extent to which authors were able to comprehend the authoring tasks required, and the way in which the system functions. Four authors were studied, in sessions lasting approximately three hours each. The authors were experienced users of ORGUE, but had never used ECAL or SHIVA before. Each subject was given one hour of training in the use of the system, including an introduction to the overall model of authoring in SHIVA, a detailed explanation of the purpose and process of creating ILO-ULM networks in PSAUME, the rules underlying the system's teaching decisions, and hands-on training in the use of the interface. The authors were seated in front of the system, with one of the evaluators seated beside them to prompt them in providing think-aloud protocols. Two video records were taken using cameras focussed on the computer screen and on the author, to record any notes made on paper or reference to documentation. Since we were only interested in evaluating the interface to ORGUE editor and PSAUME, and not the multimedia editors within this session, a set of ULMs had already been created for the purpose of the evaluation. The domain for the course was described to the authors, and they were given a list of suggested keywords with which to describe the concepts involved in the course. (This is in fact realistic, since most courseware production is done in teams, where the actual content of the course has already been specified in some way by a member of the team, and a specialist author is given the task of producing the courseware from this specification) Authors were then asked to : recreate flowcharts in ORGUE, create ILO-ULM maps in PSAUME (keywords provided), to predict the teaching sequence in the student environment, and to make some pedagogical assessment of the coherence of the teaching sequence. Where authors did not find the presentation sequence to be pedagogically "reasonable," they were asked to modify the course using PSUAME in order to achieve their preferred outcome.

11.4.2 Pilot Courseware Production Studies

We confronted the methodology of courseware design implied by SHIVA with two very different domains and learning situations. The SHIVA-Géographe project involved didactical analysis of pilot courseware, produced for teaching a specific area of geography (systematic hydrology) in a university context. In the SHIVA-Westmill project pilot courseware was produced in the context of professional training closely targeted at French-speakers and to linguistic abilities required by tasks connected with the job-function of the learner. These two case studies have been carried out with partners external to the AAT project group - geography teachers at the Institut de Géographie Alpines and the Centre Informatique et Applications Pédagogiques (Joseph Fourier University, Grenoble) in the case of SHIVA-Géographe and the Westmill Business-English company (Paris) in the case of SHIVA-Westmill. These projects enabled us to identify the extent to which SHIVA could be applied to different domains, given that the system was developed with the aim of "domain independence."

The SHIVA-Géographe course emphasised teaching the dynamic aspects of the processes involved, using a *systems* approach. This approach treats knowledge from a point of view which is neither strictly declarative (or "encyclopaedic") nor procedural, as is often the case of tutors in geography. The ULMs envisaged therefore involved simulations and the use of multiple models of the teaching domain ("water table as bath," "as system," etc.), which poses problems for the representation of domain concepts in the PSAUME editor.

The pilot courseware produced in the SHIVA-Westmill project was designed for a commercial training rather than university teaching context. WESTMILL provide training in the use of commercial English, particularly in the Banking sector. The company has a well-defined training methodology, with a good track record of success. A specific "audit" of training needs for each job function is provided for a particular company, in terms of a set of linguistic activities (eg "speaking on the telephone," "small talk," etc.), each of which are analysed into a set of grammatical structures required, together with the precise vocabulary which would be needed. We worked with this company in order to take a small part of one of their courses for remedial English, and redesign it in terms of the SHIVA authoring methodology. This was a good choice since the ULMs created for teaching specific grammatical tenses ("time ideas" in the WESTMILL methodology) could be reused in other courses, and adapted to other clients. This re-design resulted in a pilot production of SHIVA courseware (of approximately 30 minutes duration). The course contained: written booklets which explained the time ideas, together with short exercises, several hours of videos containing examples of time ideas with accompanying question and drill booklets using client-specific examples, audio cassettes for practising pronunciation and aural comprehension and CAL drill programs for basic tenses, produced in-house by WESTMILL.

11.5 Implications for Automating Instructional Design

11.5.1 Automating Instructional Design in SHIVA

SHIVA automated only part of an existing course design model, largely because of limitations on the technological "state of the art." Since course design involves planning instructional situations and strategies, it is clear, however, than even given technological advance, instructional design methodologies developed for one set of situations - such as face-to-face classroom teaching - must be *transformed* to take account of new interactive teaching media. The questions arise therefore, as to which elements of instructional design transfer to intelligent multimedia environments, which new elements need to be added, and how elements transferred need to be transformed. In the case of SHIVA we can approach these questions by making the following distinctions:

Distinction 1. Elements of the P&R course design method incorporated in the SHIVA functional model of authoring are distinguished from elements which were not incorporated, and from new authoring tasks incorporated in SHIVA which are not in the P&R model ;

Distinction 2. Within the SHIVA functional model of authoring, authoring tasks for which system support is provided (interface tools, programs) are distinguished from those which are required but for which no system support is provided.

Distinction 3. Within authoring tasks for which SHIVA provides explicit support, task which are performed by the system are distinguished from tasks performed by the author and tasks which are shared between author and system.

These distinctions are summarised in Figure 11.4 below.

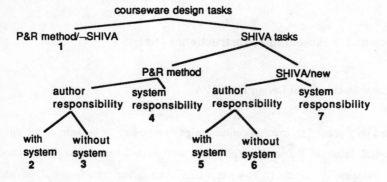

Fig. 11.4. Comparision of course design tasks in P&R method and SHIVA.

We discuss evaluation results in terms of each of these distinctions.

11.5.2 Comparing Posner and Rudnitsky with SHIVA

Design of courseware with SHIVA requires almost all elements of the P&R course design methodology. Although the system is restricted to concept ILOs ("cognitions"), the author must nevertheless be able to separate these out from cognitive, affective and psycho-motor skills for a given course. Identifying what counts as a "concept" ILO in fact turned out to be a major problem, as identified in pilot courseware production. In the case of SHIVA-Géographe authors had difficulty in deciding whether in the case of keywords such as "water table" these corresponded to learning objectives or not - should the student simply learn the names of objects? In fact, this domain uses a vocabulary belonging to different lexical and language levels, corresponding on one hand to the fact that teaching takes into account the passage from the students' "commonsense" knowledge to that of geography, and subsequently to the integration of the systemic model, and on the other hand to the hierarchical organisation of geographical knowledge.

Similar problems in authoring ILOs arose in the WESTMILL project where authors had difficulty in deciding whether an ILO was a concept or a cognitive skill. For example, authors were relutant to view grammatical tenses as concepts to be learned, since they not usually taught explicitly in their method, but rather by way of example. WESTMILL have a number of different ways of conceptualising or categorising the training domain, given its direct application in a commercial training context: they combine grammatical concepts at a number of hierarchical levels (tense, past, past continuous, etc.), specific vocabularies adapted to the particular client, groups of *competences* (such as "oral presentation," "correction of documents," "speaking on the telephone," each of which may require specific communication media), and finally, recategorisation of groups of competences, vocabularies and grammatical concepts in terms of the organisation of job functions in a specific company. In SHIVA, a single "flat" conceptual representation is provided. Our finding was that it was extremely difficult to apply this representation to the language training domain, as conceived by the WESTMILL methodology. SHIVA thus appears to be not presently suitable for developing courses with a strong procedural component, usually taught by drill-and-practice, and where there are multiple and hierarchical ways of categorising the domain (this area is mostly covered by the DOMINIE-II approach. It is rather suitable for essentially "encyclopedic" domains, where a large quantity of factual information is to be learned. A more general point concerns the fact that SHIVA incorporates a single interaction style - the system makes decisions about which declarative knowledge should be communicated - whereas learning in most complex domains requires a combination of styles for teaching declarative knowledge, flexible control over the learning sequence, and even drill and practice of learned procedures.

A second major limitation of SHIVA in comparison with the P&R method concerns the range of specific learning materials and teaching strategies (interaction styles) incorporated. It is clear that teaching activities such as "visit to a museum," envisaged by P&R can not be directly incorporated into an intelligent multimedia learning system. However, the simple question/response interaction style of ULMs in SHIVA proved to be insufficient. In the case of SHIVA-Géographe authors conceived of the course as essentially *simulation-based* - a feature not incorporated in SHIVA - and in the WESTMILL project, facilities for incorporating client-specific texts, around which drill-and-practice exercises are based, were lacking.

A related point concerns the independence of ULMs. Since SHIVA determines pedagogical seqencing automatically, ULMs must be designed as completely independent of one another. Whilst being willing to relinquish control of frame presentation order within units, authors were reluctant to allow SHIVA the control to present units after they had established a sequence for them themselves, including the decision as to which unit must come first. Since ULMs had each to be independent of the other, this led to a lack of thematic and media coherence between units. Authors felt the strong need for an explicit explanation of the relations between successive units to learners. Although SHIVA imposes no limits on the size of ULMs, its pedagogical sequencing is most effective with as small a grain-size as possible (this permits finer-grained student modelling). However, in response to the problems stated above, authors tended to create very large ULMs in order to retain control over the teaching sequence.

There are two respects in which SHIVA incorporates functionalities which are not anticipated in the P&R model, in response to the specificities of interactive multimedia with limited AI techniques. The first concerns the provision of simulation tools for enabling authors to "envision" interaction with learners. The second concerns the provision of a specialised editor for integrating different media (MULTIMEDIA editor), and the design of separate editors for each media in order to facilitate the work of authoring *teams*.

11.5.3 System Support for Authoring Tasks

In the standard CAL courseware design methodology [13] conception of a course is performed on paper by a design team, which is then implemented on the machine. In part, this separation of functions was due to the necessity for programming skills in authoring languages, and the difficulty of modifying courses once implemented. One of the design goals of SHIVA was to integrate these two design phases, by supporting authors in the conception phase, and facilitating on-line modification of the course. However, a large part of the authors' task in designing courseware with SHIVA still needs to be performed off-line. In general, it is assumed that a curriculum has already been defined and that the difficult task of identifying concept ILOs has been performed. Although this process may involve creating concept maps, with different types of relations, this is not a task which the author can carry out since the concept map is calculated automatically.

An apparently "incidental" element of the P&R method is the specification of a *pedagogical rationale* for the course, related to *educational goals*. However, this proved to be a problem for authors with respect to SHIVA, since no explanation of the rationale for its pedagogical decision-making rules was anticipated in the system. As shown from our HCI studies, authors thus found them difficult to understand and accept.

11.5.4 System and Author Responsibility for Tasks

The major tasks which the system performs for the author are the creation of a relational network linking concept ILOs, and the dynamic planning of the presentation sequence as a function of it, the student model and the dialogue model. However, this raises a number of problems, related with author acceptance and understanding of the system's decisions. Authors need to understand the decision-making rules in order to be able to modify ("debug") the course so as to produce a general result which is acceptable to them. When the rules were explained to authors during the training session of our HCI studies, authors also found the pedagogical rationale for each of the rules difficult to comprehend and accept. Nevertheless we found that the authors we studied were surprisingly good at anticipating which ULM would be presented next, given the structure they had created in PSAUME. When asked to explain how they had made their predictions, authors did not use the teaching rules and decision algorithm, even though a printed summary was made available to them. They rather relied on general characteristics of the visual layout of ILO-ULM maps in PSAUME. For example, "a concept with more links to frames is more important, and so will be presented first." However, this was a relatively small course and it is not clear whether a larger course would be so predictable using such "rule-of-thumb" methods.

One way out of the dilemma of deciding whether the system or the author should carry out a task is to attempt to *share* responsibility for achieving it between author and system. We did in fact attempt to implement this principle to some extent in response to feedback from authors in the pilot studies. For example, whilst the the concept relation map is derived automatically by SHIVA, we included the possibility for authors to define pre-requisite links between concepts, and in the case of student modelling, we were driven to providing authors with the possibility of specifying concepts to be decremented within ULM flowcharts by the necessity for finer-grained student modelling in large ULMs.

11.6 Conclusion

Automating instructional design in intelligent tutoring systems which incorporate interactive multimedia teaching materials is a problem that has received little attention in the intelligent tutoring systems community, with some recent exceptions [4; 18; 22]. The basic approach which was adopted in this research was to provide tools for supporting curriculum planning and some aspects of instructional planning (creating teaching materials to achieve curriculum objectives), leaving instructional delivery planning to the system, as a function of the students' responses. Evaluation results suggest that this way of sharing responsibility for instructional design between authors and system is not without problems, largely due to the fact that curricula are planned with a view to achieving educational goals by the means of specific teaching strategies. If authors can not understand how intended learning outcomes are to be achieved by instructional strategies , they will not be able to design courses so that the intended learning takes place. If authors do not understand the pedagogical rationale underlying dynamic instructional planning decisions, they will not be able to plan curricula in accordance with that rationale.

There are two main ways in which these requirements may be satisfied. One is by designing IMA systems which themselves understand *how* and *why* automated pedagogical decisions have been made, and which thus facilitate the generation of *explanations* for authors in terms of a coherent *pedagogical rationale*. The other is by allowing authors and systems to *collaborate* in defining the bases on which decisions are made. These alternatives are not, of course, mutually exclusive. If we look at other AI applications, such as expert systems, we find that the need for explanation facilities in expert systems has been widely accepted during the previous decade, as well as the need to implicate experts in problem-solving processes. Given the greater complexity of problems arising in the design of IMA systems, it is hardly surprising that these conclusions should be reached somewhat later in this field.

Finally, let us try to sketch what this point of view on explanation and author collaboration implies for IMA system architectures. Roschelle and Behrend [19] define collaboration (to be distinguished from *cooperation*) as "... a coordinated, synchronous activity that is result of a continued attempt to construct and maintain a shared conception of a problem [19, p. 1]." If an IMA system is to engage in *collaboration* with authors this implies that courses should be designed *incrementally*, and that both system and authors should be able to *jointly contribute* to each incremental step. This is to be distinguished from a view of an IMA system as automating and explaining some subpart of the course design process, and leaving the rest to the authors. In order to collaborate, an IMA system must possess much more higher-level knowledge of *general constraints* on course design, related to a pedagogical rationale. This knowledge should be used by the system within a process of *negotiation* [1] with authors at each proposed course design step, rather than in making unilateral pedagogical decisions. Given that some such general constraints may be abstracted from existing course design methods (for example, coherence, generality and non-redundancy of ILOs, general size of units and coherence of their sequencing, as described earlier in our discussion of Posner and Rudnitsky's method), and current advances in generating person-machine dialogues, such IMA architectures are realistic future possibilities. Our most general conclusion, therefore, is that *instructional design should not be automated* (even partially): it should be carried out as part of *collaborative activity between system and authors*.

Acknowledgements

This chapter is based on research conducted by members of the AAT project, and was supported by the European Economic Community DELTA Program, project no. D1010.

References

1.   Baker, M.J.: Towards a cognitive model for negotiation in tutorial dialogues. In M. Elsom-Cook, & R. Moyse (Eds.), Knowledge negotiation. London: Paul Chapman Publishing: London 1992
2.   Baker, M.J.: Negotiating goals in intelligent tutoring dialogues. In E. Costa (Ed.), New directions for intelligent tutoring systems. NATO ASI Series F, Vol. 91. Berlin: Springer-Verlag 1992
3.   Barker, P.: Author languages for CAL. London: MacMillan 1987
4.   Bierman, D.: "Intelligent" authoring systems: Towards better courseware. Proceedings of the Conference on Computers, Education and the Child. USSR: Urgench 1988
5.   Brooks, P., Schmeling, A., & Byerley, P.F.: A multimedia intelligent tutoring system for human-computer interaction procedures. In H.J. Bullinger (Ed.), Human aspects in computing (pp. 959-963). Amsterdam: Elsevier 1991
6.   Card, S.K., Moran, T.P., & Newell, A.: The psychology of human-computer interaction. Hillsdale, NJ: Lawrence Erlbaum 1983
7.   DELTA Project D1010.: Advanced authoring tools, Workpackage 8, Deliverable 1: Authoring for ITS. London: The Open University. Workpackage 1, Deliverable 2: Authoring for CAL. Lyon: CNRS-IRPEACS 1990
8.   DELTA Project D1010.: Deliverable 1.: Authoring requirements for advanced CAL. D1010. 1990
9.   DELTA Project D1010.: Deliverable 2.: Authoring requirements for ITS. 1990
10. Elsom-Cook, M., & O'Malley, C.: ECAL. Bridging the gap between CAL and ITS. CITE Report No. 67, I.E.T. London: The Open University 1989

11. Elsom-Cook, M., & Spensley, F.: Knowledge representation in a tutoring system for procedural skills. CITE Report No. 36, I.E.T. London: The Open University 1988

12. ESPRIT Project 1613: Evaluation of an intelligent tutoring system shell for industrial/office training. Deliverable 10: Final Report 1987

13. Guir, R.: Conception Pedagogique: Guide Methodologique.   Lyon: L'Association Régionale pour le Développement de l'Enseignement Multimédia Informatisé 1986

14. Howes, A., & Payne, S.J.: Display-based competence: Towards user models for menu-driven interfaces. Report of Alvey/SERC Project GR/D 60355. Lancaster University, UK: British Telecom plc 1989

15. MacKnight, C., & Balagopalan, S.: An evaluation tool for measuring authoring system performance. Communications of the ACM, 32, 1231-1236 (1989)

16. O'Malley, C., Elsom-Cook, M. & Ridwan, E.: The ECAL authoring environment. CITE Report No. 67, I.E.T. London: The Open University 1989

17. Payne, S.J., & Green, T.R.G.: Task-action grammars: A model of the mental representation of task languages. Human-computer interaction Vol. 2 pp. 93-133. Hillsdale, NJ: Lawrence Erlbaum 1986

18. Pirolli, P. & Russell, D.: Towards theory and technology for the design of intelligent tutoring systems. Proceedings of the International Meeting on Intelligent Tutoring Systems (IMITS-88). Montréal, Canada, 1988

19. Roschelle, J., & Behrend, S.D.: The construction of shared knowledge in collaborative problem solving. In C. O'Malley (Ed.), Computer supported collaborative learning. NATO ASI Series F. Berlin: Springer-Verlag (in preparation)

20. Russell, D., Moran, T., & Jordan, D.: The instructional design environment. In J. Psotka, L. Massey, & S. Mutter (Eds.), Intelligent tutoring systems. Hillsdale, NJ: Lawrence Erlbaum 1988h

21. Posner, G.J., & Rudnitsky, A.N.: Course design: A guide to curriculum development for teachers, 3rd Edition. New York: Longman 1986

22. Spensley, F.: Generating domain representations for ITS. In D. Bierman, D. Breuker, & J. Sandberg (Eds.), Artificial intelligence and education. Amsterdam: IOS Publishing 1989

12

Plan-based Sequencing of Problems for Introductory Programming

Hein P. M. Krammer and Sanne Dijkstra

School of Education, University of Twente, P. O. Box 217, 7500 AE Enschede, The Netherlands

Abstract: Rules for sequencing problems via an Intelligent Tutoring System for introductory computer programming are specified within four criteria of instruction: providing problem solving opportunity; providing solvable problems; opportunity for knowledge construction; advancing applicability of concepts learned. Aims of an introductory course are specified in terms of goals and plans: to decompose a problem into a structure of programming goals, to produce a solution consisting of a structure of programming plans, and to translate the structure of programming plans into executable code. Measures of the four criteria are presented based on goal/plan analyses of the problems in the ITS's knowledge bases.

Keywords: intelligent tutoring systems (ITS), instructional planning, problem solving, computer programming, goal/plan analysis

12.1 Introduction

An important phase of instruction is the presentation of problems to the student for practice in problem solving or discovery of concepts and rules. How an optimal sequence of problems can be determined for instruction is not yet solved. As far as content planning has been solved it is related to the learning of concepts and rules, not of problem solving. For sequencing the problems only general rules of thumb have been formulated which do not lend themselves for control of a content planner in an Intelligent Tutoring System (ITS). Well known ITS's for introductory programming like PROUST [5, 6] and the Lisp-Tutor [10] have no built-in control of the planning of problems; they leave the choice of problems to the student or the textbook. The only programming tutor in which the sequencing of problems is automated in order to optimize student learning is BIP-II [12].

The goal of this study is the specification of rules governing the content planner for problems in an introductory programming course. It is assumed that the instructional system has available a set of problems from which the content planner will select problems to be presented to the student. The selection of problems used to remedy misconceptions is left out of consideration.

In this chapter, after the specification of general principles for the sequencing of problems a concrete elaboration will be presented for introductory programming instruction.

12.2 General Principles for the Sequencing of Problems

When a student has solved a problem the instructional system should select as the next problem that problem which is the most instructive for that student at this time. If learning takes mainly place through the solving of problems--which is often the case if procedural skills have to be learned--those problems are considered the most instructive which offer the student a real problem-solving experience and further the construction of relevant knowledge. Halff [4] mentions three criteria for the selection and sequencing of exercises and examples by which procedural skills are taught. As an extension, four criteria for instructiveness will be specified below.

All four criteria are associated with problem difficulties and student abilities. To overcome the difficulties associated with the criteria special help should be given to the student. As the amount of help given is a measure of student ability, the criteria are also related to the learning history of the student.

12.2.1 Genuine Problem Solving Opportunity

The problem offers the opportunity for genuine problem-solving skill training. The solution structure of the problem is sufficiently new for the student that the solution is not obvious. This does not mean that new concepts or rules should be applied in the problem; it only says that the structure into which the concepts and rules have to be combined should be new to the student.

The problem difficulty associated with this criterion is that the solution structure of the problem is different from the earlier solved problems. Typical help to the student refers to similar, earlier solved problems. Students who overcome this type of difficulty with few help have the ability to transfer from one solution structure to another.

12.2.2 Solvability

Instruction that offers real problem-solving experiences is designed in such a way that the student is successful in solving most problems. The selected problem should fit with the knowledge of the student, so that the student is expected to be able to solve the problem. This means that the problem does not require the discovery of many new learning elements by the student.

The problem difficulty associated with this criterion is lack of prerequisite knowledge. In case of difficulty, help mainly contains hints to discover the requisite concepts or rules. High ability students discover the requisite knowledge with few help from the system.

12.2.3 Knowledge Construction

The problems presented to the student should further the construction of new knowledge by the student. Whereas the first criterion is directed towards the development of problem-solving strategies this criterion has to do with content in a narrower sense: the concepts and rules. This criterion means that solving the problems should advance the acquisition of concepts or rules, by stimulating the student to discover a concept or rule--by himself or with hints or other assistance from the tutor--or by offering an opportunity to exercise with recently learned concepts and rules. In a sense, this criterion is the opposite of the solvability criterion because that criterion states that there should not be too much unknown requisite knowledge, while this criterion states that there should be some addition to the acquisition of knowledge, this is that the pace of newly required concepts and rules is not too fast.

Associated to this criterion is the problem difficulty of the application of knowledge which is learned earlier but not yet fully trained. Typical help is recalling earlier learned knowledge. Students who overcome this difficulty are able to apply concepts and rules which have only few times been seen in a formerly solved problem. Students of low ability need much more exercises before they can apply the newly acquired knowledge.

12.2.4 Applicability

Problems presented to the students should be situated in meaningful contexts [2]. The problems presented should further the insight in the general applicability of earlier learned concepts and rules in a variety of contexts. To achieve this, the problems should vary in such a way that the student can abstract from one context to another context constructing an abstract formulation of the general problem. A sequencing of problems with too little variation in context may not further the abstraction from the specific context, whereas a sequencing with too great variation in context may prevent the student to discover the similarity between the problems.

This criterion is associated with the problem difficulty that the solution structure is concealed behind the context. Abstraction from a context is the special ability required from the student and the special help is directed to this abstraction.

12.3 Problem Solving Skill and Knowledge in Introductory Programming

Generally, in introductory programming courses the students are not required to perform all detailed steps in the software engineering methodology used by professional programmers. Nevertheless, in nearly all introductory courses students are trained in the three main steps of the procedure, namely the analysis of the problem, the design of an algorithm, and the implementation of the solution.

In a growing number of courses these main steps are related to programming goals and plans [1, 5, 9, 11]. We assume the aims of an introductory course to be specified in terms of programming goals and plans. A course should pursue at least the following three learning aims. First, the students should learn to decompose a problem into a structure of programming goals. Second, the students should learn to select appropriate programming plans to each goal and to produce an algorithmic solution consisting of a composition of programming plans. Third, the students should learn to translate the structure of programming plans into executable code.

Thus, it is assumed that all problems can be solved by reaching a finite set of programming goals. Associated to each goal is a small set of programming plans by which the goal can be reached. Each programming plan is stated in terms of the syntax of the language used.

Two important attributes of a problem are its structure and its context. The structure of a problem is the result of the decomposition process, this is a structure of programming goals. Each goal is directed to the manipulation of one or more variables. The decomposition as the result of this process exists of a network structure in which programming goals are connected by means of their variables. There are three kinds of connections: a variable may be identical to a variable of another goal, a variable may be a predicate about a variable of another goal, and a variable may be directly linked to another goal. In Figure 1 the decomposition of the Rainfall problem from Micro-PROUST [5] is depicted in such a network structure.

Henceforth, we will equate a problem with its decomposition structure. Each connected part of (the decomposition of) a problem will be called a part-problem. It can easily be seen that MicroPROUST's Average problem forms a part-problem of the Rainfall problem.

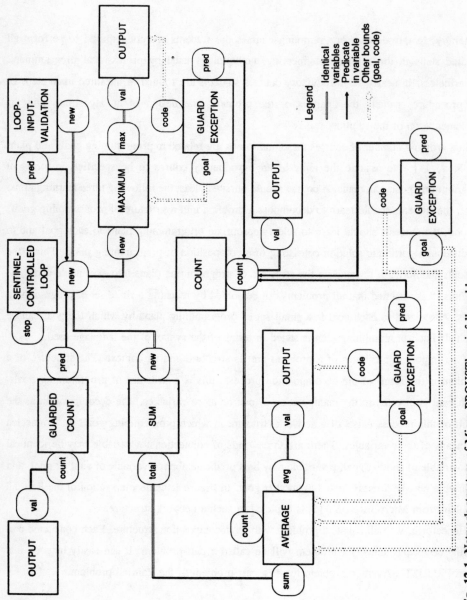

Fig. 12.1. Network structure of Micro-PROUST's rainfall problem.

The context of a problem is the situation in which the problem is presented. Problems with the same structure may not be recognized as such by the student because of the difference in context between the problems. For instance, the following problem has the same structure as MicroPROUST's rainfall problem:

> Write a program that prompts the user to input numbers from the terminal. Each number stands for the test result of a student on a specific test. Test results can not be negative, so the program should reject negative numbers. Your program should compute the following statistics from the data: (1) the average test score of the class, (2) the number of students in the class, (3) the number of valid inputs (including any invalid data that might be read in), and (4) the maximum score of the class. The program should read data until the user types a number greater than 100; as test results can not be greater than 100, any value greater than 100 is a sentinel value signalling the end of input. Do not include this value greater than 100 in the calculations. Assume that if the input value is non-negative and not greater than 100, then it is valid input data.

We assume that learning will take place mainly through the solving of problems. The student has available - in a textbook or as on-line help at the computer - a description of programming goals and the associated plans. The first confrontation of the student with a programming goal will take place in a problem to be solved. When the student has solved the problem, if necessary with help from the tutor, the student will receive information on the programming plans associated with that programming goal.

12.4 Measurement of the Criteria for Instructiveness

Programming goals and plans not only are supposed to organize the curriculum, as described in the previous section. Also, the ITS is assumed to have access to a knowledge base of goals and plans and goal decompositions of the available problems. This knowledge can be used by the system to measure the instructiveness of candidate problems, as will be shown below.

12.4.1 Genuine Problem Solving Opportunity

Based on the amount of correspondence between the decomposition structures, a distance function is defined between a candidate problem and the set of already solved problems, as explained below.

The complexity of a (part-)problem is the sum of the number of goals and the number of the internal connections within the (part-)problem, i. e. the connections between goals belonging to the (part-)problem. For instance, the complexity of the Rainfall problem is $14 + 20 = 34$, and that of the Average problem is $7 + 10 = 17$.

The difference between two problems is the sum of the complexities of what remains from the first problem if all part-problems which are maximally identical to part-problems of the second problem are deleted. To determine the difference between the Rainfall and Average problems, the whole Average problem should be deleted from the Rainfall problem. Moreover, the part-structure consisting of a guard-exception and an output should be deleted once more. The result is a set of four part-problems with a total complexity of $3 + 1 + 1 + 1 = 6$. Determining the other difference of these two problems, the difference of the Average and Rainfall problems, is much easier. Now, everything has to be deleted from the average problem. So, the difference becomes 0.

The distance between two problems is defined as the sum of the two differences between the problems. So, the distance between the Rainfall and Average problems is $6 + 0 = 6$. It can be easily proved that this concept satisfies the requirements of a mathematical distance function.

Using the distance between problems a more precise statement can be made of the principle that governs the sequencing of problems in order to warrant genuine problem-solving skill training. The distance between the next problem and all problems which the student already solved should be greater than a certain threshold value, dependent of the student's ability.

The student's ability should be determined from the learning history of the student. It depends on the amount of help associated with this criterion. How the threshold value depends of the student's ability should be investigated by empirical studies.

12.4.2 Solvability

To each programming goal is associated a set of one or more programming plans by which the goal can be reached. The programming plans to be learned in an introductory course can be organized in a hierarchical structure of a part-whole relationship. In order to learn a new plan, most students will need to know already the plans which form the parts of that new plan. Only gifted students will be able to skip a level in the part-whole hierarchy. So, this hierarchy can be interpreted as a prerequisite hierarchy of the subject matter.

This hierarchy can be used to specify the second sequencing principle. Each problem is via its goal decomposition associated with a set of plan structures. We are not just talking of one associated plan structure, because any goal may be associated with more than one plan. Each associated plan structure forms a different algorithmic solution to the problem.

Each solution can be compared with the set of plans the student already masters. The number of plans in the solution that are not yet mastered is a measure of the solvability for this student. To this also belong all those plans 'skipped' in the part-whole hierarchy. Probably, most students will discover without help only solutions with one new plan at the most.

The second sequencing principle reads as follows. The maximal solvability of the solutions of the next problem should exceed a specific threshold value, dependent of the ability of the student. Again, this threshold value should be detected by empirical research, and the ability associated with this criterion should be determined by the learning history in a way sketched in the former section.

12.4.3 Knowledge Construction

The third sequencing principle is that the problem should further the acquisition of knowledge. In case of introductory programming instruction this means that the solution of the problem adds to the acquisition of one or more programming plans.

This principle can be specified using the concept of pace. This is the mean number of programming plans learned per problem. The pace of learning programming plans should be kept close to an optimal value depending on the student's ability. Again, the ability is determined by the amount of formerly needed help associated with the criterion of knowledge construction.

12.4.4 Applicability

The selection by the student of programming plans from which the solution can be built may be more or less hampered by the terms used in problem text. First, the terms used in the text by which is referred to specific programming plans may differ more or less from the application cues used in the instructional material in which the plans are explained to the student. Second, terms may be used in the problem text which describe a specific application context but are irrelevant for the selection of programming plans.

Based on the terms used in the texts of a candidate problem, the formerly solved problems and the instruction on plans, the application 'distance' can be defined for a candidate problem. The fourth criterion leads to the following principle. The application distance should be greater than a threshold depending on the student's ability. As before, the ability is meant to be the special ability associated with this criterion determined by the amount of special help needed.

12.5 Conclusion

Four sequencing principles for problems in an automated introductory-programming tutor were presented and criteria for candidate problems were constructed. These four criteria fence the set of possible candidate problems. The set of candidate problems is highly dependent on the student history, namely the amount of help needed in earlier solved problems.

The four criteria are associated with four goals of instruction, namely the acquisition of problem-solving strategies, the experience of success in problem solving, the acquisition of the student may meet, four student abilities required to overcome the obstacles, and four types of help which the system may provide.

This model for the selection of problems is being implemented is an Intelligent Tutoring System for learning COMAL-80/Turtle Graphics. This research forms part of a project called ITSSEL (Intelligent Tutoring Shell System for Executable Languages) directed to the development of a shell system for the generation of Intelligent Tutoring Systems handling diverging instructional models [3, 7, 8].

References

1. Bonar, J, Riggs, P., Weil, W, & Jones, R.: Programming plans workbook (Draft version) 1987
2. Brown, J.S., Collins, A., & Duguid, P.: Situated cognition and the culture of learning. Educational Researcher, 18, 32-42 (1989)
3. Dijkstra, S., Krammer, H. P. M., & Maaswinkel, R. M.: The study of problem characteristics of programming tutors. In S. Dijkstra, H.P.. Krammer, & J.J.G. van Merriënboer (Eds.), Instructional models in computer-based instructional systems. NATO ASI Series F, Vol. 104. Berlin: Springer-Verlag 1992
4. Halff, H. M.: Curriculum and instruction in automated tutors. In M. C. Polson & J. J. Richardson (Eds.), Foundations of intelligent tutoring systems (pp. 79-108). Hillsdale, NJ: Lawrence Erlbaum 1988
5. Johnson, W. L., & Soloway, E.: Micro-PROUST. YALEU/CSD/RR#402. Yale University, Dept. of Computer Science 1985
6. Johnson, W. L., & Soloway, E.: PROUST: An automatic debugger for Pascal programs. In G. Kearsley (Ed.), Artificial intelligence and instruction: Applications and methods (pp. 49-67). Reading, MA: Addison-Wesley 1987
7. Krammer, H. P. M.: Instructional models for ITSSEL. Memorandum ITSSEL-90-2. Univ. of Twente, Dept. of Computer Science, Dept of Education 1990
8. Maaswinkel, R. M., & Offereins, M.: Preliminary design of the architecture of an intelligent tutoring system. Memorandum ITSSEL-90-4. Univ. of Twente, Dept. of Computer Science, Dept of Education 1990
9. Marco, R. E., & Colina, M. M.: Programming languages and dynamic instructional tools: How to address students' knowledge base. In S. Dijkstra, H.P.. Krammer, & J.J.G. van Merriënboer (Eds.), Instructional models in computer-based instructional systems. NATO ASI Series F, Vol. 104. Berlin: Springer-Verlag 1992
10. Reiser, B. J., Anderson, J. R., & Farrell, R. B.: Dynamic student modeling in an intelligent tutor for LISP programming. Proceedings of the International Joint Conference on Artificial Intelligence-85, Vol. 1 (pp. 8-14). Los Altos, CA: Morgan Kaufmann 1985

11. Soloway, E., Spohrer, J., & Littman, D.: E unum pluribus: Generating alternative designs. Paper for invited panel at the Cognitive Science Conference, Seattle 1987
12. Wescourt, K., Beard, M., & Gould, L.: Knowledge-based adaptive curriculum sequencing for CAI: Application of a network representation. Proceedings of the 1977 Annual Conference, Association for Computing Machinery (pp. 234-240). New York: Association for Computing Machinery 1977

Part 3 Summary: Implementation

Begoña Gros

Implementation is the last stage in the development of technological materials. The solution to most problems presented during this phase should be integrated into the entire development process. This is an idea that I argue throughout my summaries and that is also relevant to this part summary. Nevertheless, there are some specific topics related to this stage of instructional development. I will follow a similar structure to the previous summaries, dividing the discussion into three steps: First, I will identify the main questions that arise during the implementation process; second, I will discuss the main controversial issues and, finally, I will make some suggestions regarding future research.

The Problem of Implementation

There exists an enormous variety of ways in which computers can support the learning process. Instructional development methods can be used to produce drill and practice, tutorial systems, simulations, hypermedia, intelligent tutoring systems, interactive learning environments, etc.

This variety introduces the first problem that we have to resolve in the implementation phase. This concerns the selection of the most appropriate way of supporting the kind of learning and instruction desirable. This selection is not easy because there is not enough knowledge about the most appropriate ways of establishing interaction with the learner according to the outcomes we want to achieve.

To sum up, problems over implementation involve decisions about the delivery media related to the planning and design process of the system.

The main research and discussion about the use of expert systems and intelligent tutoring systems in the automation of instructional development has been focused in the planning and development process. Minimal research has been done into the incorporation of the different varieties of ways of supporting learning and the interaction between the system and user. In fact, in many prototypes, the authors seems not to be very concerned about the user interface and these products are sometimes not very "friendly" compared to computer-based instructional systems. However, this aspect is very important from an educational point of view, because an excellent tool would fail if the delivery system is not appropriate.

As Baker points out, the automation of instructional development which incorporates interactive multimedia teaching materials can be an interesting approach to providing more useful tools. Although the development of this material has received little attention, other tools for developing software, such as authoring systems, are incorporating a lot of facilities to create interactive multimedia materials. For this reason I think that the uses of expert systems and intelligent tutoring systems should also help to create tools to develop interactive and multimedia courseware.

Main Controversial Issues

During my discussion of the production of the automation of instructional development, I mention different technical approaches centered on three areas: simulation, intelligent tutoring systems and expert systems. I point out the main contributions of each of these approaches and will, therefore, not repeat them here. However, to follow the discussion, it is important to remember that each of these approaches introduces differences that affect delivery systems.

Intelligent tutoring systems have become widespread over the last few years, and most of the chapters on implementation concentrate on discussion of the uses of these systems to support the automation of instructional development.

The proposal of Krammer and Dijkstra follows the same idea. The authors consider that it is possible to use artificial intelligence techniques to produce tools to automate instructional development. These authors propose the employment of instructional systems to provide an learning environment focused on the presentation of problems to the student in order to practice problem-solving strategies.

Other systems proposed, such as SHIVA, ORGUE, ECAL, etc., are concerned with the production of authoring systems to support instructional development.

According to Baker, the main problem with this approach seems to be that several tools provide a system to support curriculum planning or some aspects of instructional planning, but instructional delivery planning is made by the systems as a function the students' responses. As Baker points out, "...if authors can not understand the pedagogical rationale underlying dynamic instructional planning decisions, they will not be able to plan curricula in accordance with that rationale."

To conclude, the main problem is how to create materials that can satisfy these requirements. As Tennyson suggests, it is necessary to create exploratory tools and visualization support in order to understand how and why the decisions are made and to facilitate an explanation for authors. It is also important to allow authors and systems to collaborate in decision making and defining the bases on which decisions are made.

The Development of Interactive Multimedia Authoring Systems

Most authors seem to agree with the idea that it is necessary to develop interactive multimedia authoring systems for authoring courseware. The main problem is that there are few well developed methodologies for developing these interactive systems.

Most traditional ISD models are developed for traditional teaching. However, the design of courses for multimedia systems presupposes specific media for the materials to be presented, and a specific delivery system for presenting them. So, the main question is to develop instructional development methods that can provide a framework for the design of interactive multimedia authoring systems.

In the chapter by Baker, there is a description of one specific attempt to incorporate an instructional development method in an interactive multimedia authoring system known as SHIVA.

During discussion of this proposal, the main problem pointed out by Baker concerns the instructional development model used by SHIVA. The system follows the course design method of Posner and Rudnitsky, which was developed to create "traditional" instructional materials. This instructional development model establishes a separation between curriculum and instruction, and the processes and products of planning. As Goodyear (Ch. 2) and Tennyson (Ch. 3) both state, this separation can create some problems because it is not clear that we can separate the representation of concepts from assumptions about how they will be used. We therefore need to elaborate specific theories of instructional development to produce interactive multimedia materials.

Evaluation

In relation to the evaluation of the implementation process, it is necessary to establish a distinction between the evaluation of the system from the author's view from that of the learner. Both types of evaluation are necessary, but there ae few examples of them.

Baker used a formative evaluation program to evaluate SHIVA. This evaluation focused on the authors who produced courses using the system. The pilot courseware productions study developed is very interesting but there are still a lot of questions to resolve regarding the methodology for evaluating the use of the system by instructional design experts.

As Krammer and Dijkstra, and Muraida suggest, the study of the differences between expert and novice designers seems to be an interesting way to continue evaluation the author's capability.

Few evaluations focus on the learner and the effectiveness of the instructional materials. However, the effectiveness of these systems depend on the final results in the instructional process. In other words, there is the need to evaluate such important aspects as the learner's progress, motivation, and degree of satisfaction.

Future Research

I have attempted to summarize the main questions concerning the implementation phase. Many questions and problems remain unanswered, and I have chosen two of these as follows:

- What implementation issues are involved in creating effective and adaptive delivery modalities?
- When are computer-based modalities and multimedia presentations useful and instructionally effective?

The answer to these questions is not simple. Some proposals are made by the authors of this book. However, a lot of research needs to be carried out into the relationship between the different ways offered by the computer to support learning and the effects of them on the designer and the learner.

13

Integrating Instructional Science, Learning Theory, and Technology

J. Michael Spector

Armstrong Laboratory, AL/HRTC, Brooks AFB, TX 78235-5601 USA

Abstract: Interactive technologies provide the basis for computers to provide effective platforms for the delivery of complex instruction. These technologies, combined with object-oriented design techniques, can be used to enhance courseware authoring efficiency and improve student learning. This chapter presents an extended argument for taking an integrated approach towards optimizing the use of these new interactive learning technologies. The integration that should occur involves the traditional multi-phase instructional system development model, learning theory, and the variety of technologies available. Each of these areas interacts with the other, and overlooking the interactions is likely to result in suboptimal learning systems.

Keywords: automated instruction, automated learning, instructional systems, interactive instruction, learning theory, multimedia, object-oriented design, student modeling

13.1 Introduction

About 500 years ago a terrible inquisition occurred. The motivation behind that inquisition was not to find answers to questions. The motivation was social and political control of a population -- control to the extreme ends of lack of tolerance and respect for individual differences. Happily, that era is now closed and behind us. We have come of age. Socially and politically we have become more tolerant and respectful of differences. However, our educational systems do not always reflect this same understanding of the value and significance of individual differences. The argument that threads through this chapter is that instructional computing systems need to come of age and reflect the significance of individual differences in learners and integrate this with an understanding of new interactive technologies. At the same time, it will remain paramount to retain the worthwhile aspects of careful instructional planning built around specific learning objectives [6].

The basic question that I would like to address in this chapter is what it would mean for instructional science to catch up with modern technology and come of age, so to speak. I realize that this is an ambitious undertaking, especially because it is somewhat vague and may appear to commit the fallacy of complex question -- assuming an answer to a logically prior question that may also be in contention. Nonetheless, in this chapter I shall argue that attempts to create automated learning environments have created a crisis of sorts. More specifically, attempts to automate the design and development of computer-based instructional materials have tested the limits of our knowledge about how advanced interactive technologies can best be used in support of human learning. The crisis is that we still have limited knowledge about how individuals learn various knowledge types and skills in particular situations. If we hope to use technology to improve education and training, then we must push forward our knowledge of human learning.

It is a commonplace saying and all-too-frequent occurrence that as soon as children learn to speak we start telling them to shut up and be quiet. While there are occasions when silence is desirable, it is surely true that the natural inclination of a child (and any learner) is to engage actively in communication. One premise of this chapter is that such interactivity must be planned into the design of instruction if it is to be effective. Coming of age for a child includes having acquired a self-monitoring sense for which questions to ask, when to ask them, and what kinds of answers to expect. Psychologists call this sensibility metacognitive knowledge, and they argue that good instruction should provide support and encouragement for this ability [5, 9, 19]. Coming of age for automated learning environments will include providing support for these very same metacognitive learning strategies.

13.2 Integrating Instruction and Learning Theory

Since this chapter is about integrating instructional science, learning theory, and technology, it is appropriate to begin with a short discussion of what such an integration might be like. I shall first describe the classical view of such an integration to be found in the dialogues of Plato, and extract from it what I believe to be the critical elements of a useful integration.

Plato had an elaborate and well developed theory of knowledge. That theory of knowledge had implications for how human learning occurred, which in turn had implications for how teachers should teach. While we are likely to reject the particular aspects of each of these three areas of Plato's thought, the holistic understanding of human knowledge and learning toward which Plato aspired and the resulting attempts to integrate his views are worth considering. In Plato's epistemology (see Theaetetus, for example) knowledge involved certainty and universality and pertained to things which did not change [16]. Plato believed that the soul was immortal and survived many rebirths. Since souls had been around for such a long time, they had come to know everything. However, the process of being born was traumatic and caused the soul to forget what it already knew. So, learning was a process of being reminded [16]. The teacher's job, then, was to remind students of things they already knew. Supposedly, Socrates did this as well as anyone, although some would argue that Socrates failed to remind the Athenians about the meaning of justice.

In addition, Plato argued that moral knowledge was to be assessed on the basis of performance. If one failed to act in accordance with a moral principle, then clearly one did not understand that principle [16]. Understanding goodness implied the inability to act in a manner not in accord with goodness. Perhaps Plato's is the first recorded account of the need for performance-based evaluation criteria.

What is worth retaining in this fanciful recreation of Plato's educational philosophy? First, one should begin with a coherent view of what it is to be a person. Then, one should develop a consistent account of what persons can come to know. Then, effective instructors are those who structure the experiences of students in a way which is likely to cause the learning to occur. The first step in the Socratic process was to get the learner's attention by a reminder that a critical piece of knowledge was missing. Gaining attention is also Gagné's first event of instruction [10]. Gagné's eighth event of instruction is to assess performance. As already indicated, performance (in accordance with moral principles) was a critical concern in Plato's view.

Perhaps the most significant aspect of Plato's view of learning is that it is centered around the view of what constitutes a person (viz., an immortal soul). We are more inclined to look to cognitive psychology for this information. A person is someone with sensory receptors and associated short-term sensory storage mechanisms, with a capability for language, with long-term memory, with working memory, and with storage and retrieval mechanisms to move items between these types of memory. In this abbreviated cognitive view, a person is someone without a personality and without a culture. An integrated account of human learning should account for a person who is integrated into a society. People have a social context, and consequently personalities and cultures play key roles in making sense of this context. Surely we need to account for personality and cultural factors when planning instructional interactions.

Second, we need to combine the view of a person integrated into a setting with the knowledge that instructional goals are integrated in a meaningful but often complex setting [12]. We now have two complex factors to consider in our instructional planning: persons and learning tasks. Learning tasks are embedded by nature in enterprises -- complex human activities which are directed toward some purpose, such as analyzing chemicals into component elements or calculating stress factors for structures or developing software to control a piece of equipment [12].

Third, we need to begin at the beginning, by being sure that we have the learner's directed attention. Attention can easily be misdirected, especially by technological wizardries. Gain the learner's attention and focus it on the learning task at hand is a lesson to be carried forward from both Plato and Gagné.

Finally, automaticity with regard to procedural tasks is a common goal found in the cognitive learning literature [36]. If the behavior is not automatic then there is more to be learned. Plato surely thought this about moral behavior. What remains to be done with rigor in automated learning environments is to provide proper support and opportunities for achieving automaticity for complex procedural tasks. Moreover, assessment is an issue that must be addressed throughout the instructional development process, as suggested by Tennyson [30].

We have used Plato as a guidepost, to give us an idea of what we are looking for in integrated learning environments. We seek to construct and implement learning environments which:

- treat humans as integrated into a society and culture;
- encourage those who are trying to learn to perform complex enterprises;
- take into account the many conflicting interests of learners;
- assist learners in focusing on particular situations; and,
- assess knowledge in terms of performance on tasks resembling those which are likely to be encountered in non-learning situations.

13.3 Constructivism and Instructivism

Before addressing the separate areas of instructional science, learning theory, and interactive technologies, an integrative comment on the constructivist debate [23] is in order. I make this comment because I believe that much of this debate has served to fragment the community of learning theorists and educational psychologists and this fragmentation is not helping us build better learning systems. The constructivist view is that we impose meaning on the world, and, as a consequence, learning means constructing a view of the world. In this sense, teachers do not teach students; rather, students teach themselves. In the constructivist world, teachers are not unlike Socratic gadflies who buzz about trying to get students activated into building their own views of the world. Clearly, the focus in constructivist writings is on the activities of the learner much as the Socratic interest was in the behavior of the Athenian citizen [25].

The contrasting view is sometimes called the objectivist view [8]. The objectivist view assumes that there is a world out there independent of our internal mental constructions, and it is that external reality which is the subject matter of various pieces of instruction. There is a philosophical debate that parallels this dispute in learning psychology. That epistemological debate also served to fragment the philosophical community with very little good resulting from centuries of brow and breast beating.

The truth seems to be that meaning exists neither solely in the external world apart from individuals nor in individuals apart from their existence among other individuals. After all, meanings are expressed in a language which is inherently a product of culture. I choose to refer to the objectivist view as instructivism. Instructivism focuses on the activities of the instructor or the instructional system. Clearly there is a need to plan and organize activities to be presented to learners.

In short, constructivists are right to emphasize the importance of learner activities and constructions, but they would be wrong to ignore the need to arrange experiences for learners that are likely to be efficient in creating useful constructions. Instructivists are right to emphasize the need for plans and organized sets of activities, and they would be wrong to ignore the need for learners to make their own constructions.

13.4 Learning Theory

One of the odder aspects of the twentieth century is that in spite of great progress in our knowledge about learning, countless educational reforms have yet to establish noticeable success. Nonetheless, there has undeniably been remarkable progress concerning our knowledge of learning, especially concerning how language skills are acquired and how experts perform various kinds of tasks [13]. We know, for example, that:

- comprehension is an active;
- learning occurs by extending existing knowledge;
- the organization of knowledge in memory determines accessibility and depth of understanding;
- learning is enhanced when acquired in a specific context;

- problem solving is a strategic (not rule governed) process;
- metacognition is an important component of learning;
- knowledge acquisition is a social process;
- higher-level thinking depends on automaticity at lower levels;
- learning is enhanced through immediate qualitative feedback; and,
- content should fit individual learner needs.

Other similar lists could be constructed. For example, Wilson and Cole [36] reviewed nine cognitive teaching programs in terms of the features found in the cognitive apprenticeship model. They found a diversity of features and approaches, but the following trends were noted:

- most models were oriented to problem-solving as opposed to skill acquisition;
- most models incorporated a detailed cognitive task analysis as opposed to a broad or behavioral analysis;
- most models favored authentic contexts over academic contexts;
- most models allowed a fair amount of learner control; and,
- some models are error-driven while others are error-restricted.

In order to establish a baseline, it is worth reconstructing the features of cognitive apprenticeship that inspired the analysis cited above. According to Wilson & Cole (1992), these are as follows:

- teach tacit as well as textbook knowledge;
- teach knowledge and skills in contexts that reflect the way the knowledge and skills will be used;
- show how a process unfolds and explain why it happens that way;
- observe students as they work and provide hints as needed;
- have students reflect on and analyze their own work;
- encourage students to try out different strategies and hypotheses; and,
- sequence instruction from the simple to the complex and teach global skills before local skills.

When these cognitive learning principles are presented at such an abstract level, they appear quite similar to what instructional designers have been saying for a long time, as the next section will illustrate.   Clearly there is a strong emphasis on the student, and this is appropriate. Clearly there must be some attention paid to individual differences.   However, what requires more research is just how much attention should be paid and what kinds of differences and in which learning situations these individual differences are crucial.   In some cases, the answer is obvious.   If instruction is to be delivered aurally in a particular language, then the learner must be fluent in understanding that spoken language.   In many other cases, especially those involving scaffolding for mental models and visualization support, the role played by individual differences is far from clear [24].

13.5 Instructional Science

Gagné, Briggs, and Wager [11] argue that since the purpose of instruction is to bring about effective learning that instruction must be made to influence the internal processes of learning. They identify the following processes:

- reception of stimuli by sensory receptors;
- registration of information in sensory registers;
- selective perception for short-term memory storage;
- rehearsal to keep information in short-term memory;
- semantic encoding for long-term memory storage;
- retrieval from long-term memory to working memory;
- response generation to appropriate muscle groups;
- performance in a particular environment; and,
- exercise of some control over these processes.

These processes are, of course, closely related to Gagné's nine events of instruction [11]. Gagné et al. [11] have summarized instructional design knowledge in terms of the following 12 principles:

- different learning objectives require different instructional strategies;
- there are five different types of learning objectives (verbal knowledge, concepts, procedural rules, motor skills, and attitudes);
- begin with an event that sustains and arouses learner interest;
- communicate clearly what the learner must learn to do;
- stimulate recollection of previously learned relevant knowledge;
- make the stimulus aspect of the task readily perceptible;
- present rule and example followed by practice;
- guide the learning through elaborations;
- verify initial learning by performance;
- provide varied practice with corrective feedback;
- communicate the relation between what is to be learned and how it will be used; and,
- arrange occasions that require retrieval.

It should not be surprising to find very similar instructional design principles running through the literature on instruction since these principles are well-established and accepted by most learning theorists. Yet another sample can be cited from Larkin and Chabay [18] in their design guidelines for teaching science in the schools:

- develop a detailed description of the processes the learner needs to acquire;
- systematically address all knowledge included in this description;
- arrange for most of the instruction to occur through active work on specific tasks;
- give timely and informative feedback;
- provide repeated opportunities for practice and review; and,
- limit the demands placed on students' attention.

This discussion of instructional science would be incomplete without providing a short review of the instructional development process alluded to above.

13.6 Instructional System Development

Models of instructional design and models of design in other domains undeniably exist. The most prevalent instructional   models are based on an engineering approach to curriculum (Instructional System Development or ISD). There are a number of these models in use today [1, 30]. They typically divide the process of developing instruction into the five stages outlined in Table 13.1.

The problem with typical ISD models is that they often fail to account for relevant cognitive aspects of the learning task. For example, a behavioral ISD model for performing task analysis for troubleshooting might include a description of the particular procedures carried out by the troubleshooter, but it would leave out of the account the mental model that guides the troubleshooter through the maze of procedures. Tennyson provides a detailed description of an ISD model and then elaborates ways to refine the analysis and design phases to include relevant cognitive science principles [31].

13.7 Modeling of Courseware Authoring

Tennyson (1989) has argued that there is a need to attend to the specific authoring activities in each instructional development phase. We agree with Tennyson and maintain that following his guidance results in a more useful model of the instructional design process. The usefulness resides in its emphasis on human activities (what instructional designers do) as opposed to the idealized results of those human activities. For example, a superficial ISD model for CBI might make reference to the creation of a lesson storyboard. What may be needed, however, is a specific treatment of how effective storyboards are created and used in a particular environment.

Table 13.1. Conventional ISD Model

ISD PHASES	TYPICAL GOALS
ANALYSIS	Define training requirements. Analyze target population. Establish performance levels.
DESIGN	Specify instructional objectives. Group and sequence objectives. Design instructional treatments. Specify evaluation system.
PRODUCTION	Develop learning activities. Develop test items. Perform formative evaluation.
IMPLEMENTATION	Implement learning activities. Administer test items. Assess student results.
MAINTENANCE	Revise content materials. Revise test items. Assess course effectiveness.

Tennyson's model attempts to specify **what** actions the designer must take to create conditions conducive to learning. A model which tells the practitioner what to do should be based on a model specifying **how** to do it. The latter implies a model that explicitly describes **how** the designer does (or should) organize thoughts about instructional design. A complete model of courseware authoring should account for the instructional designer's thinking, planning, use of schemata, and metacognition during the evolution of a courseware design [22].

Making the instructional designer the primary unit of analysis in the model immediately introduces an additional complicating factor: levels of expertise. What the expert designer does may differ radically (in both order and substance) from what the novice designer may do. It is widely acknowledged in cognitive psychology that experts perform differently than novices (e.g., Glaser [13]). Experts achieve levels of automaticity with regard to common procedures. Evidence also indicates that experts chunk problems much differently than novices. As a consequence, novice designers are more likely to implement instructional designs at a superficial level, failing to address subtle instructional issues [22].

In addition to the need to account for relevant instructional design experience, a complete model of the computer-based instructional design process will need to take into account how and whether various design activities are supported within a particular automated instructional design system. That is, do the tools available to a particular instructional designer augment or impede the process of instructional design?

13.8 Implications for Courseware Authoring

One implication of our view is that particular courseware authoring features will need to be represented as parameters in any model of the automated instructional design process (see the process column in Table 2 below). Van Merriënboer, Jelsma, & Paas [33] make a distinction between recurrent and non-recurrent skills that can be used to illustrate this point. Recurrent skills are those which are performed in a similar way across a variety of problem situations, whereas non-recurrent skills vary significantly with the problem situation. What is a recurrent skill in one authoring environment may not be a recurrent skill or even occur in another environment. For example, many CBI designers currently create lesson storyboards. Some CBI design environments, however, obviate their use (e.g., transaction shells, [2, 14, 21].

Likewise, Tennyson's analysis of complexity can also be used to make the same point [32]. Different authoring environments differ in levels of complexity. One environment may require developers to use an operating system to find files or to be familiar with a particular instructional theory or vocabulary. Another environment may hide the operating system and provide analogous functionality via pull-down menus and, as a consequence, place less demand on the user with regard to familiarity with a particular operating system.

However, other approaches should also be studied and appropriate models elaborated for those environments. Duchastel [7] contrasts instructional design expert systems (Merrill's ID Expert) with critiquing systems (his own proposed ID Workbench). Expert systems are faulted for being too restrictive or unpalatable for experienced users.   Our argument supports Duchastel's general view that different kinds of authoring environments are appropriate for different kinds of authors. However, we go further in that we hypothesize different elaborated models and human activities for the experienced and the inexperienced users of particular systems.

Duchastel mentions a third kind of possibility for an automated instructional design system -- an intelligent tutoring system (ITS). Tennyson also proposed the possibility of an ITS for instructional design [31]. There are still other possibilities. Progressive Learning Systems is developing a system called ID Advisor for the Armstrong Laboratory as part of a Phase II Small Business Innovative Research proposal. ID Advisor is a case-based instructional design advisor, rather than a rule-based system of the type criticized by Duchastel. Robert Gagné, a Senior Research Fellow at the Armstrong Laboratory, is pursuing a dialogue-based guided approach to instructional design. Gagné's system offers the novice instructional designer worked examples of applying the nine events of instruction [11] to CBI similar to that which the user is tasked to design.

13.9 Integrating Technologies

One central problem remains before drawing any conclusions concerning the integration of instructional science and learning theory, and that problem is determining how to optimize the use of interactive media in support of learning in automated environments [34]. First, however, it is necessary to indicate exactly what is meant by advanced interactive technologies or multimedia and to state the critical factors of analysis.

Kozma [17] has proposed identifying both a symbol system and processing features for each media to be used in support of learning. The advantage of this is that the semantic encoding associated with the symbol system is taken into the planning strategy. In addition, cognitive demands and attentional and affective factors can also be accounted for in terms of Kozma's twofold definition. Finally, because the processing features of a media include the mode of access, the choice of media which incorporate the same symbol system might be made on the basis of another characteristic (viz., whether or not non-sequential processing is feasible).

There has been a debate whether media have any influence on learning. Clark [4] has argued that media do not influence learning, and that strategies and learner characteristics are the only relevant considerations. Kozma [17] rejects this argument and calls for additional research to optimize the use of multimedia in support of learning. Clark's conclusion is hasty and dogmatic. It is much more likely that all of the following factors require analysis and study when planning instruction:

- instructional designs and strategies;
- media and delivery mechanisms;
- subject matter and knowledge types; and,
- learner characteristics and desired constructions.

Numerous individuals have cited the effects of interactivity on instruction [3, 15, 20, 26]. Four basic levels of interactivity can be identified: (1) physical interdependence, (2) action-reaction interdependence, (3) interdependence of expectations, and (4) genuine interaction. Although this list predates most CBI, it is worth noting that the term 'interaction' is with held until the situation is fully bidirectional and conversational. The first level corresponds to the 'PUSH ANY KEY TO CONTINUE' interaction. The second level corresponds to a user choice and subsequent branch in the instructional delivery. The third level involves some modeling by the system of the student as well as some modeling of the knowledge being acquired by the student. The fourth level includes all of the previous types of interdependence as well as a qualitative simulation and two-way communication.

I [27] argue that interactions should be analyzed in terms of their receiver specificity, response contingency, and directionality. Likewise, I [28] contend that the relevant factors for evaluation of the quality of an interaction include the following: immediacy of response, access modality, adaptability of response, timeliness and correctiveness of feedback, flexibility of options, directionality, and grain size or duration. In addition, we should be concerned to analyze the quantity and variety of interactions, especially with regard to cognitive loading (acknowledging that individual differences play a role here).

13.10 Conclusion

In short, it is my argument that these new technologies (digitized audio and video, hypermedia presentation systems, object-oriented design environments, etc.) can help provide the integration needed between instructional science and learning theory. On the one hand, by building automated environments that can be used to quickly prototype lesson materials, we can more readily determine the way that individual characteristics, media, strategies, and knowledge type interact in a learning situation. This research will help augment what we know about how knowledge is acquired and accessed.

On the other hand, these new technologies afford us with a new opportunity to construct learning environments which include human-computer conversations (recognizing that this is a computationally complex problem) that are goal driven and fully supported by multisensory learning experiences. By emphasizing the applied side of the equation we might make the educational reforms (or revolutions) of the future more effective.

References

1. Andrews, D. H., & Goodson, L. A.: A comparative analysis of models of instructional design. Journal of Instructional Development, 3(4), 2-16 (1980)
2. Canfield, A. M., & Spector, J. M.: A pilot study of the naming transaction shell (AL TP-1991-0009). Brooks AFB, TX: Armstrong Laboratory 1991
3. Carter, J.: The interactive courseware decision handbook. (Contract No. F41689-89-D-0252). Randolph AFB, TX: HQ ATC. 1990

4. Clark, R.: Reconsidering research on learning from media. Review of Educational Research, 53, 445-459 (1983)
5. Derry, S. J., & Murphy, D. A.: Designing systems that train learning ability: From theory to practice. Review of Educational Research, 56, 1-39 (1986)
6. Dick, W., & Carey, L.: The systematic design of instruction. Glenview, IL: Scott Foresman 1985
7. Duchastel, P. C.: Cognitive designs for instructional design. Instructional Science, 19, 437-444 (1990)
8. Duffy, T. M., & Jonassen, D. H.: Constructivism: New implications for instructional technology? Educational Technology, 31(5), 7-11 (1991)
9. Flavell, J. H.: Metacognition and cognitive monitoring: A new area of psychological inquiry. American Psychologist, 34, 906-911 (1979)
10. Gagné, R. M.: The conditions of learning (4th ed.). New York: Holt, Rinehart, & Winston 1985
11. Gagné, R. M., Briggs, L. J., & Wager, W. W.: Principles of instructional design. Orlando, FL: Harcourt, Brace, & Jovanovich 1992
12. Gagné, R. M., & Merrill, M. D.: Integrative goals for instructional design. Educational Technology: Research and Development, 38, 23-30 (1991)
13. Glaser, R.: Expertise and learning: How do we think about instructional processes now that we have discovered knowledge structures? In D. Klahr, & K. Kotovsky (Eds.), Complex information processing: The impact of Herbert Simon. Hillsdale, NJ: Lawrence Erlbaum 1989
14. Goel, V., & Pirolli, P.: Motivating the notion of generic design within information processing: The design space problem. AI Magazine, 10(1), 18-36 (1989)
15. Gustafson, K., & Reeves, T.: Idiom: A platform for a course development expert system. Educational Technology, 30(3), 26-31 (1990)
16. Hamilton, E., & Cairns, H. (Eds.): The dialogues of Plato, including the letters. New York: Pantheon Books 1966
17. Kozma, R. B.: Learning with media. Review of Educational Research, 61, 179-212 (1991)
18. Larkin, J. H., & Chabay, R. W.: Research on teaching scientific thinking: Implications for computer-based instruction. In L. B. Resnick, & L. E. Klopfer (Eds.), Toward the thinking curriculum: Current cognitive research. Chicago: University of Chicago Press 1989
19. Lohman, D. F.: Predicting mathemathanic effects in the teaching of higher-order thinking skills. Educational Psychologist, 21, 191-208 (1986)
20. Merrill, M.D.: An expert system for instructional design. IEEE Expert, 2, 25-37 (1987)
21. Merrill, M. D., Li, Z., & Jones, M. K.: Second generation instructional design (ID-2). Educational Technology, 30(2), 7-18 (1990)
22. Nelson, W. A., Magliaro, S., & Sherman, T.: The intellectual content of instructional design. Journal of Instructional Development, 2, 29-35 (1988)
23. Perkins, D. N.: Technology meets constructivism: Do they make a marriage? Educational Technology, 31(5), 18-23 (1991)

24. Pirolli, P.: On the art of building: Putting a new instructional design into practice. Proceedings of the 2nd Intelligent Tutoring Systems Research Forum, 129-141 (1989)
25. Rowe, H. A. H.: Problem solving and intelligence. Hillsdale, NJ: Lawrence Erlbaum 1985
26. Russell, D. M., Moran, T. P., & Jordan, D. S.: The instructional design environment. In J. Psotka, L.D. Massey, & S. A. Mutter (Eds.), Intelligent tutoring systems: Lessons learned. New York: Wiley & Sons 1988
27. Spector, J. M.: Designing and developing an advanced instructional design advisor (AFHRL-TP-90-52). Brooks AFB, TX: Armstrong Laboratory 1990
28. Spector, J. M., & Muraida, D. J.: Evaluating instructional design theory. Educational Technology, 31(10), 29-35 (1991)
29. Spector, J. M., Muraida, D. J., & Dallman, B. E.: Establishing instructional strategies for advanced interactive technologies. Proceedings of the Psychology in the DoD Symposium, 12, 347-352 (1990)
30. Tennyson, R. D.: Cognitive science update of instructional systems design models (Contract No. F33615-88-C-0003). Brooks AFB, TX: Armstrong Laboratory 1989
31. Tennyson, R. D.: Framework specifications document for an instructional systems development expert system. (Contract No. F33615-88-C-0003). Brooks AFB, TX: Armstrong Laboratory 1990
32. Tennyson, R. D., Elmore, R. L., & Snyder, L.: Advancements in instructional design theory: Contextual module analysis and integrated instructional strategies. Paper presented at the annual meeting of the American Educational Research Association, Chicago, IL (April, 1991)
33. van Merriënboer, J. J. G., Jelsma, O., & Paas, F. G. W. C.: Training for reflective expertise: A four-component instructional design model for complex cognitive skills. Paper presented at the annual meeting of the American Educational Research Association, Chicago, IL (April, 1991)
34. Weller, H. G.: Interactivity in microcomputer-based instruction: Its essential components and how it can be enhanced. Educational Technology, 28(9), 23-27 (1988)
35. Wilson, B. W., & Cole, P.: A review of cognitive teaching models. Educational Technology: Research and Development, 39(4), 47-64 (1992)
36. Winograd, T., & Flores, F.: Understanding computers and cognition: A new foundation for design. Norwood, NJ: Ablex 1990

Author Index

Subject Index

adaptive 5, 75-77, 131-133, 136-138, 167, 189, 235, 241

AIMS 89, 90, 199, 212, 224, 228

artificial intelligence 1, 26-28, 35, 38, 43, 45, 47, 77, 109, 110, 112, 156, 160, 187, 189, 193, 197, 223, 234, 235, 238

assessment 21, 22, 33, 35, 37, 49, 54, 56, 129, 130, 133, 194, 213, 247

authoring 8, 1, 3, 11, 23, 26-28, 30, 31, 35, 36, 38, 39, 43, 45-57, 94, 129, 131, 132, 135, 136, 147, 152, 155, 163, 164, 169-172, 177, 180, 188, 191, 197, 198, 205, 206, 208, 212-219, 222, 223, 238, 239, 243, 252-255

authors 4, 5, 2-4, 6, 62, 75, 98, 101, 114, 120, 132, 139-143, 145, 147-149, 151, 153, 154, 158-160, 176, 177, 179, 195, 198, 208-213, 216-222, 238-241, 255

automated instruction 1, 31, 59, 79, 86, 93, 129, 243, 254, 255

automated learning 5, 243, 244, 246

automating instructional development 7, 1, 3, 131, 156

automation 7, 1-4, 7, 9-12, 18-20, 47, 67, 79, 80, 83, 86, 88, 91, 93-97, 100, 103-108, 111-115, 118, 127, 129, 130, 131, 137, 163, 164, 168, 169, 171, 172, 187, 188, 191-193, 195, 197, 198, 205, 212, 237, 238

behavioral 29, 31-39, 43, 56, 112, 121, 144, 249, 252

behaviorist 99, 112

CAI 18, 25, 77, 104-106, 119, 129, 132, 133, 136, 235

CAL 79, 80, 206, 215, 219, 222

CASCO 61, 63, 67, 74-76

CBT 19, 28, 79, 80, 138

coaching 35, 54, 135, 141, 142, 147, 148, 151, 152, 154, 158, 167

cognition 3, 1, 14, 27-29, 58, 81, 90, 96, 119, 137, 139, 234, 259

cognitive complexity 51

cognitive science 6, 10, 28, 29, 31, 33, 43, 57, 77, 102, 113, 139, 235, 252, 259

cognitive theories 66, 93, 100

complex problems 79, 82, 102

computer programming 7, 38, 61, 62, 66, 75, 76, 224

computer software 46, 139, 158

computers in education 92, 117

concept 4, 13, 14, 27, 31, 37, 50, 57, 99, 119, 141, 146, 158, 159, 166, 173, 200, 203-206, 209, 216, 217, 219, 220, 226, 231, 233

constructivism 2, 51, 101, 109, 110, 247, 258

constructivist theories 93, 101

content 4, 32, 33, 36, 38, 39, 43, 45-47, 50, 52-54, 56, 57, 67, 93, 94, 97-101, 103, 104, 106, 107, 116, 123, 135, 136, 138, 140-142, 144, 147-149, 151, 153, 155, 156, 159, 163, 172, 173, 175, 180, 186, 189, 190, 191, 202, 204, 213, 224-226, 249, 253, 258

contextual 34, 43, 48, 51-53, 113, 114, 144, 193, 259

  knowledge 34, 48, 51, 113, 193

  skills 52

courseware 7, 1, 2, 7, 9-12, 15, 17-25, 27, 28, 76, 94, 95, 98, 109, 131, 132, 134, 138, 155, 170, 176, 191, 194, 197, 198, 206-208, 212-216, 219, 222, 238-240, 243, 252-254, 257

  engineering 7, 9, 12, 19-25, 206, 207

creative processes 35, 52

creativity 151

cultural 117, 122, 127, 246

curriculum 27, 76, 77, 104, 122, 123, 126, 128, 133, 139, 170, 175, 176, 180, 186, 199-201, 206, 209, 219, 220, 223, 230, 234, 235, 239, 240, 252, 258

declarative knowledge 35, 112, 113, 217

delivery 3, 4, 1, 2, 4-12, 17-19, 32, 39, 45, 46, 51, 52, 56, 67, 69, 79, 89, 113, 129, 155, 167, 169, 187, 191, 197, 198, 220, 237-239, 241, 243, 256

DELTA 2, 7, 9, 20, 24-28, 88, 177, 188, 189, 198, 206, 212, 222, 261

development 3, 4, 7, 8, 1-12, 16, 18-22, 25-40, 43, 45-48, 50, 51, 54-58, 76, 79, 80, 88, 94-96, 98, 99, 101, 106, 109, 111-115, 117-120, 123-126, 129-142, 144-148, 153-161, 163, 164, 168-172, 180, 187, 188, 191, 192-195, 197, 199, 206, 209, 211, 223, 226, 234, 237-240, 243, 244, 247, 252, 257-259

diagnosis 35, 43, 46, 48, 49, 54, 76, 124, 135, 142, 143, 148, 149, 153, 154, 159, 172, 193, 202

Printing: Weihert-Druck GmbH, Darmstadt
Binding: Buchbinderei Schäffer, Grünstadt

NATO ASI Series F

Including Special Programmes on Sensory Systems for Robotic Control (ROB) and on Advanced Educational Technology (AET)

NATO ASI Series F

Including Special Programmes on Sensory Systems for Robotic Control (ROB) and on Advanced Educational Technology (AET)

NATO ASI Series F

NATO ASI Series F

NATO ASI Series F

Including Special Programmes on Sensory Systems for Robotic Control (ROB) and on Advanced Educational Technology (AET)

NATO ASI Series F